'Of the happy moment in the I Ching that foresees a fortunate future for work brought to completion by someone who has given a project all that it deserves, Richard Wilhelm comments, "No one knows himself. It is only by the consequences of his actions, by the fruit of his labors, that a man can judge what he is to expect." In *The Plural Turn in Jungian and Post-Jungian Studies*, students from Professor Andrew Samuels' decades at the University of Essex, who include editor and major contributor Stefano Carpani, are given their chance to show how much this analytic teacher has allowed post-Jungian thought to take root in minds that have been taught by him to deploy critical thinking and critical feeling to get to the heart of any opinion. This *Festschrift* takes the long view: the harvest on display is a harbinger of the fertility of the ideas it advances. Andrew has every reason to expect that his way of joining the personal with the political – a poly-directional relational position aimed at preserving the openness of the psyche itself – will continue to correct, for educational generations to come, the orthodoxies that perennially threaten both academic settings and analytic schools.'

– John Beebe (MD), author of *Integrity in Depth*

'From the creative mind of Stefano Carpani comes a brilliant and fine book that captures in form and content the deeply relational spirit with which Andrew Samuels has carried out his work as mentor, teacher and theorist, through the fruitful encounter with the plurality of minds of his PhD students. Masterfully – and mutually – cultivated, their voices express themselves in a novel way on a wide variety of themes. Such meetings have left a profound trace in the people and the cultural humus of analytical psychology, generating something deeply new and peculiar, the Jungian branch of the Essex school of psychosocial studies.'

– Monica Luci (PhD), Jungian Psychoanalyst and Scholar

'*The Plural Turn in Jungian and Post-Jungian Studies* reveals the transformation of Jungian studies by one extraordinarily creative figure, Professor Andrew Samuels. As a distinguished analyst, innovative theorist and pioneering teacher, he has rejuvenated the legacy of Jung and inaugurated generations of scholars while taking psyche into politics and beyond. This book gathers the work of his PhD students who continue to thrive in the pluralism he proposed. By creating the critical stance of the Post-Jungian, Samuels and his "Essex School" bring rigour and liveliness to Jungian scholarship.'

– Susan Rowland (PhD), Pacifica Graduate Institute

The Plural Turn in Jungian and Post-Jungian Studies

This unique book showcases the cutting-edge work of researchers in Jungian and post-Jungian studies, focusing on the advances being made at the University of Essex, UK, and operating as a *Festschrift* for Professor Andrew Samuels.

The Plural Turn in Jungian and Post-Jungian Studies includes contributions from innovative authors who specialise in Jung but incorporate ideas from other psychoanalytic schools and from a range of disciplines. The book includes chapters which shed new light on concepts including alchemy, archetypes and individuation and which examine art, relationships and politics. It both honours the work of Andrew Samuels and sets the foundations for an 'Essex School' of Jungian studies.

A wide-ranging collection, this book will be essential for academics and scholars of Jungian and post-Jungian studies. It will also be a key title for all readers with an interest in the work of Andrew Samuels.

Stefano Carpani M.A. M.Phil., is a Psychoanalyst and a Sociologist (graduate of the C.G. Jung Institute Zürich, Switzerland and the University of Cambridge, respectively), and a Ph.D. candidate at the Department of Psychosocial and Psychoanalytic Studies, University of Essex, UK. He works in private practice in Berlin, Germany.

The Plural Turn in Jungian and Post-Jungian Studies

The Work of Andrew Samuels

Edited by
Stefano Carpani

LONDON AND NEW YORK

First published 2021
by Routledge
2 Park Square, Milton Park, Abingdon, Oxon OX14 4RN

and by Routledge
52 Vanderbilt Avenue, New York, NY 10017

Routledge is an imprint of the Taylor & Francis Group, an informa business

© 2021 selection and editorial matter, Stefano Carpani; individual chapters, the contributors

The right of Stefano Carpani to be identified as the author of the editorial material, and of the authors for their individual chapters, has been asserted by them in accordance with sections 77 and 78 of the Copyright, Designs and Patents Act 1988.

All rights reserved. No part of this book may be reprinted or reproduced or utilised in any form or by any electronic, mechanical, or other means, now known or hereafter invented, including photocopying and recording, or in any information storage or retrieval system, without permission in writing from the publishers.

Trademark notice: Product or corporate names may be trademarks or registered trademarks, and are used only for identification and explanation without intent to infringe.

British Library Cataloguing-in-Publication Data
A catalogue record for this book is available from the British Library

Library of Congress Cataloging-in-Publication Data
A catalog record has been requested for this book

ISBN: 978-0-367-52506-4 (hbk)
ISBN: 978-0-367-52507-1 (pbk)
ISBN: 978-1-003-05821-2 (ebk)

Typeset in Times New Roman
by Newgen Publishing UK

*I am convinced not only that what I say is wrong
but that what will be said against it will be wrong as well.*
                                                    Robert Musil

Contents

Preface by Kevin Lu   xi

Introduction – Andrew Samuels: Plurality, politics
and 'the individual'   1
STEFANO CARPANI

PART I   13
From the PhD theses

1   An enquiry into psychological aspects of recovery from
dependence on psychoactive substances   15
MARY ADDENBROOKE

2   The tabloid Trickster: a post-Jungian evaluation of early
twenty-first century popular British newspaper journalism
characterised by that of The Sun   26
JAMES ALAN ANSLOW

3   Laws of inheritance: an archetypal study of twins   38
ELIZABETH BRODERSEN

4   From emancipation to liberation: a neo-Jungian critique
of Theodor Adorno   57
STEFANO CARPANI

5   A spatial rapprochement between Jung's technique of
active imagination and Desoille's *Rêve éveillé dirigé*   71
LANER CASSAR

6   A critique of containing space in therapeutic work   86
MARTYNA CHRZESCIJANSKA

7	Alchemy and individuation CLARE CRELLIN	100
8	Pan stalks America: contemporary American anxieties and cultural complex theory SUKEY FONTELIEU	113
9	Personal myth and analytical psychology PHIL MCCASH	129
10	On the spirit and the self: Chagall, Jung and religion J.A. SWAN	143
11	Marriage as a psychological relationship in China HUAN WANG	159

PART II   179
Andrew in 1000 words

12	Mary Addenbrooke	181
13	James Alan Anslow	183
14	Elizabeth Brodersen	186
15	Stefano Carpani	188
16	Laner Cassar	191
17	Martyna Chrzescijanska	195
18	Clare Crellin	198
19	Sukey Fontelieu	200
20	Phil McCash	202
21	J.A. Swan	205
22	Huan Wang	208

PART III   211
Psychoanalysis in the 21st Century

23	Stefano Carpani and Andrew Samuels in conversation	213

List of contributors	231
Index	243

Preface

Stefano Carpani has accomplished a Herculean task, bringing together the works of many PhDs supervised by Professor Andrew Samuels across the years. Stefano has brought to the job his experience as both an academic and clinician to provide a measured view of the exciting and creative topics that, together, cement the Department of Psychosocial and Psychoanalytic Studies at the University of Essex as a centre of excellence and innovation. I have been involved with several of these projects in some capacity: as a co-supervisor, supervisory panel member and internal examiner. Reading through these contributions brought back fond memories and reminded me of how far our discipline has come. The rapid development of the field since the publication of Andrew's *Jung and the Post-Jungians* (1985) has led Stefano to posit the existence of an *Essex school* of critical Jungian studies. This is a provocative idea that will no doubt be a topic of debate in the years to come. But we can all agree that the work of one man will stand as a central pillar (amongst many) in these future discussions. Indeed, it is a rare occurrence that one individual receives two *Festschrifts* in recognition of his/her contribution to a field of endeavour. And yet here we are.

It would not be hyperbole to state that Andrew Samuels has, singlehandedly, been the architect of an entire discipline. My aim in this preface is not to enumerate a list of Andrew's achievements and accolades. This has been done elsewhere and, in all honesty, the word limit to which I must work would not suffice. Rather, I have two goals in mind. First, I wish to highlight the ways in which Andrew has intuited the directions of a field of study and how he continues to do so. It would be wise for all those who consider themselves Jungians and Post-Jungians – broadly defined – to take notice. Second, I want to comment on Andrew as a PhD supervisor. There may be many 'formulas' to successfully guiding PhD candidates, but as a witness to his approach (Andrew was my mentor when I first started supervising PhDs and together, we have guided three PhDs to completion), I can attest that the alchemy behind the transformation he facilitates lies not in an adherence to any one style, but his ability to read a relational matrix and to mobilise a *persona* (and not in the pejorative sense) that is required in any given moment of a PhD 'life cycle'. In many ways, his ability to adapt therapy thinking to diverse contexts has been his 'calling card', and I have been fortunate enough to observe the ways in which he has enriched student lives in the potentially stultifying context of neoliberal higher education.

In his seminal paper, 'The Future of Jungian Studies: A Personal Agenda' (1996), Andrew reiterates a definition of what it means to be 'Post-Jungian', first outlined in his *Jung and the Post-Jungians* (1985). If Jung's ideas are to be taken seriously in the academy – and certainly, this is a site in which his psychology might flourish – then we need to be his 'critical friends'. In essence, a balancing of tensions is required, where we openly acknowledge a connectedness to Jung's ideas while establishing the need for critical distance. This increases the possibility of generating new knowledge and building bridges to other academic disciplines with which Jung engaged, albeit to varying degrees and with different levels of success. Here, I am reminded of Karl Popper's (1957/1961) dictum, 'For if we are uncritical, we shall always find what we want: we shall look for, and find, confirmations, and we shall look away from, and not see, whatever might be dangerous to our pet theories' (p. 134). Andrew's intentions in mapping out parameters of inquiry have injected 'traditional' Jungian Studies, which some may define as an approach to analytical psychology underpinned by a myopic dedication to 'the master', with some serious academic rigour and scholarship. The MA Jungian and Post-Jungian Studies at Essex, which was initiated by both Andrew and Professor Renos Papadopoulos in 1996 with the generous support of the Society of Analytical Psychology, is a testament to this.

The contents of this book are further evidence that the critical eye Andrew has compelled us to cast upon the study of Jung's psychology was the appropriate direction upon which to embark; indeed, it was the only path possible if Jung's ideas were to survive in academia. The areas of research that Andrew (1996) highlighted requiring our attention over twenty-three years ago have been addressed and continue to be topics of concern: the social and cultural location of analytical psychology; the relationship between analytical psychology and psychoanalysis; the epistemological and methodological challenges presented by Jung's understanding of the psyche; and the utility of applying Jung's ideas to the human sciences, the arts and religious studies. All chapters in this book speak to at least one, if not several, of these themes simultaneously; these areas have become, metaphorically, the landscape, terrain and setting from which every PhD journey in Jungian and Post-Jungian Studies begins. And, as our colleague Dr Gottfried Heuer (2010) rightly notes in his own Introduction to Andrew's first *Festschrift*, 'hardly any texts that deserve to be taken seriously in the field can be said not to be directly or indirectly influenced by his [Andrew's] work' (p. 1).

Not one to rest on his laurels, Andrew's (2017) article on the future of Jungian analysis updates his mission statement on the direction of analytical psychology in its many forms, be it as an academic discipline, theoretical lens, clinical practice or lynchpin for social justice initiatives. While we should celebrate and continue to develop our strengths – which include the eclecticism of Jung's psychology and its growing importance to political discourses, its applicability to neuroscience, the potential contribution it makes to the relational turn in psychoanalysis, and its unique position to speak to shifting gender identity norms and relationship styles – he is also keen to point out the potential pitfalls or, in Jungian terms, the *shadow*. His ability to resist being blinded by the discipline's blind spot not only acts as a clarion call to all scholars to be aware of the unconscious in their research, but also constitutes areas of research in and of themselves. These include Jung's prejudices (in particular, issues surrounding race and racism), the fear of elitism and esotericism that are still evoked when Jung's psychology is utilised, and the residual effects of Noll's (1994) characterisation of Jung as a charismatic leader. My point in briefly summarising Andrew's recent article is this: his ability to see the field from a plurality of perspectives, to celebrate its achievements while noting its limitations (warts and all), to embody the voice of reason and to be the voice of caution, make him a pillar of our community and a leader in an enterprise we call Jungian psychology.

It is no surprise, then, that Andrew's recognition as a leader in our field reflects his success as a PhD supervisor, where he helps others to create new knowledge that pushes the boundaries of the discipline to which he has committed his life. The sheer breadth of research covered in this book indicates Andrew's wide-ranging expertise and diverse interests. What I am more concerned with here, however, is his approach to supervision and his role as a metaphorical 'midwife'. The suggestion may seem odd at first, but I hope the following explanation justifies its use as a quintessential archetypal image that encapsulates the many ways Andrew has impacted the field, in visible ways and others of which some may not be aware.

Terry Gatfield (2005), reflecting on PhD supervisory dynamics, suggests that a supervisor's supervision style is determined by the emphasis he/she places on the *structure* and *support* he/she provides to the candidate. Structure entails how the supervisor organises and manages the research project, while support indicates the way in which a supervisor sustains the candidate's morale throughout the research project. When structure and support are brought together in dynamic tension, four different supervisory styles emerge: *laissez-faire*, *pastoral*, *directional* and *contractual*. A supervisor of the laissez-faire style is non-directive and not committed to high levels of personal interaction. The pastoral style entails a low emphasis on structure, but stresses high levels of support. A directional style supervisor plays a prominent role in structuring the work, but avoids non-task-related issues and interactions. The contractual style combines high levels of structure and support. Here, the supervisor manages the project while simultaneously cultivating a strong interpersonal bond with the student.

Any educational model that seeks to understand the dynamics of PhD supervision will have benefits and drawbacks. Gatfield's research provides a useful point of orientation regarding what supervision entails and, indeed, alerts us to what is missing in terms of appreciating the psychological nature of the relationship that develops. When reflecting on Andrew's own style, I am struck by his uncanny ability to know which style is required at a particular point in the supervision cycle. At times, students will need a directional style; at others, they won't need Andrew to be the font of knowledge but rather, they'll need the compassionate role model who cultivates the emotional fortitude required to complete a PhD. Sometimes students don't want to engage at all and they want their supervisor to leave them alone, and that's acceptable, especially if they're in the all-consuming process of writing up. Does this mean that Andrew has got it right every time and that he hasn't made some mistakes along the way? Far from it. He will be the first to admit that he can be grumpy and, on occasion, can be a bit short with candidates. Yet he is quick to apologise and to repair relationships where ruptures have occurred. But on the whole, I've seen Andrew embody all these styles at one point or another to the greatest effect. His intuitive grasp of the PhD supervision process is that it must be fluid and lived in relationship with the student. This, in turn, reflects the plurality and relational ethos of his approach (Samuels, 1989; Loewenthal and Samuels, 2014). His supervisory style or, in Jungian terms, the persona he dons, needs to be whatever the student requires him to be so that this crucial step in another's *individuation* process may be facilitated.

When seen in this way, analysis and academia don't seem to be worlds apart. Indeed, if I were to characterise Andrew's style, I would call it 'mercurial'. He is both analyst and academic, one of the few who are able to straddle these identities faithfully and with integrity. He is a taskmaster, sounding board, critic and friend. His ability to balance all of these personas, and more, defines him as one of the most successful, humane and celebrated scholars in Jungian and Post-Jungian Studies and beyond. What sets him apart and indeed, what is missing from Gatfield's otherwise insightful analysis, is the alchemy and transformational potential of the supervisory relationship itself, which can boil down to a supervisor's ability to see the *telos* of the relationship from a larger perspective. Perhaps this is a reason why Andrew may come across as being impatient at times. He sees what students and their projects can become, and he's eager to get them there.

The Hermes-like function Andrew serves as a PhD supervisor is not only to help students achieve a coveted title, but to also help them manage this moment of liminality and period of unknown possibilities. It is both truly terrifying and liberating, and it takes a unique person who is willing and able to shape-shift – to don these multiple masks and roles – in accordance to someone else's needs. The significance of this is only heightened when we gauge the reality of Andrew's situation – he is playing this role for multiple students at any given time, alongside his teaching and administrative duties, research, clinical practice, speaking engagements, his commitment to activism and above all else, his dedication to his family. In the spirit of Jung (1941/1959), a student learns because of who the teacher is, not by what he/she says.

To return to the image of the midwife, Andrew is not only nurturing a student's research and facilitating its birth into the world, he's also nurturing the development of the student. Every PhD will have that moment when they hit the pit of despair, when their respective *superegos* tell them that they are frauds, and that their research will never be 'good enough'. And it is at this precise moment that Andrew springs into action like no other can. Having co-supervised PhDs with Andrew and others, I can say in all honesty that when we come to this crucial point in the PhD life cycle, no one is better than Andrew.

I want to end this preface with a personal vignette of my initial image of Andrew, which was quickly laid to rest when I forged a real relationship with him. As an undergraduate at the University of Toronto, I remember picking up a copy of *Jung and the Post-Jungians* (1985) from Robart's Library. After reading it, I was astounded as to how far Jungian thinking extended beyond the reaches of what Andrew terms a 'classical' approach. In particular, his distinctions between various 'schools of thought', however controversial, provided a useful framework from which I began to grasp the reality of Jungian Studies – there wasn't a unified way of research and understanding Jung, only a multiplicity of perspectives reflecting the very plurality for which he was arguing. When I began my PhD at Essex in 2006, I had an idealised image of an authoritative leader in the field who demanded respect, which in turn coloured the way I interacted with him. But he was very quick to 'kill' this image. As a student, he told me to call him by his first name; as a newly appointed member of staff, he took me aside and said, 'Stop it with this deference. You belong here, end of story.' Usually, a *complex* arises because of an inevitable gap between an ideal and the real. In this instance, however, the reality was much better than the fantasy.

Andrew sees the psychological aspect in all things, and proactively mobilises his vast knowledge and experience to help and enable others. He hasn't achieved what he has achieved by being a 'shrinking violet', that much is true. But equally, he is a sensitive and kind individual who has gone out of his way to launch the careers of several other prominent members of our field, be it within the clinical or academic domain, or both. I have seen firsthand his unwavering commitment to students and his concern for the future and advancement of our discipline. I have seen him push back against policies he thought would disadvantage PhD students, and I've seen him win these battles. Andrew is not so worried about how posterity will judge him, but only that his work – and the research he has inspired and supervises – contributes to a critical appreciation of analytical psychology for which he has tirelessly fought his entire working life.

At the beginning of 2019, Andrew retired from the Department of Psychosocial and Psychoanalytic Studies. I think it is fair to conclude that things aren't quite the same. But to my colleague and friend, I'd like to say that I hold on to the lessons you've imparted and that I keep your ethos to education in mind. If a university is a business at all (a thought that fills me with dread and absolutely breaks my heart), then we're in the 'business' of enriching lives through research. Thank you for reminding me of this.

Dr Kevin Lu
Senior Lecturer
Department of Psychosocial and Psychoanalytic
Studies, University of Essex

References

Gatfield, T. (2005). "An Investigation into PhD Supervisory Management Styles: development of a dynamic conceptual model and its managerial implications" in *Journal of Higher Education Policy and Management*, 27(3), pp. 311–25.

Heuer, G. (2010). "Introduction: a plural bouquet for a birthday celebration in print" in *Sacral Revolutions: reflecting on the work of Andrew Samuels – Cutting edges in psychoanalysis and Jungian analysis*. London and New York: Routledge, pp. 1–4.

Jung, C. G. (1941/1959). "The Psychology of the Child Archetype" in *The Collected Works, vol. 9i: The archetypes and the collective unconscious*. Sir Herbert Read, Michael Fordham and Gerhard Adler (eds); R. F. C. Hull (trans). London: Routledge & Kegan Paul, pp. 151–81.

Loewenthal, D. and Samuels, A. (2014). *Relational Psychotherapy, Psychoanalysis and Counselling: appraisals and reappraisals*. London and New York: Routledge.

Noll, R. (1994). *The Jung Cult: origins of a charismatic movement*. Princeton, NJ: Princeton University Press.

Popper, K. (1957/1961). *The Poverty of Historicism*. New York and Evanston, IL: Harper & Row Publishers.

Samuels, A. (2017). "The Future of Jungian Analysis: strengths, weaknesses, opportunities, threats ('SWOT')" in *Journal of Analytical Psychology*, 62(5), pp. 636–49.

———. (1996). "The Future of Jungian Studies: a personal agenda" in Martin Stanton and David Reason (eds), *Teaching Transference: on the foundations of psychoanalytic studies*. London: Rebus Press, pp. 15–26.

———. (1989). *The Plural Psyche: personality, morality & the father*. London and New York: Routledge.

———. (1985). *Jung and the Post-Jungians*. London and New York: Routledge.

Introduction – Andrew Samuels
Plurality, politics and 'the individual'

Stefano Carpani

This book is quite unique. It is a *Festschrift* for Andrew Samuels, written by his own PhD students and, furthermore, it is Andrew's second *Festschrift*. Therefore, this book is a tribute to Andrew, *the teacher, the man, the mentor* and *the theorist*. It is a tribute to Andrew as – as the Germans would say, in one word – *Doktorvater*.

Andrew, as *Doktorvater*, wrote about the father in almost all of his books: the plural father, the father of whatever sex, the wounded father (as something to be healed), the father's desire to be loved (and not only as an a-emotional or un-emotional security provider); therefore, the father as the new man, which he described as a 'loving and attentive father' and a 'sensitive and committed partner of whatever sex'.

This is a book that, for the very first time, reunites some of Andrew's PhD supervisees – scholars trained at the Centre for Psychoanalytical Studies[1] at Essex University who have specialised in Jung studies but whose passion for psychoanalysis goes beyond Jung's theory. Therefore, those scholars – whom I call *Neo-Jungians*[2] – employ Jung (in a new fashion) along with other schools and traditions of psychoanalysis (and beyond psychoanalysis), which mutually contaminate and enrich each other.

I sense this book might also help to acknowledge what could be called the *Essex School*, which is a particular approach to the study of Jung and Psychoanalysis and finds its centre of gravity – with distinctions – in Andrew himself and Renos Papadopoulos. An example of this, apart from this book, is Elizabeth Brodersen and Pilar Amezaga's book titled *Jungian Perspectives on Indeterminate States: Betwixt and Between Borders* (Routledge, 2020), which includes six papers (out of 15) from Essex graduates.

Now, before diving into the themes and the authors who contributed to this work, I would like to briefly investigate Andrew's own work on plurality, politics and 'The Individual'.

In his 1985 book *Jung and the Post-Jungians*, Samuels claimed that there are three main post-Jungian traditions – the 'classical', 'developmental' and 'archetypal'. It may now be time to add a fourth: the plural. This approach, encompassing eclecticism and integration, is rooted in Samuels' work and aims to restore and enhance Jung's work and analytical psychology at the core of depth psychology, by studying the psyche as plural and, therefore, as political.

As a writer who blends Jungian with relational psychoanalytic and humanistic approaches, Samuels is not a 'classical', 'developmental' or 'archetypal' Jungian analyst, and his work can be divided into two different but linked elements, 'the plural' and 'the political', underpinned by an interest in psychosocial studies.

Samuels' 'plural' period was solidified in the late 1980s with the publication of *The Plural Psyche* (1989), the first in a series, of which the second and third books *The Political Psyche* (1993) and *Politics on the Couch* (2001), marked his 'political' period. These were followed in 2015 by *A New Therapy for Politics*.

According to Samuels, the plural psyche is a concept necessary to both analytical and depth psychology to 'hold unity and diversity in balance', because pluralism is an 'instrument to make sure that diversity need not be a basis for schismatic conflict' (Samuels, 1989: 1). This is, in my opinion, what makes of Samuels a relational psychoanalyst *ante litteram*. He also examines the post-1989 world (communism vs. capitalism) from a merging perspective, in suggesting that the 'fostering of competitive bargaining between conflicting interests produces creative rather than destructive results' (Samuels, 1989: 1).

Therefore, as the Cold War world (1989) was ending, Samuels suggested 'reconciling our many internal voices and images of ourselves with our wish and need to feel integrated and speak with one voice' (Samuels, 1989: 2). This applies to both depth psychology and the socio-political sphere, and Samuels emphasised that pluralism can serve as a political metaphor.

Samuels' political interest heightened, as Peay (2015) has underlined, in the early 1990s when, during and after the Gulf War and Iraqi invasion, he noticed patients bringing war-inspired dreams into the analytic hour. He also realised that not only do psychotherapists 'have little time for politics' but that, in turn, many politicians 'scorn introspection and psychological reflection as a waste of time' (Samuels, 2001: 3).

Examining the plural and political psyche thus enabled him to work both within and outside of the consulting room, as a successful consultant for politicians, organisations, activist groups, etc. In contrast to Hillman, Samuels actively demonstrated 'how useful and effective perspectives derived from psychotherapy might be in the formation of policy, in new ways of thinking about the political process and in the resolution of conflict' (Samuels, 2001: XI) and claimed that 'our inner worlds and our private lives reel from the impact of policy decisions and the existing political culture'. In considering why policy committees do not include psychotherapists, Samuels notes that 'you would expect to find therapists having views to offer on social issues that involve personal relations' (Samuels, 2001: 2). This is Samuels' most innovative aspect: to see psychoanalysts (as well as individuals) as activists, with a fundamental role to play within society.

Samuels suggests that within both the microcosm of an individual and the macrocosm of the global village, 'we are flooded by psychological themes' and that 'politics embodies the psyche of a people' (Samuels, 2001: 5). Thus, he reminds us that 'the founders [of psychoanalysis] felt themselves to be social critics as much as personal therapists' (Samuels, 2001: 6) and in this respect, recalls Freud, Jung, Maslow, Rogers, Perls, the Frankfurt School, Reich and Fromm. He also notes that in the 1990s, psychoanalysts such as Orbach, Kulkarni and Frosch began to consider society once more, but notes that although 'the project of linking therapy and the world is clearly not a new one [...] very little progress seems to have been made'. Thus, he stresses that today 'more' therapists than ever want psychotherapy to realise the social and political potential that its founders perceived in it, but is aware of the 'large gap between wish and actuality' (Samuels, 2001: 7). I propose that psychosocial studies might fill this gap.[3]

In his 2014 paper titled "Appraising the Role of the Individual in Political and Social Change Processes: Jung, Camus, and the Question of Personal Responsibility – Possibilities and Impossibilities of "Making a Difference"", Samuels opened the discussion on the role of the 'individual in contemporary progressive and radical political discourse', engaging with Giddens, Beck and Beck-Gernsheim, who are also key to my own work. In his paper,[4] Samuels – concurring with Jung – underlines that 'individuals are socially constructed, even when they believe themselves to be autonomous and inner directed entities' (Samuels, 2014: 100). Therefore, referring to Giddens, Beck and Beck-Gernsheim on the so-called 'self-invented identity,'[5] cut off from traditional context' (Samuels, 2014: 100), he claims that although challenging and useful, these authors offer only an 'experience distant' perspective (Samuels, 2014: 100), and adds – quoting Layton (2013) – that 'sociologists today [...] have reached the conclusion that individuals need to be better theorised, though this is usually in order to make a deeper and more fecund contribution to their own discipline of sociology' (Samuels, 2014: 100).

This is reminiscent of Durkheim's dispute between what constitutes psychology and sociology, and I also sense that Samuels here is attempting to 'repair' Hillman's error in leaving the consulting room in order to theorise, without considering societal development and the claim of individuals. Instead, for Samuels, the psychosocial turn is imperative for its ability to approach the *individual* from a psychological and social standpoint. Examining the individual through this lens, Samuels sought to recover the aim of the founders of psychoanalysis: to examine the individual within the social environment and the complexities arising from this relation. Therefore, he has worked to regain the revolutionary *quid* of psychoanalysis and to remind us – as alchemy suggests – that *our Art* comprises both theory and practice.

Samuels comments that 'the sociological individual of the past twenty-five years' is 'interested mainly in her or his life issues, and not in the life of the times and its issues' (Samuels, 2014: 100). I see this interest 'mainly in her or his life issues' – or what Beck and Beck-Gernsheim called individualisation (2002) – as a fantasy[6] exercise, the fantasy of fulfilling one's own fantasies. Once such a fantasy has developed, however, it must be grounded in reality to avoid neurosis. In this regard, Freud is key, since he theorised that the cause and symptoms of neuroses are rooted in wishes (not memories), which have an impellent and (partly) unconscious need to be satisfied (Wollheim, 1977: 19).

Perhaps individualisation, as a fantasy of fulfilling one's own fantasies[7] – as I underlined elsewhere (2020) – turns into *broken individualisation*, which corresponds – as Italian sociologist and media anthropologist Chiara Giaccardi noted[8] – to 'the betrayed promise of freedom and happiness for all'.

Hence, the difference between today's electronically advanced society (Carpani, 2019) and the previous advanced industrial society (Marcuse, 1986) is that, today, everyone can fantasise about developing, as Beck and Beck-Gernsheim puts it, 'your do-it-yourself biography' (2002), unchained from tradition, gender or class certainty, due to the changes in Western society since the fall of the Berlin wall. However, this is where sociologists fail, since this so-called detraditionalisation cannot eradicate emotion *tout court*. Thus, Samuels refers to this as 'self-invented identity, cut off from traditional context' (Samuels, 2014: 100). In this regard, an example could help.

Let us take the case of a young couple meeting their couple counsellor for the first time. She is 35 years old, a mother, wife, and manager in a multinational company. However, she is dissatisfied with her well-paid job, with the city they live in, and with her social relationships. Additionally, she always feels tired and sleeps badly. She is anxious and upset about her husband's job situation and angry each morning when her husband takes their kids to school while she goes to work. He is 33 years old and has been unemployed for a year because his company relocated elsewhere and made him redundant. In the interim, he has decided to undertake postgraduate training in a field he has always dreamt of. He is happy with his studies but also feels guilty for not contributing a good enough salary (as he used to do). Does sociology consider this, and if so, what proposals would it make? I sense that it does not, although Giddens (1992), Beck and Beck-Gernsheim (1995) as well as Bauman (2003) wrote extensively about it. I say it does not because these authors claim that everything in a second modern (Beck and Beck-Gernsheim, 2002) reflexive (Beck, Giddens, and Lash 1994) society must be negotiated and that nothing is certain. In my view, this couple cannot yet negotiate because they are trapped in their own emotions – unable to transform them into feelings or to express them – projections and complexes towards the other, as well as in the need to transition between a society based on sociological certainties and a post-certainty society. With the help of psychosocial counsellors, they could examine both societal demands and their current emotional state (Asper, 1993: 61) and work towards developing 'a positive, loving relationship with oneself and a more tolerant attitude toward others'. This also means 'a "coming to light" of possibilities that were previously inhibited and overshadowed' (Asper, 1993: 66) This, in my opinion, is what psychosocial studies aim at – the merging of aspects of societal development with individuals' emotions.

Paraphrasing Layton (2013: 139), Samuels notes that 'individualization is not just about the expansion of autonomy to an ever-widening portion of the population, but rather has been about the creation and extension of a certain version of subjectivity and autonomy'. He adds that 'the sociologically perceived narcissism and plasticity of that kind of individual actually potentiate her or him as far as political activism is concerned' (Samuels, 2014: 100). I agree and also claim that, in Jungian terms, individualisation is a compensation (of the individual inferiorities), and therefore stems from centuries of patriarchy, tradition, gender and class certainty.

Thus, following Samuels, I propose examining individualisation from a psychosocial approach because I also believe that individuals 'are embedded and constructed by and in social relationships, communal networks, task-oriented groups and ecosystems' and 'if Jungian psychology could refashion its approach to the individual, then it could become a sort of support and inspiration to embattled citizens whose experience of their battles is often that they are in it on their own' (Samuels, 2014: 101).

Structure of the book

Having briefly addressed Andrew's work on plurality, politics and 'the Individual', I wish to introduce the structure of this work. This book is divided into three parts. The first is primarily academic. Each contributor provided a chapter of her/his thesis and adapted it for this work.

The second part of this book is a portrait of Andrew from the supervisees' points of view. Titled 'Andrew in 1000 words', each piece comprises a personal memoir.

The third and conclusive part is a conversation between Andrew and myself. This final part is divided into three broad sections. First, it focuses on Andrew's personal biography, then on his intellectual biography and his own contribution, and finally on psychoanalysis in the twenty-first century.

In Chapter 1 of Part I, 'An Enquiry into Psychological Aspects of Recovery from Dependence on Psychoactive Substances', Mary Addenbrooke proposes a grounded theory study of the video- or audio-recorded interviews of 27 former patients of an NHS addiction treatment service, highlighting the cessation of drug and/or alcohol use leading to recovery in 21 respondents, contrasted with stasis or deterioration caused by ongoing addiction in six respondents. The specific drug use was injectable heroin, but all of these patients also used a variety of other drugs and alcohol. In the literature on addiction, evidence based on the words of addicted people or those who have left addiction behind is scant. The words of the respondents in this study illustrate the influences leading to cessation of addiction; the experience of cessation; the vulnerability of those who have recently quit compared with the situation of those who have remained abstinent for at least five years; and factors observed in the resumption of development after leaving addiction behind. Rather than a sociological or medical approach, Mary views the findings from a psychoanalytic/post-Jungian perspective. Evidence emerges of the positive influence of Alcoholics Anonymous and Narcotics Anonymous. Development of the personality, which tends to be arrested during addiction is resumed and she highlights elements involved in this process.

James Alan Anslow investigates 'The Tabloid Trickster'. James's contribution is a personal reflection of his experience as one of Andrew Samuel's PhD charges. It seeks to relate some of the dynamic of their relationship to one of the key explorations of his doctoral thesis: the Trickster principle, as discussed by Carl Jung and others. James's attempt to identify that archetypal energy within the phenomenon, practices and psychosocial impacts of journalism, notably the tabloid variety, seemed to him to be enhanced by his sometimes challenging, but always productive, relationship with Andrew.

Recalling some of their telling interactions, and only now relating them to the Trickster, James discusses how his experience as a journalist on Britain's disruptive, libidinous *Sun* newspaper, and Andrew's often provocative roles in the theatre, academia and the consulting room, intermingled to fuel an unlikely PhD thesis, whose survival, and ultimate success, owes much, possibly all, to its Tricksterish overseer.

The published passage from James's PhD thesis draws on two sub-chapters from its concluding chapter, Tabloid Trickster, Tried and Rebooted. One relates the eponymous archetypal potential to the technological convulsions currently shattering the press in its myriad forms, and the other identifies the Trickster's journalistic contribution to the public sphere.

Elizabeth Brodersen's 'Laws of Inheritance: An Archetypal Study of Twins', examines the evolutionary development of two inheritance laws as archetypal, twin, overlapping, conflictual structures of socio-economic, distributive interaction: firstly, matrilineal (Eros) as inclusive, undifferentiated, horizontal, communal land usage, based on subsistence; secondly, patrilineal (Thanatos) as differentiated, goal orientated, conical/vertical usage based on property ownership and distributive surplus. She begins with anthropological evidence of Palaeolithic–Neolithic matrilineal communal kin structures before the introduction of patrilineal primogeniture around ca. 3000–5000 BCE. Elizabeth asks why the first-born male as rightful, sovereign heir to property was historically promoted over earlier matrilineal communal inheritance. She traces how second-born and other male offspring and all women were disinherited as legal owners of property in favour of first-born males. She speculates upon the socio-economic reasons behind the changeover, analysing the all-male creationist ideas of the Genesis Myth as a rationalising attempt to legitimise the transfer of property from female to male lineage.

Elizabeth discusses the profoundly negative effect primogeniture has exercised on the socio-economic lives of women as the second, disinherited, 'other' twin sex, exploring the historical ramifications of the missing 'other' through feminist psychoanalytical writers who link the subjugation of women to depression and other guilt-ridden, self-harm manifestations of an oppressive misogyny. Radical feminists, however, have moved beyond these parameters to access their own innate, inherited properties, free from a daughter's apparent 'lack' and the need of the father's blessing as an idealised, signifying compensation. Her perspective of the 'other' twin emphasises this academic work, accomplished outside the legitimised frame of patrilineal psychoanalysis.

Stefano Carpani turns to the Frankfurt School in his contribution titled 'From Emancipation to Liberation: A Neo-Jungian Critique of Theodor Adorno' in which he examines Adorno's critique of Freud and psychoanalysis and its relationship with society. He proposes that Adorno took Freud and his dogma as the only source from which to draw in the context of psychoanalytic investigation. He also proposes that Adorno omitted any other view (e.g. Jung and Adler as well as the post-Freudians) and made of Freud and his dogma a model (paralleled by Marx's view of society) that afforded no space to pluralism or to other emerging views in line with the developments of society and within psychoanalytic theory's own development. Therefore, Stefano claims that Adorno paired Marx's theory with Freud's to build a theory of emancipation in the pursuit of happiness, but failed to take into consideration that psychoanalysis does not simply equal Freud and does not lead to happiness. This view and approach, Stefano claims, have been the mainstream in sociology up to the present day. To redress this, Stefano employs C.G. Jung and Mary Watkins as a possible alternative when examining society. In so doing, he proposes that, today, emancipation from authority cannot occur due either to its internalisation and acceptance as proposed by Adorno or due to its mutuality, as proposed by Jessica Benjamin (1977). Instead, (the process of) clarification and knowledge is key. In this spirit, he proposes – as an alternative to Freud's and Adorno's views – examining Jung's approach in his essay 'Stages of life' (*CW* 8: 749/795) in which he proposes that instincts correspond to a state which he calls *natura primitiva* (when humans are unconscious).

Therefore, Stefano proposes examining Mary Watkins's concept of liberation (2003), instead of Adorno's emancipation. Watkins suggests replacing the term 'development' with 'liberation', because 'with regard to economic and cultural progress, "development" of one group seems often to require an oppression of the other' (2003: 3). She also adds that 'a dominant culture's idea of development is too often imposed on a culture, depriving it of undertaking its own path of development' (2003:).

Laner Cassar focuses on 'A Spatial Rapprochement Between Jung's Technique of Active Imagination and Desoille's *Rêve Éveillé Dirigé*'. His contribution starts by exploring historically the concept of inner self-knowledge or interiority and describes how it has been developed by various disciplines, including philosophy, spirituality and literature. It also throws light on how these notions have influenced the emphasis on an inward focus on oneself in C.G. Jung's and Robert Desoille's work. Laner's chapter investigates the spatial metaphors used by C.G. Jung in his active imagination and by Robert Desoille in his directed waking dream. The spatial exploration exemplifies the classical mythological heroic plots in which the individual/hero discovers his identity by moving through space. Different spatial metaphors seem to characterise the two approaches. While Jung insists on facing the depths in one's unconscious, Desoille has a preference for the heights. For Jung there are no heights without first bearing the abyss. In fact, for Jung, his descent into the unconscious is a *descensus ad inferos*. To the contrary, Desoille offers a more benevolent kind of descent into that nether realm. Desoille offers his patients support and ways to emerge unharmed from the precipitous depths. Jung chooses to bear fear in his journey to the unconscious since creative expression can only be born through great suffering.

Martyna Chrzescijanska proposes 'A Critique of Containing Space in Therapeutic Work'. Her chapter focuses on a critique of the traditional concept of containing space that can be found in different theories of space in depth psychology. The presented work discusses the contexts and different understandings of boundaries and borders, including the ambivalence of keeping in/out related to putting boundaries in place. This is followed by a discussion on the social and historical contexts of the idea of the 'contained self'. It also reflects on the possibly defensive use of boundaries in psychotherapy.

Clare Crellin looks at 'Alchemy and Individuation'. In her chapter she outlines how Jung's work on alchemy is often regarded as a deviation from his psychological purpose. She argues that Jung's 50-year fascination with alchemy lies at the heart of his thinking and she proposes that a full understanding of the subtleties of meaning of the main concepts and theoretical constructs in his theory of personality is impossible without first understanding the alchemical ideas that helped to shape these concepts.

She asserts that any attempt to encapsulate Jung's theory by enumerating his main concepts leaves half of the story untold. Its unique aspect is the fusion of Jung's psychological concepts with his knowledge of religious and cultural history. The typology is often thought of as 'Jung's theory of personality', but it is not the core of his personality theory. The core is individuation, a position of balance and unity.

Her chapter introduces alchemy and cosmology and shows the specific ways in which alchemical ideas and images shaped Jung's approach to therapy and his concept of the collective unconscious with its intimations of immortality.

Sukey Fontelieu's 'Pan Stalks America: Contemporary American Anxieties and Cultural Complex Theory' is a revision of the introduction to her book *The Archetypal Pan in America: Hypermasculinity and Terror* (2018). It is a significant exploration into archetypal causes for anxieties and ethical dilemmas in the US. Since the turn of the millennium, violent attacks perpetrated by rapists and both homegrown and foreign terrorists have increased in tandem with a rise in a type of hypermasculine leadership, a neo-conservative movement now in full display under the current president, Donald Trump. The amount of reported serious mental disorders in the country have also sharply increased. Relying on C.G. Jung's theory of the applicability of myth to psychological problems and the post-Jungian theory of cultural complexes, the myths of the Greek god Pan are used as an archetypal scaffolding that informs this disastrous situation. Pan is understood as an archetypal representation of hypermasculinity as well as that of panic with all its psychological burdens. It explores how weekly random shootings, panicky xenophobia, and ongoing misogyny can be better understood when seen as reactions that were easier to ignore when the US was on the rise as a world power, but since the turn of the millennium latent complexes have been triggered and the country now reels in disarray.

Phil McCash discusses 'Personal Myth and Analytical Psychology'. This chapter focuses on a central but neglected area of Jung's late work: the personal myth. The evolution of Jung's thought in relation to personal myth is traced with particular attention paid to the influence of Adlerian ideas. The key features of the personal myth are subsequently delineated. Phil argues that it represents Jung's arrival at a definitive and integrated stance in relation to his scientific and more personal works. More generally, it is proposed that the personal myth is an evolving lifelong and life-wide project. It is an attempt to find a middle way between the twin extremes of fatalism and agency. The personal myth includes ideational and cultural material and is mythopoetic in conception. It entails coming to terms with one's distinctive life pattern and bringing it to its fullest possible expression. Overall, Phil suggests, personal myth means to carry life and weave together the golden threads that connect us all.

J.A. Swan's chapter, 'On the Spirit and the Self: Chagall, Jung and Religion', is formed of excerpts from her same-titled thesis and is now a similar-titled book (Chiron, 2019). Central to this study is the psychic process of individuation and the ways in which archetypal, or transformative, images created by artists (here, Marc Chagall 1887–1985) appear to depict the deeper changes in our collective human existence. The chapter initially explores visual imagery and the imaginal world, establishing a vocabulary and context from which to incorporate Andrew Samuels' work on symbols and the symbolic. Samuels' (1989) Post-Jungian thought, the archetypal experience as a result of an 'affect' or 'archetypal filter', is considered as a transformative dynamic – relocating Jung's archetypes to the contact experience of the imaginal within the personal unconscious's connection to life. This paradigm is furthered beyond visual art and image into a discussion of the digital realm of twenty-first-century technology, image hyper-saturation and its psychic mechanisms. The chapter concludes with an imaginal exploration of the self: Chagall's self-portraits as Christ. In Chagall's oeuvre, the most prominent example of the transformative metaphor is the Crucifixion, which Chagall revisited in various forms and materials from 1909 until his death in 1985.

Huan Wang, in her chapter titled 'Marriage as a Psychological Relationship in China', looks at how the concept of integration has been welcomed in the realm of psychotherapy in China. A similar attitude to integration suggested panacea for marital difficulties. It represents an inclusive attitude, with its underlying ideology of collectivism emphasising similarities, cooperation and the sameness within the group while ignoring individual differences and conflicts between individual members. However, young Chinese people realise that integration will bring many painful and intolerable issues to their marriages. Thus the idea of 'integrity' has emerged. Integrity focuses primarily on the self; it stands for individual differences and one's best judgements, and values personal autonomy and boundaries. Hence, listening to one's inner voice, standing by one's best judgement, and taking responsibility for one's own choices will be a new approach for couples who meet difficulties in their relationships. Further, the difference between the two spouses in a marriage is not due to the difference between men and women but due to the differences between individuals, and the conflicts that occur are due to the fact that each is a distinct and separate human being. It is natural for them to have disagreements. However, simplification places both integration and integrity in a dangerous position; with moral imagination, which places our moral choices in an imaginative space, an open and ambivalent space, dialogue between different voices are facilitated. In such spaces, integration does not simply combine everything, and integrity is not a single criterion; hence, people can find their individual positions within a collective context.

Notes

1 Renamed in 2018: *Department of Psychosocial and Psychoanalytical Studies*.
2 Not to be confused with Robert Moore's 'Neo-Jungian Mapping of the Psyche'
3 Please see Carpani, S. (unpublished) Unpublished PhD thesis. University of Essex.
4 Which evolved into the publication of 'A New Therapy for Politics?' (2015).
5 Thus Giddens, Beck and Beck-Gernsheim, but I would also add Bauman (Liquid Modernity, 2000).
6 Fantasy in the Jungian glossary is a creative exercise fundamental for development.
7 Which is fine if confined to the teenage years.
8 Chiara Giaccardi underlined the concept of *broken individualisation* at a conference titled 'Social Generativity. What it is and what it is good for' (2018).

References

Asper, K. (1993). *The Abandoned Child Within: On Losing and Regaining Self-Worth*. New York: Fromm Intl.
Bauman, Z. (2000). *Liquid Modernity*. Cambridge: Polity Press.
Bauman, Z. (2003). *Liquid Love*. Cambridge: Polity Press.
Beck, U. and Beck-Gernsheim, E. (1995). *The Normal Chaos of Love*. Cambridge: Polity Press.
Beck, U. and Beck-Gernsheim, E. (2002). *Individualization: Institutionalized Individualism and its Social and Political Consequences*. London: Sage.
Beck, U., Giddens, A. and Lash S. (1994). *Reflexive Modernization: Politics, Tradition and Aesthetics in the Modern Social Order*. Cambridge: Polity Press
Benjamin, J. (1977). "The End of Internalization: Adorno's Social Psychology" in *Thelos*, 77(32), pp. 42–64.
Carpani, S. (2020). "The Consequences of Freedom" in E. Brodersen and P. Amezaga (Eds), *Jungian Perspectives on Indeterminate States: 'Betwixt and Between' Borders*. London and New York: Routledge, pp. 221–239.
Carpani, S. (unpublished). Unpublished PhD thesis. University of Essex.
Fontelieu, S. (2018). The Archetypal Pan in America: Hypermasculinity and Terror. London: Routledge.
Giaccardi, C. (2018). *Conference titled 'Social Generativity. What it is and what it is good for'*. Milano, Universitá Cattolica del Sacro Cuore.
Giddens, A. (1992). *The Transformation of Intimacy: Sexuality, Love and Eroticism in Modern Societies*. Cambridge: Polity Press.
Jung, C.G. (1992). *Collected Works*, Vol. 8. London: Routledge and Kegan Paul.
Layton, L. (2013). *Who's That Girl? Who's That Boy?: Clinical Practice Meets Postmodern Gender Theory*. London: Routledge.
Marcuse, H. (1986). *One-Dimensional Man*. London: Ark Paperbacks.
Peay, P. (2015). *America on the Couch: Psychological Perspectives on American Politics and Culture*. New York: Lanter Books.
Samuels, A. (1985). *Jung and the Post-Jungians*. London: Routledge.
Samuels, A. (1989). *The Plural Psyche*. London: Routledge.
Samuels, A. (1993). *The Political Psyche*. London: Routledge.
Samuels, A. (2001). *Politics on the Couch*. London: Profile Books.
Samuels, A. (2015). *A New Therapy for Politics*. London: Karnac.
Samuels, A. (2014). 'Appraising the Role of the Individual in Political and Social Change Processes: Jung, Camus, and the Question of Personal Responsibility – Possibilities and Impossibilities of "Making a Difference"' in *Psychotherapy and Politics International*, 12(2), pp. 99–110.
Swan, J.A. (2019). *On the Spirit and the Self: The Religious Art of Marc Chagall*. Ashville: Chiron.
Watkins, M. (2003). "Dialogue, Development, and Liberation" in I. Josephs (Ed.), *Dialogicality in Development*. Westport, CT: Greenwood.
Wollheim, R. (1977). *Freud*. Milano: Rizzoli Editore.

Part I

From the PhD theses

Chapter 1

An enquiry into psychological aspects of recovery from dependence on psychoactive substances

Mary Addenbrooke

My study is based on the qualitative analysis of a set of tape recorded interviews of twenty-seven ex-patients of a local substance misuse service formerly treated for dependence on alcohol or injectable drugs, primarily heroin. In the majority of cases, abstinence had lasted between five and twenty-four years whereas six informants, who were originally treated in the 1970s were still addicted, providing a comparison group.

I reflected upon the significance of Jung's link with the founding of Alcoholics Anonymous and examined precursors to the cessation of drug and alcohol use and the mode of their quitting and both the short and long-term challenges of living without alcohol or drugs.

Methodology

The theoretical perspective of the enquiry developed through the study of psychoanalytic literature, recall of patients' material in my own analytic practice, and through contact with colleagues in the hospital team. Recently, questions of legitimation have been raised as to whether it is actually possible for researchers to capture lived experience directly, or whether such experience is created in the text written by the researcher. This can be seen to arise partly from the debate over the possibility of obtaining an objective view of experiences which are subjective in character, that is, between a positivist and a constructivist perspective. As Denzin claims, "We create the persons we write about, just as they create themselves when they engage in storytelling practices" (Denzin 1989 82). This question is a difficult but important one for a psychoanalyst and my interpretations of the words of my informants speak from that perspective, rather than from a sociological or behavioural one. As an analyst I am continually in touch with the quality of mutuality in forming or discovering interpretations of patients' states of mind, in a setting where analyst and patient are joint creators in the enterprise. My aim in this study has been to try to enter imaginatively the world my informants inhabit as I listen to their words. Yet I am aware that it is not my own world.

When informants speak of recovery, or, conversely, of a turgid entrapment in their addictions, I may empathise with the struggles they describe, but the empathy derives from imagination rather than memory. Some aspects of the challenge to build a different life after addiction are universal and would not be unfamiliar to the experiences of, for example, displaced people in a new land, or of the bereaved or of the terminally ill, all of whom find themselves metaphorically in a new landscape. Thus, as a researcher, I grapple continually with the challenge of trying to understand the world of the 'other', while being aware of the presence of the 'other', the unconscious, within myself.

The sources of the methodology are:

- Grounded theory, a branch of qualitative research, which rests upon field work employing observation and recording of words and actions of a sample selected for its applicability to the phenomenon in question.
- Psychoanalytic research based upon single or cross-case reporting from a series of sessions in the consulting room, observed and reported upon, usually, though not invariably, by the analyst. Its focus is the psychological development and functioning of the individual in depth.

Still addicted after 25–30 years

The interviews of six individuals still addicted to drugs and/or alcohol were studied. The overriding factor remains their relationship with the drug. This is no longer seen as pleasure-giving or life-enhancing. Their predominant attitude is dissatisfaction and ambivalence towards their drug dependence. There is a striking preoccupation with a balancing act between how much they need, how much they want, and how much they wish to jettison their drug dependence completely. Methadone is used as something to be boosted from other illicit sources or as a salve to the conscience. It is as if they can tell themselves that they are doing *something*. Here four people speak about their situations:

> I know in myself I can stop drinking if I go back to A.A. At the moment I don't want to put down that last drink. I haven't got the wolves at the door. I haven't lost face. I've not got run over in a drunken stupor and woken up with broken legs. None of these things have happened to me – yet. I mean, I've caused riots with people, and I'm a nasty piece of bloody work when I've been drinking ... At the treatment centre, I bullshitted my way through, I've got to admit it now. I was very clever, because I didn't have to open up. I knew exactly what they wanted out of me, and I gave it to them.
>
> I've always been drug orientated since I've been sixteen years old, and it's always an easy way out of any mental problem. I don't really see old mates, because I don't think they're mates anyway. They want to have more people involved with them, because they don't want to be on their

own. For somebody to put any addictive drug, any opiate, in any shape or form, in front of me, he's not a friend. It's the only way they keep you, well, it's like being on a leash.

I hate boredom in my life. I like things to be boom, boom, boom. But I also like to have the odd swerved ball in there, as long as I'm the manipulator of that swerved ball. That sounds like I'm doing an armed robbery or something like that. It's something where you have the control. It's against the *run of the mill* thing.

There's no *best* time. I'm not very content. I do get quite emotional. I think that's depression. I just wish things could be better. And I don't feel very well, all the time. And I get fed up with that, and I just wish things could be different. There's no point in looking back because it's too late. I can't see much in the future at the moment. I'm just plodding on day to day, hoping everything'll stay in place.

There is little evidence of a sense of confidence in being able to spring the trap of dependence or indeed to affect what happens in any way in their lives. Well-known sources of self-help are mostly regarded with scorn as useless and there is equally little sense of a hopeful outcome of treatment within the statutory services. In general, outside sources of help are criticised as inadequate or failing. A passive, fatalistic attitude prevails. In some people this extends to a sense of despair, blame or angry bravado. Yet all except one have had periods of abstinence, sometimes extending over several years. They have proved that they can quit and can exist without drugs. The reasons for their relapses in the past are not uniform or consistent, but are as varied as their personalities.

All have deviated far from the flow of mainstream society in their aspirations and their thinking. Those who are drawn to deviance and live on the brink of the criminal world express no hope of enjoying the fruits of the materialistic culture. Experimenting with drugs which started as exploratory and part of a varied picture of deviance has overtaken them and grown to be an all-pervasive influence in their lives, dictating their actions and aspirations. No part of their lives is untouched by this now. The imperious lure of 'must have' rules their lives, so that they have come to live within an archetypal tyranny. Several of them speak of drug use as an escape, especially from emotional problems, but what has happened is that having escaped up a particular track, they now feel demoralised and imprisoned there. No longer is drug-taking an activity that brings a sense of belonging to, and identifying with, a chosen group as it was at the start. On the other hand, now each person has one 'accomplice'. The quality of life of these people is not only poor, but diminishing in terms of health, morale and relationships. None have any legitimate employment or any significant interests beyond the chemicals on which they are dependent, although at the time of the interviews the amounts involved were not vast. All illustrate a lack of mutually satisfying relationships, either being isolated in ways they regret or being unhappily dependent on the aid and support of others.

Quitting

There are invariably multiple factors which drive drug-dependent people to change. Fears, even of death, are only a part of what motivates change, as can been seen in some of the informants still addicted. They seem able to deny or ignore their fears. It is when a level of desperation is reached that the time comes. The persuasion of others had little effect in many cases, which accords with the Alcoholics Anonymous belief that the decision has to come from within. Informants recall their experiences of cessation in vivid detail, however many years ago this took place. The experience had great significance in the flow of their lives and the descriptions resemble those of survivors of wars speaking about the battles and personal escapes which colour their perception of the world for ever after. This informant's story illustrates the power of narrative:

> The turning point actually was, I phoned up a man, not in the caring profession, a man in Alcoholics Anonymous. I thought I was going to drink again. I had planned to have a drink again, because I still thought I could control it. I still thought I could handle it. Cut down! Just have one or two drinks, like a normal person. I phoned this man up, and I said, 'I want to beat this thing, you know?' And he said, 'Pal, you won't beat it. It will beat you into the ground. Nobody has beaten it yet. A chemical will beat any human being. Alcohol is a chemical. It will beat you into the ground. You have to accept defeat. Accept that alcohol has beaten you. I know how you feel.' He said, 'You're like the picture of a prize fighter who has been the champion. It's like you're the champion of the pub – the raconteur – the storyteller. Great adulation. "Lovely to see you again." Terrific. Great, like a prize fighter. He was the champion. He's been around some time, and gradually he's taken a few hits, and he doesn't win. He loses. But he's going to make a comeback. So he goes back in the ring again. They say, "Lovely. Great to see you back." So you go back into the pub. The guy goes back in the ring and gets knocked down. You suffer. You go in the pub. You have a drink. It'll last a little while, maybe a few days, maybe a few weeks. You'll be sick again. You think, "The hell with that." So you pack up. But at the back of your mind you're going to make a comeback. You're going to try it again, you know? And you try it again. And the prize fighter goes in again. Great. The spot lights up. But this time he gets a bigger hiding than ever. So he still comes out again and he goes in the pub. You're welcome again. "Lovely to see you; like old times …"' 'And somehow at the end of the day,' this guy told me, 'You've got

three choices. You can die in the ring, or you can die from alcohol. You can finish up punch drunk, incoherent, don't know what you're doing half the time. You can finish up with a wet brain, as he called it, in a psychiatric hospital – somebody feeding you with a spoon and you're saying, "Good pud." Or you can recover. So if the prize fighter wants to recover, wants to stay good – keep out of the ring. Your choice is to stay away from alcohol and you can recover.'

'For the rest of my life?'

'No,' he said, 'Just for one day.'

The A.A. approach fitted the needs of this man who had had many detoxifications in private hospitals at great expense, all of which had resulted in a rapid return to drinking. At one point he fell downstairs drunk, and broke his neck – even this didn't cause him to stop drinking. His employers had offered him every chance of help and support. His description of the A.A. response to his call demonstrates the power of narrative, which he is recalling many years later with great clarity. The words have a magic quality for him. He himself is metaphorically a 'prize fighter', left in an orphanage at an early age with his brother because his parents were destitute. In an intuitive way, his A.A. phone respondent tuned in to this. The juxtaposition of the fighter, lord of the battle in the ring, with the Korsakoff's sufferer with a 'wet brain' totally abject and childishly helpless, is a dramatic tour de force. His respondent uses narrative to bring him into tune with his vulnerability. He had had a long affair with alcohol, the mistress, and was loath to let go, but he tuned in to the terror of the threat of the helplessness he had experienced as a little boy, deserted by his parents. The A.A. member told him that he should know when to retire gracefully from the ring, because his life was more important than his audience's entertainment. Just as his parents gave him and his brother up for the sake of their survival in the face of destitution, so he has given up something he loved – alcohol – so that he can survive and flourish.

His life story illustrates several enantiodromia. From being left in a children's home, he pulled himself up, first to look after his younger brother and to win the support of his school teachers by his feisty style, and then went on to lead an exciting and challenging life as a soldier. At the crisis point he reached with the destructiveness of his alcoholism, he was able to listen and accept and act on the advice from a recovering alcoholic who recognised his omnipotence. He became an avid member of A.A. and said of his current situation,

> I'm off on holiday shortly. My wife said to me the other day, 'The children asked me if you were going to start drinking again on holiday'. I told them, 'Don't worry, your Dad won't drink'.

The first five years of abstinence

Here two people describe their state when they stopped using drugs, heroin in the first case, and alcohol in the second:

> I was terrified. I actually couldn't function – doing up my shoe laces, or whether I'd get a pair of shoes, or where did I get them? Endless. My head was just a complete mess. You've got no way emotionally of coping with just everyday stuff. I mean – are you going to burst into anger? Are you going to cry one minute and be up in the air the next?
>
> I had no self-respect. I couldn't function, and I was full of fear. I was frightened I was going to drink. There was this over-riding terror, that everything was going to cave in on me and I'd be left with nothing.

The challenges facing people who quit chronic addiction are great: the physical and psychological aftermath of the addiction, the attitudes of family members, the disturbing effects of other drug users or drinkers, the re-emergence of former problems, guilt and shame, apart from cravings and temptations to lapse. Strategies to alleviate the situation in the early days involve learning – listening to the words of others, learning about one's own nature, and discovering what is effective in relation to the task in hand, which is basically building a life in a different pattern from the old addicted lifestyle. If quitting the drug-dependent lifestyle is to be more than temporary, then the individual must rise to the challenge of radical change. Use of the substance during the addiction is a defence, and now the individual is faced with the problem of abandoning it, of substituting the drug-dependent lifestyle by one free of drugs, and meeting unforeseen difficulties as they arise, as well as the emotional turmoil inevitably occasioned by change. Of the resources which were experienced as useful, paramount was the group experience, either the A.A. or N.A. or in the statutory services, followed closely by help from individuals, most notably from the true 'experts', ex-addicts.

The process at work within the individual striving to stay abstinent at this stage can be seen as a growing discernment. In order to stay free of the drug, it is necessary for the individual to become watchful as to what is helpful and what is not, what is realistic and what is not, and most of all, to become self-aware. Most respondents speak of this development. It is a time of readjustment from the isolation imposed by the addiction towards a relationship, initially a relationship of need, necessitated by extreme vulnerability.

Abstinence in the long term

'Long term' is defined as more than five years, and fourteen informants fell into this category. Nine people had involvement with Alcoholics Anonymous or Narcotics Anonymous, and in all but three cases, the hospital service had been involved in their detoxification.

Jung believed that addiction occurred at the deepest level of the psyche. If, as one informant says, 'Addiction is a distraction from the pain inside', then abstinence in the long term requires a changed orientation towards inner pain. The words of the informants illustrate the many ways they found of maintaining a changed attitude of openness and acceptance both to the vicissitudes of life and to their own vulnerabilities. Seen in terms of surrender, the defensive function of addiction is abandoned in favour of an orientation towards acceptance – acceptance, for example, that change is gradual, that it is the human condition to be happy for only 'a fair chunk of the time'.

For some informants, becoming less beholden to their fierce superegos allowed them to accept what they saw as an improvement in facing challenges, rather than the 'all or nothing' stance of either achieving success or experiencing failure. Others discovered the pointlessness of blaming others or life itself, which in Kleinian terms indicates negotiating an overriding shift from the paranoid-schizoid towards the depressive position. In the early days after cessation, when these informants learned to be self-aware in order to look out for triggers to lapsing, they discovered an inner strength that proved to be a lasting gift. In this way, times of great adversity can lead to a spiral of growth.

It is as if the extreme of degradation that these informants fell into in the final stages of their chronic addiction highlights their continuing sense of not only being well grounded within reality, but also their pleasure in having survived – and thrived. The new orientation they struggled towards in finding a place in a world faced without the help of alcohol or drugs was no fleeting phenomenon. Trust in the inner resources they discovered, either with the help of their membership of A.A. or N.A. or of other reference points – their therapist, or their group – seems to have proved itself more satisfactory and satisfying to them in the long term than their former dependence on the chemical. Only through the journey of finding a way to clamber out of the trap of their addictions into a renewed relatedness with others did they discover their own strength – or perhaps the journey itself evoked and developed that strength.

From it came the sort of rewards that are not ephemeral and are not dependent on good fortune, but that sustain life even when it shows its harshest demeanour. Treatment by long-drawn-out substitute prescribing is aimed in theory at making cessation a more seamless and painless process. I wonder how much it deprives people of learning about their strengths, for it implies distrust in their potential. The words of these two informants illustrate a changed orientation:

> I have a better understanding of who I am, where I am, what I am. I'm not struggling to be what I think somebody else thinks I should be. I take what my own expectations are. I was always a bit of a ducker and diver. I was always prepared to see an angle whereby none of the blame would have been attached to me. But now I'm happier just to say, 'Yea, I screwed

up.' And the world doesn't stop. The fact that I'm actually able to sit here and talk to you like this is also another change.

'I think the very core of a good recovery is having each segment within a circle balanced. You take your recovery in different forms. You do some voluntary work, you take an active part. Or you are interested in things that could make a difference. You have a home life that you develop and grow within. I think we continue to grow within our own family. Relationships have to be more honest. If I know I'm wrong, I'd remove myself from the situation, I would go downstairs, out in the garden and have a cigarette. I'd think about whether it was me, whether it's them or whether it's both of us. And then, once my cigarette was finished, I'd come back and I'd tackle it. Whereas I could not have done that before. I couldn't have even looked at the fact that maybe I was wrong, or maybe they were wrong. It was just a mess. I think a marriage is like that, you're continuously in a process of confronting things you're not happy about. – Whatever the years are that you miss out on, when you're drinking, whatever development is suppressed, I must have caught up, in some way or other. Maybe I had to go through what I went through, in order to be where I am today. My family has to have been the centre of what was going on, but I have to have been the centre as well. In a way, I have to have believed that I was important, otherwise, I wouldn't have been able to do the things that I was able to do. What I do and how I can help someone else is also important. Just helping other people, I help myself really. That helps my recovery profoundly.

A life disrupted by a period of addiction is not a lost cause, and the threads can be picked up again. Even people who had had little well-being or 'life achievement' prior to experimentation with drugs and then proceeded to become addicted were able to build lives of singular purpose and contentment after cessation. We are wrong to assume that the 'addict' subpersonality is the whole person. People can and do rebuild their lives afterwards. It became clear that the influence of the philosophy and practice of A.A. and N.A. was overwhelmingly positive. Not only had they been helped in their efforts to achieve and maintain abstinence, but they had actually built lives which are impressive in terms of maturity.

The enquiry identified some elements intrinsic to recovery, by examining the words of the informants in the light of psychoanalytic and particularly Jungian theory. Those individuals who come to a point of abandoning the use of drugs or alcohol changed radically. From a situation of degradation they were able over time to create lives that they find satisfying in spite of fresh setbacks. Instead of living in the blur of the addicted life, self-awareness becomes essential after cessation to avoid relapse, and in itself, it brings rewards. This is the development of ego-consciousness. The essence of the enantiodromia is a turning away from an exclusive dependence upon inanimate substances towards relationship with people, with all the difficulties and rewards that entails. Elements of their subsequent lives found to be rewarding included a growth of tolerance, achieving mutuality in relationships and enjoying the creative aspect of reparation for the harm caused in their addiction by becoming wounded healers.

Therapeutic implications

The questions raised by the findings are of immense practical relevance to those who are involved in the treatment of substance misusers. Nothing can rule out the part played in addiction by the role of conditioned responses. However, the somewhat mechanistic models, for example of relapse prevention, can become a template for failure for those who cannot live up to its demands, unless tempered with an attempt to understand the individual as unique. In treating addicted people, the basic rule should not be forgotten: search for the strengths as well as the weakness and concentrate on a 'whole person' approach. The addict subpersonality is only one part of an individual, who may espouse a lifestyle and adopt its persona wholeheartedly, yet other parts are lying dormant and are only temporarily obscured from view. Therapists need to keep awake to this.

When clients are in the full grip of an addiction it is hard for a therapist to be ignored and treated in a cavalier fashion, as they often are. Yet it is clear from what the informants say, that they recall clearly what therapists have said to them, even if they are dismissive at the time or do not maintain contact. The psychodynamic perspective is invaluable for throwing light on actions of clients that contravene the 'rules' as set out by therapists. Yet little of this aspect is incorporated in nursing and medical trainings. This can lead to a misguided kindness in glossing over gross breaches of 'etiquette', which could rather be used as starting points for a more honest statement of the point of having boundaries.

The isolation of addiction and the solitude of spirituality

Jung's view was that addiction was a misguided search for spirituality, but this was a view he said he was reticent to express openly for fear of being misunderstood (Jung 1976 624). In this enquiry, two different manifestations of the concept of spirituality can be seen. In following the path of the Twelve Steps, members of the Fellowships of A.A. and N.A. are living according to the mainstream tradition of spirituality, as has been illustrated by Naifeh (1995), in which there is a continuing acknowledgement of a power greater than the individual, both within and outside oneself, a search for honest acceptance of shadow aspects of the personality, and an ongoing search for ways to make reparation. Paradoxically, this path is entered on in the company of others, yet it is an individual path. A spiritual orientation in life implies a capacity for appreciating solitude in the interests of allowing awareness of the presence of God, of deeper aspects of oneself. This is in stark contrast to the isolation of addiction, which is, as it were, forced upon the addict by the imperious nature of the transference on to the substance and the shame and secrecy that so often ensue. Such isolation is the real cost of addiction. The addict is imprisoned in it.

Seen from a wider perspective, a spiritual approach to life is also a vital part of what this enquiry has disclosed in the approach of the informants. Two of the informants who were still addicted spoke of a void in their lives, which they felt that they must fill if they were to abandon their addiction. While they have increased this void by the lifestyle of their addiction, it is apparent that there was also a void in their lives, which they were trying to fill in the first place. For some of the informants, the search was initially for an escape from boredom, distress or pain, for others it was an attempt to solve the problems of becoming an adult, containment for the ambivalence of wanting to rebel, yet longing to conform.

The informants who became abstinent came to face their pain and inadequacies and to accept them. They discovered that the act of accepting help is not weak and despicable, but strong. As well as discovering an inner strength, they used this to help others in turn, and many found a quality of mutuality in their relationships. Those abstinent in the long term did not appear to be on the brink of slipping back into drug dependence. They built secure structures for themselves in their relationships with others and with themselves. They were not glib evangelicals or fanatics, but tended to take responsibility for, and in, their lives and appreciate a spiral of rewards. The paradox is that the self-imposed limitation on their lives, their continuing abstinence, promoted richness and strength.

To conclude, an informant who had no contact with A.A. or N.A. wrote to his former therapist:

> I would like to think that something of my experience may prove useful to other people. The reason I am writing is partly to clarify some of what I told you face to face, but also to reveal the truth that the task has not yet been completed. Is it ever? The struggle is to remain true to that in me which is essential.
>
> Our giving up addictions has to be placed in a meaningful context. We have to rediscover our essential goodness, and to do this we have to honour our vulnerability: it is what makes us human. I am still in the process of learning to do this.

References

Denzin, N.K. 1989 *Interpretive Biography*. Newbury Park, CA: Sage Publications.
Jung, C.G. 1976 *Letters Volume 2*. London: Routledge and Kegan Paul.
Naifeh, S. 1995 Archetypal foundations of addiction and recovery. *Journal of Analytical Psychology*, 40(1): 133–159.

Chapter 2

The tabloid Trickster: a post-Jungian evaluation of early twenty-first century popular British newspaper journalism characterised by that of The Sun

James Alan Anslow

Media metamorphosis

The tabloid Trickster is a manifestation of the media Trickster, but it retains an existential distinction from its parent category: it does not reflect to its subscribers 'the broken nature of modern lifestyles and the confusing diversity of choices' (Bassil-Morozow 2015: 133). That is how many of its externally positioned detractors view the paradigm, because they see its content and, by extension, the practice and culture generating that content, as an unworthy project in a developed society in the twenty-first century. For McGuigan, 'The *Sun* is, arguably, symptomatic of and contributory to a political culture in which popular pleasure is routinely articulated through oppressive ideologies that operate in fertile chauvinistic ground. It is populist in the worst sense' (McGuigan 1992: 184). However, for a *The Sun* practitioner, who feels 'love' for that project, the role of the tabloid Trickster is to mediate Bassil-Morozow's 'confusing diversity of choices'. *The Sun* Journalist A.[1] who, as her interview attests, is not an ideologically oppressed agent, puts it thus,

> I ... think that people are trying to edit down what they see ... they've got so much information being thrown at you ... I think people need and want the same as they always have ... an edit, someone telling them what's important, what's of interest.

The 'trick' of this bricoleur and her colleagues – to make meaning of information and collective feelings in the postmodern media landscape – is characteristically an unintended outcome of the Trickster's inherent disruptiveness.

The Sun readers, as evidenced by their continued purchase of the newspaper, appear to support *The Sun* Journalist A.'s analysis. As construction worker Mustafa, 27, told a focus group:

> Well, I will sometimes look at the Mirror. But the Sun, they summarise everything, in a nice way. Yeah. In the Mirror, the pages are so many! The

pages are many, and then you get lost. Sometimes when you read something else, you don't know what to look for ... Maybe if there's no Sun around, then I'll go for the Mirror.

(Johansson 2007: 127)

Shop-fitter Adam, 28, puts it thus in the same focus group, 'Like on the bus to work, you're tired, and you just wanna be entertained. You know, get the latest on the sports, get a peep into the glamour world [laughs]. So the *Sun* is good for that' (ibid.: 141).

The tabloid Trickster's existential challenge is to retain this collating, psycho-culturally filtering function in a rapidly transforming techno-cultural landscape that has removed the 'mass' from media by presenting myriad methods of 'throwing' information at a subject, to co-opt *The Sun* Journalist A.'s term. The existential challenge to the tabloid Trickster's transgressiveness, and hence its entire archetypal integrity, was exemplified by the Leveson Inquiry, and any regulatory restrictions engendered by that process. The new media landscape presents a co-equal challenge to the manifestation of archetypal energy examined by this work, and one that can be characterised by the Trickster trait of commerce. Tabloid journalism, in its printed newspaper form, demands payment in return for curating, customising and re-presenting psycho-culturally appropriate information and entertainment. The technologically driven shift that threatens to make that transaction redundant is the iteration of the Internet, extant at the time of writing, which reflects a development of user-generated content (UGC) published and shared via more accessible and faster connections on social media platforms such as *Facebook*, *Twitter*, *YouTube*, *Instagram* and *Snapchat*. In 2016, 56 per cent of UK journalists thought that the influence of 'audience generated content such as blogs' had 'strengthened or increased a lot ... over time', and 80 per cent thought the influence of social media such as *Twitter* and *Facebook* had similarly increased (Thurman et al. 2016: 36).

In 2015, two-thirds of British adults owned an Internet-enabled smartphone capable of capturing still images and audio-visual content, and of publishing it on the internet within seconds (Ofcom 2016). These devices are employed in moments of crisis or scandal, utterly transforming the dissemination of 'news' and enabling so-called 'citizen journalists' to publish it as well as 'professional' communicators. As Shirky notes, this has forced newspapers to 'think the unthinkable' (Shirky 2008). Some tabloid journalists have embraced these technological developments and, as true Trickster-like bricoleurs, 'throw spaghetti at the wall to see what sticks' (Brock 2013: 201). *The Sun* Journalist B. enthuses '[You] always want a reaction from the reader ... especially now [they are armed with smart phones with instant interactive online access] because you want to engage them more ... so they can contribute to the story'. *The Sun* Journalist A., too, is confident that 'the entertaining way ... we project news with attitude can work across smart phones, tablets, on the internet'. Other redtop practitioners are more pessimistic about the tabloid Trickster's reconfiguration in the social media age; *The Sun* Journalist C. claims, 'Our problem is we can't see beyond the medium ... we cannot contemplate a world without that medium'.

Different types of newspaper have responded to the problem of monetisation posed by the Internet in different ways: paywalls, micropayments and 'freemium' online models. However, the tabloid Trickster faces the biggest problem of all because so much of its commercial value is invested in its revelatoriness and hypersexuality, both of which are rendered far less exclusive by freely available UGC. In the first half of 1989, the average paid-for daily circulation of *The Sun* was 4,173,265; in July 2016, it was 1,544,535. In the same month, the average number of daily 'unique browsers' to its recently opened website (in contrast to its previous paywall) was 2.584 million, much less than the 55.8 million scored by the world-beating *MailOnline* in 2014 (*ABC*), a figure which itself is dwarfed by the 1.59 billion people actively using *Facebook* throughout the world in December 2015. As has often been observed, if *Facebook* were a country it would be the most populous in the world (*AdWeek* 2016). An analysis of 27 countries, including the UK, in 2016 shows that over half of all web users treat social media as a news provider (Newman et al. 2016: 7–11). However, it is not lack of readers per se that threatens the existence of the tabloid Trickster in its current configuration but the fact that more than three million businesses worldwide now advertise on *Facebook* 'and most of them are small and medium-sized businesses that used to buy newspaper space' (Greenslade 2016a).

The conclusion of this investigation is that the confluence of regulatory pressure on the tabloid Trickster, notwithstanding its contemporaneous 'escape' from the recommendations of the Leveson Inquiry (Part 1), and the diminution of advertising income and readership by rapidly increasing social media use, is creating a 'perfect storm' for popular newspaper journalism in Britain and some other parts of the world beyond the scope of this investigation. The tabloid paradigm relies on its collating, curating cultural nous, or feeling, to select and feedback content to its subscribers who have to be prepared to pay for that service if it is to survive. Increasingly, it appears that, with the aid of analytic selection and 'nudging',[2] imperceptible to the consumer, the subject becomes her own curator of news and online entertainment, explicitly or implicitly choosing cultural and commercial search destinations. In other words, through *Facebook*, *Twitter* or other social media platforms the celebrities, sports clubs and activities enjoyed by the consumer are fed to her without the need for a curating intermediary. This can be fairly characterised as an example of editorial enablement. However, it is an individual editorial choice that does not have a share in a collective compendium. The individual items of news and entertainments are indeed shared with like-minded consumers, but not the collective whole.

Paradoxically, this enabling of the individual through social media, at the cost of the collective, may, as Charles warns, 'divorce citizens from the desire for social and political agency which is traditionally viewed as essential to democratic citizenship' (Charles 2012: 200). As Brock puts it, the public sphere 'is now a diverse collection of overlapping spheres of fluid shape and varying size' (Brock 2012: 3), or, in Charles' interpretation, a 'new paradigm of a hypermediated reality' (Charles 2012: 19). McLuhan presciently observed in the 1960s that 'it is impossible to understand social and cultural change without a knowledge of the workings of media' (McLuhan and Fiore 1967: 8) and appears to anticipate the coming of the media Trickster by citing one of its dozen traits identified by this work: 'our time is a time for crossing barriers, erasing old categories' (ibid.: 10).

Culturally aware contemporaneous psychoanalysts, such as Balick, observe that 'online social networking sites are an important locus through which the psychodynamic functions … are often mediated' (Balick 2014: 27). Furthermore, such platforms, and the activities they engender, cannot accurately be described as 'new'. My own *Twitter* page reminds me that I opened it almost eight years ago at the time of writing;[3] in other words, the activity has embedded itself in my psychological habit and that of millions. It shows no signs of being a transient mode in which I, and millions, nay billions, of others interact psychosocially.

Bassil-Morozow and I note that 'lifestyle choices characterising postindustrial societies are supposed to assist individuals in discovering their new – and unique – identity'. We warn, 'This does not mean, however, that each and every individual is equally capable of assembling this unique identity from a variety of fragments offered by the capitalist system and mass media' (Bassil-Morozow and Anslow 2014: 9). I would revise, or at least amplify, that assertion now in the knowledge that 'mass media' in the sense discussed by McLuhan and Fiore (McLuhan and Fiore 1967) and Curran (Curran 2003), has altered beyond recognition, at least in the developed world, largely due to the impact and ubiquity of social media. The editing, or curating, of cultural information lauded by construction worker Mustafa and shop-fitter Adam, 14 years before the time of writing, and the importance ascribed to it by *The Sun* Journalist A. are judged by this work to be irreversibly diminishing, notwithstanding critics' qualified approbation of *The Sun*'s redesigned website (Greenslade 2016c).

By the time of writing, Mustafa and Adam, whom this investigation has not traced, will (extrapolating from their recorded responses and from national statistics) be filtering their own cultural content via *Facebook* and other social media. 'Sex, sport and competition', the editorial trilogy promised by Rupert Murdoch at the launch of his redtop *The Sun* (Sandiford 2002) are no longer required to coexist in the 'redtopped casket' of delights. Topless Page 3 'girls' are only available for view on a platform[4] separate from *The Sun* and their sexual explicitness is chaste compared with the nature and size of online pornography. One international pornography site alone claims it received 21.2 billion visits in a single year (Drucker 2016).

Meanwhile, 'instant' online dating smartphone applications such as *Tinder* have made potential sexual encounters just a 'swipe right'[5] away. Live sports results, augmented by audio-video material accessed through smartphones, is instantly available, at no extra cost in Britain through the *BBC*,[6] and *The Sun* has launched a separate platform *SunBets* to capture those 'punters' wanting to compete with bookmakers over sporting results.[7] Typically, Mustafa and Adam, and consumers sharing their interests, can, at the time of writing, edit their own newsfeeds in a way unthinkable when they were taking part in their focus group in 2004, the year *Facebook* was created. A dozen years later, in 2016, that social media company is valued at $314.8 billion and has a net annual income of $1.51 billion (*Forbes* 2016). Has *Facebook*, and competing platforms, rendered the function of the tabloid Trickster, as developed in the second half of the twentieth century, redundant? This thesis suggests it has not, but it has left it utterly transformed and transformation is integral to the Trickster function.

Mercurius Britanicus (note the name's Trickster associations) was an anti-royalist 'London newsbook' which, on 4 August 1645, asked mischievously, 'Where is King Charles? What's become of him?' (Macadam 2011). The publication was 'informally licensed and vetted by an official of Parliament', and its editor Marchamont Nedham 'delighted in evading these controls' (Brock 2013: 15). It is not difficult to liken this aversion to state control of journalism with both those contemporaneous newspaper editors opposed to accepting the imprimatur of a royal charter, as well as journalistic Internet-based entrepreneurs, for example Nick Denton (whose US-based tabloid revelatorial site *Gawker* was driven to bankruptcy by a libel suit (*BBC* 2016)) and Paul Staines (whose *Guido Fawkes* Tricksterish political blog[8] worked in partnership with *The Sun* for three years (Fawkes 2016)).

Thus, the spirit of the Trickster infused text-based popular journalism from its earliest days and through multiple technological transformations. However, its latest, and most transformative, metamorphosis, into the amorphous nexus of connections and modes of publication (e.g. smartphone, tablet, laptop) that reflects any internet-based 'news-and-views' brand (e.g. *MailOnline*), is the one that is most existentially challenging to that manifestation. For, as Brock correctly tells us, 'journalism requires a community to work in' as well as a 'means to circulate information and opinion' (Brock 2013: 8). Where does tabloid journalism go when it loses its audience, when that audience is fragmented into silos relating to this or that celebrity, this or that sport, or club, or this or that subculture often international in scope? The curator of our entertaining news, or infotainment,[9] was once, exclusively, a mighty redtop brand. However, in 2016, that curator is the individual which can access its own media Trickster, enabled by social platforms such as *Facebook* – a facilitator, not mediating 'mass media', a term so many social scientists, including Bassil-Morozow and I, have sometimes appeared reluctant to leave behind in the twentieth century (Bassil-Morozow and Anslow 2014: 6).

The self-editing, self-curating tabloid consumer of 2016 and beyond does not share a generic brand, red-topped or otherwise. An individual armed with 'selfies' and profiles on *LinkedIn*[10] and *Facebook* must brave accusations of narcissism (Bassil-Morozow and Anslow 2014) to create attractive social media presences. Some digital proselytisers anticipated this rise of personal, or 'micro' news-and-views brands; for example, Negroponte declared in 1995, '[T]he monolithic empires of mass media are dissolving into an array of cottage industries'. Sixteen years on, when the commercial behemoths of *Facebook*, *Google* and *Amazon* bestride struggling 'legacy media',[11] the predicted demise of such empires can rightly be challenged. This work, however, suggests that these technologically facilitated social platforms, however commercially pre-eminent, are not 'mass media' as characterised by Curran (Curran 2003) and others, because they are neither editing nor editorialising vehicles in the manner of newspapers and television news channels.

In the transformed new media landscape, the Trickster, it seems, really does make this world as Hyde (1998) suggests. In 1995, Negroponte anticipated the self-curating brand and dubbed it The Daily Me (Negroponte 1995: 153). In this way, this thesis argues, the tabloid Trickster is metamorphosing into a psycho-culturally democratic manifestation that continues to reflect its underlying principle. Negroponte interprets, with some justification, the tectonic change in commercialised communications thus: 'the medium is no longer the message' (Negroponte 1995: 61).

In the judgement of this investigation, Curran is uncharacteristically, culturally short-sighted to dismiss Negroponte, Rheingold (Rheingold 1994), their critique, and that of others, of the fundamental impact of internet-enabled news amplified through social media. He attacks 'sweeping generalisations … presenting simple ideas in elliptical prose that conveys the impression of profundity'. Moreover, he sneers at the notion that the Internet is 'allegedly inaugurating a new era of "netizen" cyberdemocracy because it is facilitating "many to many" communication through channels that transcend structures of geo-political power and control' (Curran 2003: 53). Some of the writing styles of those Curran cites, indisputably, do not match his own in elegance or scholarship. I, however, suggest their central thrust exposes the fundamental flaw of his own underestimation of the transforming psychosocial effect, and affect, of the new media landscape. This work agrees, instead, with the feeling underlying the assertion, if not with the unequivocal nature of its accompanying prediction, that

> there will always be a market for news and comments delivered in a tabloid style, and a twenty-first-century Alfred Harmsworth [the *Daily Mail*'s former successful proprietor] would doubtless be looking to new technologies to find the best format for providing it. He would note with approval that the *Daily Mail* has not only adapted confidently to the changing environment with its spectacularly successful *MailOnline* website,

but that its journalism still reliably generates controversy and *continues to infuriate critics* [italics added]. The tabloid newspaper may have been the medium of the twentieth century, but its values and approaches will continue to define the twenty-first.

(Bingham and Conboy 2015: 231–232)

Whichever forecast of the future of UK popular newspapers proves true, it is indisputable that their ancient regime, like its equivalents throughout the developed world, is being swept away, and along with it the tabloid Trickster as currently configured. However 'spectacularly successful' the *MailOnline* appears, the profitability of the print-based *DMG* (www.dmgmedia.co.uk/about/) that owns it, and supplies its journalistic and technological infrastructure, is far more questionable at the time of writing (Greenslade 2016b). As Paul Dacre, the much-reviled editor-in-chief of that organisation, which includes the *Daily Mail*, told the Leveson Inquiry,

[T]he political class's current obsession with clamping down on the press is contiguous with the depressing fact that the newspaper industry is in a sick financial state ... this demand for greater press regulation comes at a time when more and more of the information that people want to read is being provided by an utterly unregulated and arguably anarchic internet.

(Leveson 2012)

Recapitulation and recommendations

This thesis has evaluated a contemporaneous, sociocultural phenomenon shown to be of pressing importance to the British public sphere at a time, for the reasons described throughout this work, when that phenomenon faces the possibility of extinction or fundamental transformation. This evaluation has taken place within the field of depth psychology employing the insights of analytical, or Jungian, psychology, and the amplifying commentaries of post-Jungians, and associated scholars. This thesis asserts that such an investigation has not been carried out hitherto within the field, and so judges that its conclusions provide a unique contribution to post-Jungian, and, more broadly, depth-psychological, scholarship, as well as contributing a useful analysis to vexed societal discourses addressing the continued existence, in newspapers or on digital platforms, of collectively enjoyed, popular, text-based journalism, and the ethico-legal and regulatory challenges it engenders. The work suggests that its investigation has been enhanced by my own intimate occupational engagement with the subject for over 30 years and its attendant insight.

To recapitulate, I have restricted the subject of this study to early twenty-first-century, popular, British, tabloid journalism, characterised by that of *The Sun* and the *News of the World*, although, for contextual enlightenment, I have reached back to twentieth-century events, and I suggest that the investigation has international applications, worthy of further exploration. In order for the study not to get 'stuck' in an examination of a tabloid product, I trisected the subject into three dimensions, product, practice and phenomenon, so it could be explored holistically as a paradigm or praxis. My thesis evaluates the psychosocial value of the paradigm by applying Jungian insight, predominantly that connected with the archetypal, to the societal arena of media.

The methods employed by me, both to extract understanding from the subject and to impart 'knowledge' to the reader, are situated firmly on an interpretative, or hermeneutical, platform. They employ my journalistic understanding of the subject under examination, augmented by autoethnography and interviews, and blended with my interpretation of post-Jungian writing and that of media sociologists and commentators. The primary hypothesis of the work, that the subject manifests the archetypal Trickster principle, borrows an investigatory model frequently used by post-Jungian, and more broadly cultural, scholars for explorations in associated areas, notably film studies (Hockley 2007). I achieved this by re-examining and re-presenting the Trickster, concluding that, as a whole, the principle is psychosocially positive, and measuring its 12 traits, narratively, against 20 case studies drawn from all three aspects of the UK tabloid paradigm. I suggest this examination reveals a psychosocially positive function underlying the mischievous, sometimes malevolent, hypersexual, mendacious (actual or perceived), commercially focused paradigm that is British tabloid journalism.

The substantive conclusion of this work is that information about culture and society, or 'news' as it is generally labelled, for most of us 'ordinary' busy, unspecialised citizens, has to be transmitted in an entertaining and energised manner. It needs to be infused with Trickster characteristics, which, by the nature of the principle, and by the nature of the news-gathering process and the way that is perceived, frequently crosses lines transgressively. In the view of this investigation, such transgressions should be dealt with by the full force of criminal law, and be open to civil prosecution, notably for libel for which legal actions London is famously the capital of the world (Collins 2014). To embed regulations, underpinned by royal charter or other statute, in an externally imposed code upon the practice, and product, of the tabloid Trickster would diminish its archetypal effect, and affect, to the point of extinguishment. It would require the statutory defining of 'a journalist' and then, in effect, the licensing of same, a move which most liberal democrats, including me, feel does not fit comfortably in an enlightened state.

In short, if we want news, and by extension entertainment and culture, to be shared in a broadly based public sphere to which millions of engaged citizens remain subscribed, then the Trickster's services are required. Ultimately, the Trickster is best left to weigh the competing claims of 'public interest' and 'interest of the public'. In the view of this thesis, any other deciding agent, in my view, would be subject to the influence of class and politics. As Brock correctly points out, 'Any publication that establishes a connection between the provider and consumer of news becomes a platform on which a number of different motives, aims and purposes jostle for space' (Brock 2013: 8–9). In the view of this investigation, such jostling is best left to the archetypal Trickster, within the structure of the law. The intrusion of regulation beyond that law, conflated with the commercial pressures on popular journalism described throughout this thesis, will almost certainly, in my informed judgement, send us 'ordinary', unspecialised readers into online silos of interest, deserting the public sphere and leaving it populated entirely by a very small and narrow section of the establishment, unrepresentative and unknowing, of broader interest and opinion.

I offer this conclusion to the continuing debate on the regulation of the British press, and I recommend that this work's identification of Trickster energies as a necessary component of effective, entertaining and engaging text-based journalism be considered by media analysts and educators intent on 'professionalising', inappropriately in my view (Anslow 2013), through externally imposed regulation, an activity whose etymological root, self-evidently, is in the word 'journal'. Hence, a journalist is someone who 'keeps a journal' (Simpson and Weiner 1989: 280), someone whom we might reasonably call in 2016, a blogger. In opposing the 'professionalising' of journalism, with all the socially unhealthy inhibition and exclusiveness that term implies, in the judgement of this investigation, I admire, as a practitioner and educator, the core tradecraft so astutely identified by Brock: that of verification, sense making, witnessing and investigation (Brock 2013: 201–202).

As described in its introduction, this thesis has proved to be an individuating project, and one that I respectfully suggest indicates I can undertake a variety of qualitative research methods and deploy them in the development of an original idea, adding knowledge to the field of depth psychology. During this undertaking, I have realised that *The Sun* will reach its 50th birthday in 2019, and so intend to use this work as the basis of a book psychoanalysing this middle-aged presence from a post-Jungian perspective to coincide with that date, providing it does not share the fate of its Trickster partner the *News of the World* who marked its own demise with a characteristically humorous final front page. I am aware there will be critics who will judge the conclusions of this thesis to be the self-fulfilling outcome of a journalist who has spent most of his working life participating in, and teaching, the tradecraft of popular newspaper journalism. My response to such a critique is that I have been a critical subscriber to Jungian thought longer than I have been a tabloid journalist, and that, in both the fields of depth psychology and journalism, the notion of pristine objectivity was long ago dismissed as unachievable and unhelpful. I offer this investigation of a subject I know thoroughly, both as a practitioner and an academic, and suggest it is a depth-psychologically robust test of a hypothesis whose principles are embedded in the quintessentially Jungian concepts of the collective and the archetypal, housed within the broader field of depth psychology, that discipline which uniquely acknowledges the influence of the unconscious on mind, culture and society.

Finally, to those critics of the British tabloid paradigm who wish to see the end of its content, practice and cultural and societal impact, whose taste-based critique was responsible for *The Sun* Journalist B.'s university experience, '[T]here was a lot of baiting of the tabloids ... a lot of people would sneer at them', I commend, as the concluding words of this study, Jung's description of the Trickster, and precede it with what I consider to be its irresistible corollary: that this principle is always with us, and that therefore, teleologically, psychodynamically and psychosocially, it is a necessary and positive contributor to the human condition. As such, following this investigation, I am confident that the tabloid Trickster will navigate, and survive, the wildly capricious uncertainties of the new media landscape, but what reconfigured form, or forms, it will favour are yet to become clear, if they ever do:

> The trickster is a collective shadow figure, a summation of all the inferior traits of character in individuals. And since the individual shadow is never absent as a component of personality, the collective figure can construct itself out of it continually.
>
> (Jung 1954: par. 484)

Notes

1 Journalists A., B., and C. are anonymised in the passage from my doctoral thesis published here. In the original thesis they are named, with their permissions.
2 For example, *Amazon*'s private and 'personal' reading recommendations to consumers who have bought books through its service. 'Recommended for you, James'. Available at: www.amazon.co.uk/gp/yourstore/home/ref=nav_cs_ys (Retrieved 23 August 2016, and only available for viewing with my permission).
3 See https://twitter.com/jamesalananslow (Retrieved 20 August 2016).
4 See www.page3.com/sol/homepage/page3/ (Retrieved 20 August 2016).
5 Colloquial phrase 'used to describe your acceptance of something. The term was originally a reference to the Tinder app. On Tinder, swiping right means you approve of a male/female'. Available at: www.urbandictionary.com/define.php?term=Swipe%20right (Retrieved 20 August 2016).
6 See www.bbc.co.uk/sport (Retrieved 20 August 2016).
7 See www.sunbets.co.uk/ (Retrieved 20 August 2016).
8 Guido Fawkes. Available at: http://order-order.com/ (Retrieved 23 August 2016).
9 'A mix of information and entertainment that is often dismissed by commentators as a form of so-called dumbing down', Harcup (2014: 138).
10 See www.linkedin.com/nhome/ (Retrieved 20 August 2016).
11 'A term popular amongst advocates of new media, especially in the USA, to describe extant forms of media with longer histories such as newspapers, magazines, and broadcast journalism', Harcup (2014: 157).

References

ABC (2014) *National Newspaper ABC figures: 2014*. Available at: www.theguardian.com/media/2014/feb/14/abcs-national-newspapers-2014 (Retrieved 9 September 2016).

AdWeek (2016) *Here's How Many People Are on Facebook, Instagram, Twitter and Other Big Social Networks*. Available at: www.adweek.com/socialtimes/heres-how-many-people-are-on-facebook-instagram-twitter-other-big-social-networks/637205 (Retrieved 8 August 2016).

Anslow J. A. (2013) *Journalism is NOT a profession*. Available at: www.huffingtonpost.co.uk/james-alan-anslow/journalism-is-not-a-profession_b_3265272.html (Retrieved 27 July 2016).

Balick A. (2014) *The Psychodynamics of Social Networking*, London: Karnak.

Bassil-Morozow H. (2015) *The Trickster and the System*, London and New York: Routledge.

Bassil-Morozow H. and Anslow J. A. (2014) Faking Individuation in the Age of Unreality: Mass Media, Identity Confusion and Selfobjects. *Analytical Psychology in Conversation with a Changing World*, London and New York: Routledge.

BBC (2016) *Gawker Media sold to Univision in Bankruptcy Auction*. Available at: www.bbc.co.uk/news/business-37102718 (Retrieved 18 August 2016).

Bingham A. and Conboy M. (2015) *Tabloid Century*, Oxford: Peter Lang.

Brock G. (2012) The Leveson Inquiry: There's a Bargain to be Struck over Media Freedom and Regulation. *Journalism and Mass Communication Educator*, 13: 519–528.

Brock G. (2013) *Out of Print*, London, Philadelphia, PA and New Delhi: KoganPage.

Charles A. (2012) *Interactivity: New Media, Politics and Society*, Oxford: Peter Laing.

Collins M. (2014) *After the Defamation Act, London May No Longer be the Libel Capital of the World*. Available at: www.democraticaudit.com/?p=2150 (Retrieved 22 August 2016).

Curran J. (2003) *Media and Power*, London and New York: Routledge.

Drucker A. (2016) *Here's Exactly How Many Hours of Porn People Watched in 2015*. Available at: www.maxim.com/maxim-man/how-much-porn-do-people-watch-2016-1 (Retrieved 20 August 2016).

Fawkes G. (2016) *Sunday Service*. Available at: http://order-order.com/2016/01/31/sunday-service/ (Retrieved 19 August 2016).

Forbes (2016) *#188 Facebook*. Available at: www.forbes.com/companies/facebook/ (Retrieved 20 August 2016).

Greenslade R. (2016a) *Impress Draws up a New Ethical Code that is Wholly Unimpressive*. Available at: www.theguardian.com/media/greenslade/2016/aug/19/impress-draws-up-a-new-ethical-code-that-is-wholly-unimpressive (Retrieved 19 August 2016).

Greenslade R. (2016b) *Suddenly, National Newspapers are Heading for that Print Cliff Fall*. Available at: www.theguardian.com/media/greenslade/2016/may/27/suddenly-national-newspapers-are-heading-for-that-print-cliff-fall (Retrieved 29 August 2016).

Greenslade R. (2016c) *The Sun Launches a Redesigned – and Much Improved – Website*. Available at: www.theguardian.com/media/greenslade/2016/jun/08/the-sun-launches-a-redesigned-and-much-improved-website (Retrieved 18 September 2016).

Harcup T. (2014) *Oxford Dictionary of Journalism*, Oxford: Oxford University Press.
Hockley L. (2007) *Frames of Mind*, Bristol and Chicago, IL: Intellect.
Hyde L. (1998) *Trickster Makes This World*, London and New York: Canongate.
Johansson S. (2007) *Reading Tabloids*, Stockholm: Södertörns högskola.
Jung C. G. (1954) On the Psychology of the Trickster-Figure. In *Collected Works, vol. 9i, The Archetypes and the Collective Unconscious*.
Leveson L. J. (2012) *An Inquiry into the Culture, Practices and Ethics of the Press*. London: The Stationery Office.
Macadam J. (2011) Mercurius Britanicus on Charles I: An Exercise in Civil War Journalism and High Politics, August 1643 to May 1646. *Historical Research*, 84(225): 470–492.
McGuigan J. (1992) *Cultural Populism*, London and New York: Routledge.
McLuhan M. and Fiore Q. (1967) *The Medium is the Massage*, Germany: Gingko Press.
Negroponte N. (1995) *Being Digital*, New York: Alfred A. Knopf.
Newman N., Fletcher R., Levy D. A. L., et al. (2016) *Reuters Institute Digital News Report*, Oxford: University of Oxford.
Ofcom (2016) *The UK is now a Smartphone Society*. 6 August edition, London: Ofcom.
Rheingold H. (1994) *The Virtual Community*, London: Secker & Warburg.
Sandiford R. (2002) *The Sun and Me. BBC 2*.
Shirky C. (2008) *Newspapers and Thinking the Unthinkable*. Available at: https://edge.org/conversation/clay_shirky-newspapers-and-thinking-the-unthinkable (Retrieved 20 September 2016).
Simpson J. A. and Weiner E. S. C. (1989) *The Oxford English Dictionary, Vol. 8*, Oxford, New York, Toronto: Oxford University Press.
Thurman N., Cornia A. and Kunert J. (2016) *Journalists in the UK*, Oxford: Reuters Institute for the Study of Journalism.

Chapter 3

Laws of inheritance
An archetypal study of twins

Elizabeth Brodersen

Introduction to 'Historical development of the laws of inheritance as "twins": matrilineal/Eros; patrilineal/Thanatos'

I discuss (Brodersen, 2016, chapter 1, Introduction) that a recent study of same-sex twins shows that gender characteristics are fluid and interchangeable between them: the first-born twin tends to adopt the societal gender norm relating to his/her sex, while the second-born twin adopts the norm of the contra-sexual 'other' because access to the first identification is blocked. Such transfer between same-sex twins shows that gender roles are culturally imposed rather than based on innate, sexual characteristics. I show (Brodersen, 2016, chapter 2) how early creation myths display no fixed gender role allocation either, as both sexes adopt each other's creative gender activities whether Eros or Thanatos. This chapter follows by showing how the relationship between the 'first' and 'other(s)' became structured as concrete inheritance laws with the need to own and control assets, defined not only as fixed (land) but also as disposable surplus.

I have divided this chapter under five aspects: the first researches anthropological evidence (past and present) that speculates about the nature of matrilineal/communal societies before land became fixed property under primogeniture. The second discusses evidence of the changeover from the matrilineal line (female gens) to patrilineal inheritance. I emphasise the socioeconomic factors that led to this change and how it affected sexual roles and parenting. I use the twins, Eros and Thanatos, as a tool for examining the inherent dynamics behind the concretisation of property forms: one as egalitarian/communal (Matrilineal/Eros); the other as separation into hierarchical preference (Patrilineal/Thanatos). The third analyses concrete evidence that shows that the onset of primogeniture paved the way to monotheism, the acquisition of church property and monarchic absolutism. The economic institutions of slavery, feudalism, class systems plus the nuclear, monogamous family all stem from the hierarchical preference enacted between the 'first' and 'other(s).' The fourth takes Britain as a case study to show how the onset of primogeniture introduced after 1066 influenced the development of human rights for both sexes. I illustrate the corrective moves taken to ameliorate its negative effects and revert to earlier common-law socio-economic structures at a higher level. Finally, I stress the role primogeniture has played historically in allocating British women the disenfranchised aspects of the second-born, contra-sexual twin 'other.' I conclude that the 'twins' (Eros/Thanatos) are achieving a more balanced distribution of gender traits during the twenty-first century.

Author's Note: Due to the word count limitation for the *Festschrift*, I have not included aspects 3 and 4 and encourage readers to access them in the original publication, *Laws of Inheritance*, pp. 44–56. I have expanded the arguments in this chapter in my publication *Taboo: Personal and Collective Representation: Origins and Positioning within Cultural Complexes*, 2019, Routledge for interested readers.

Anthropological evidence of the matrilineal line

Mainstream anthropological debate (Harris, 1968, 2001; Kuklick, 2008) tends to sidetrack earlier speculation of the existence of an earlier matrilineal system of communal exchange when lineage and inheritance passed through the female line (Morgan, 1877). Such a claim questions the too-often undisputed, equally speculative claim made by Freud that the inherited position of the father as dominant male *always* had primacy; that women have *always* taken second place as his property. Freud postulates the following:

> The essential part ... I am about to describe occurred to *all* primitive men – that is to *all our ancestors* ... The strong male was *lord* and father of the entire horde and unrestricted in his power, which he exercised with violence. *All* the females were *his property* – wives and daughters of his own horde and some ... robbed from other hordes. The lot of his sons was a hard one; if they roused his father's jealousy they were killed or castrated or driven out.
>
> (1938, pp. 324–325; my italics)

Freud bases his main theory of psycho-sexual development on the fear of castration, expulsion or death enacted by a powerful father on any son(s) who challenge, threaten or seize his inherited property (including his wife and daughters). Freud mythologises and universalises this narrative as the Oedipus complex. The sexual basis of Freud's premise as the 'genesis' of human interaction also constitutes part of a wider debate between evolutionary and creationist theories. Freud's fixed model begins ca. 3000 BCE with the advent of 'civilisation' and is *creationist* in character, ignoring evidence of earlier *evolutionary* differing gender roles.

Freud's theory is misleading because he mixes aspects of Darwin's evolutionism with patrilineal creationist theory, doing a disservice to both humans and apes in the process. He bypasses human evolutionary processes by speculatively attaching man's primal, aggressive instincts to his animal, ape-like nature without adequately exploring diversity in the animal kingdom, particularly in the allocation of aggression, hunting skills and territory protection to male exclusivity, thereby jeopardising scientific objectivity (Reed, 1978, pp. 9–39, 63–84).

Nineteenth- and twentieth-century evolutionary anthropologists and materialist historians support Darwin's main theory (1859, 1871), namely, that humans evolved from animals (including women) and were not created from a superior, single male god as postulated in *OT* Genesis. Tylor (1871); Bachofen (1871); Morgan (1877); Engels (1884); Briffault (1931); Reed (1975, 1978); Gimbutas (1989) and Joyce (2006, 2008) amongst others, all speculate, from differing perspectives, that a matrilineal, communal clan system existing during the Palaeolithic era and extending through to the Neolithic era was the original form of social organisation where heredity passed through the female line (gens). There is nothing, therefore, innate about primogeniture, the role of the father and the inherited rights of the 'blessed' first-born male as a societal norm that posits a predetermined male hierarchy. Cultural norms develop as a response to specific socio-economic conditions. I argue that the subjugation of other sons and all women originated with the introduction of primogeniture ca. 3000 BCE, which disqualified and disenfranchised them as the unequal 'other.' My analysis of anthropological data asks whether primogeniture as an inheritance law has ever been questioned or simply accepted as the norm.

The work of classical nineteenth-century evolutionary anthropologists (Morgan, Tylor, Bachofen, Engels) has been dismissed by twentieth-century secondary critique as old fashioned and pejorative, although their hypothetical analyses of Palaeolithic matrilineal communal systems of exchange are anything but pejorative of either sex. Before discussing their critics, therefore, I want to firstly examine, chronologically, the basic tenets of evolutionist arguments. Briefly, Morgan (1877) delineates three epochs of social evolution: 'savagery,' 'barbarism' and 'civilisation.' 'Savagery' (Palaeolithic era), comprising a span of ca. one million years based on nomadic hunting and food gathering, accounts for 99 per cent of human existence. Simple garden culture developed towards the end of this period. 'Barbarism' (Neolithic era ca. 8000–3000 BCE) began with food production through to agriculture, land settlement and stock-raising which provided a surplus of food for larger populations, greater productivity and a higher culture. 'Barbarism' gave rise to the first urban populations from Egypt, Mesopotamia, India and China. The growth of Greek and Roman city states dating from ca. 3000 BCE heralded 'civilisation,' bringing the development of metallurgy and commodity production into hierarchical, patrilineal structures of exchange, which superceded earlier matrilineal communal relationships.

Morgan (1877, pp. 525–554) further elucidates how the idea of property ownership might have developed throughout the above-mentioned epochs. During the Palaeolithic era, energy was directed towards subsistence: rude weapons, fabrics, utensils, implements of stone, flint or bone and personal ornaments constituted the main forms of property, the most valued buried with the deceased for his/her continued use in the spirit world. Land or dwellings were used collectively by their occupants. Personal property that was not buried with its owner was appropriated by the nearest to him/her and remained in the horde/gens of the decedent. As Sahlins (1974, p. 12) points out, property was intentionally minimised to fit in with a nomadic lifestyle. All children inherited equally through their mother's lineage.

Both Morgan (1877) and Tylor (1881) in their analysis of indigenous cultures – Morgan, the American Indian Iroquois tribe; Tylor, the Australian aborigines – emphasise their evident egalitarian social and sexual relations, which arose from collective production and a communal use of property. In his study of Iroquois Indians, Morgan argues that there was no ruling classes or coercive state apparatus to keep clan members subjugated. Clans were, therefore, although rudimentary in form, self-governing and democratic with equality among its members, including women. Despite their childbearing function, women were allowed more productive freedom than under 'civilisation' where their role became privatised in the home.

Morgan (1877, pp. 477–478) thus suggests that the 'family' was a late arrival in history, the term being derived from the Roman *famulus* and no older than 'civilisation.' There was no family or father as such during most of the Palaeolithic era; men and women lived in individual hordes, which made up their collective clans/tribes. He adds that nomadic hunter-gatherers, past and present, had no concept of land ownership or property inheritance so there was no need for the family as an institution to protect its inherited property by the 'first' from other(s). Men and women met for procreation purposes without fixed hierarchical monogamous contracts which would make one the sole property of the other. Morgan called this system 'primitive communism' to describe the 'first' matrilineal hordes.

Morgan argues that the pejorative, patrilineal description of women during 'civilisation' as dependent, sedentary and intellectually inferior to men did not exist in pre-modern cultures. It developed as a direct result of a change in inheritance rules with the domestication of animals in pastoral and agricultural societies during the later Neolithic era. Earlier, women were physically active and authoritative in their communities, sharing jointly with men the twin archetypal properties of Eros (fusion/cohesion) and Thanatos (separation/independence). Headmen/women and councillors were democratically elected, not inherited offices, which theoretically freed up communities to look for fresh talent instead of re-inheriting the 'first.'

Bachofen (1871) recognises two forms of 'mother right,' one belonging to the Palaeolithic era, the other Neolithic; the first form as a primitive 'hetaerist-aphroditic' horde (Palaeolithic) and a second, higher phase (Neolithic) as the 'matrimonial-demetrian' or 'cereal' phrase after Demeter the Greek goddess of agriculture. He suggests that the Neolithic era was advantageous historically to women over nomadic existence because farm settlement brought more security and gave rise to the powerful, idealised mythologies of the earth goddess and their sexual analogies of begetting and birth to the sowing and harvesting of tilled, fertile soil.

It can, however, be equally speculated that the growth of agriculture led to the gradual exploitation of the feminine for profit and surplus and loss of freedom as she became fixed property. The over-idealisation of the 'feminine' as analogous to fertile, virgin land during the Neolithic epoch heralds, in my opinion, the beginning of misogyny[1] to hide the ambivalence felt about the increasing exploitation of land with the development of surplus that robbed, devalued and commoditised its symbolic value.

Briffault (1931), concurring with the research of Morgan and Bachofen, sees matrilineal communal structures as the necessary 'first' form of social organisation because the female sex visibly symbolises new birth, as seen through her venerated representation in effigies created during the Palaeolithic/Neolithic eras. He credits women with initiating the humanisation and socialisation of culture as biological mothers and as the first *active* industrial workers and teachers who developed their intellect through co-operative multi-tasking. In his view, Thanatos (separation/independence) was particularly evident in women's roles. Briffault (ibid., pp. 158–178) further contends that physical and intellectual differences between the sexes are less marked when both share common economic tasks. He notes that, in some cases, indigenous women are intellectually and physically superior to the male (p. 177) showing more physical courage and ferocity in combat (pp. 162–163) and greater shrewdness in arbitration (p. 178).

Briffault speculates (1931, p. 180) that in such societies women are independent and influential *because* they work; under primogeniture, women lose their independent status and public value by becoming little more than sexual slaves (Eros) for the production of male heirs for private ownership. As Goldenweiser (1937, p. 365) likewise argues in his study of the Iroquois tribe, women as 'counsel of matrons' have equal influence in the election of chiefs and curtailing aggressive tribal behaviour. Such evidence does suggest that in indigenous cultures, past and present, men and women both play overlapping symbolic 'twin' gender roles of containment (Eros) and separation (Thanatos) without any one sex being designated as 'first.'

Reed (1975, p. 105) further undercuts creationist theories about the 'first' as male, by contending that human beings did not start out, as Freud maintains, with a concern about incest taboo within a clan/tribe circle because no one knew who their biological father was and, therefore, could not be castrated by him. Using Morgan's research, she notes that the role of the father and family developed only gradually when the pairing family gradually displaced the position of mother's brother as initiator of offspring into wider societal norms. Malinowski (1927) earlier discredits Freud's Oedipus complex because it was not evident in his research of matrilineal families of the Trobriand islanders of New Guinea (Palmer, 1997, pp. 64–69). Unlike Reed, he fails to link the significance of the absence of Oedipal urges in matrilineal families and their presence in patrilineal cultures to the changeover to primogeniture giving exclusive rights of access to all male 'property,' including women.

Reed suggests that taboos began with the necessity to create co-operative social organisations, not as a device to swap male property of women from the father to husband. Co-operation not competition required a suppression of sexual competition and violence in the sex hunt and in the hunt for food. Reed (1975, pp. 21–42) argues that primitive taboo was a general sex taboo linked to food, which prohibited members of a fraternal organisation from mating with each other. Exogamy ensured enough food for clan members through periods of lean resources without resort to cannibalism. Taboo had a two-fold purpose: taboo against members of the same totem engaging in sexual activity and taboo against cannibalism. This explains better the genesis of ancient institutions, such as the classificatory system of kinship, exogamy and endogamy, segregation of the sexes, rules of avoidance, blood revenge and the gift exchange system, than creationist theories of property which came later.

Reed (1975, pp. 43–65) points out that under totemic law, a man could not mate with a woman belonging to his totem-kin group. Under the food clause, a man was prohibited from killing or eating totem-kin animals. The lives of members of the horde or kin community were sacred and inviolable; kinsmen could never kill or eat each other. They could only kill and eat outsiders or non-kin who were regarded as animals. To differentiate him/herself from animals and reduce cannibalism, early woman/man developed social boundaries by establishing first the boundaries of cannibalism. Those who were of the same kin were of the same kind, human beings. Outsiders, non-kin, were members of a different kind, therefore, animals. The development of the 'other' could have its roots here. Leach (1961) links the origin of taboo to sex and food, not incest, suggesting a complex system of classificatory rules of the edible/permissible and inedible/impermissible, based on boundary maintenance.

Twentieth-century anthropological paradigms (diffusionism/functionalism/structuralism) have sidetracked earlier research speculations about an original matrilineal communism because, first, it questions creationist ideals which perpetuate a patrilineal system of vested interest based on private ownership and class distinction; second, a Marxist materialist paradigm and, by association, any earlier communal structure, benign or otherwise, threatens the basis of inherited property. Finally, evidence of a prior matrilineal system of communal exchange upsets the speculative, patrilineal vision of father as 'first,' damaging the hierarchical binary division between the sexes with women created as 'second' (Reed, 1978, pp. 187–205).

Diffusionists (Perry, 1923; Smith, 1928) focus their attention on the onset of 'civilisation' ignoring evidence of Palaeolithic human fossil activity (Harris, 1968, pp. 381–382). Schmidt (1935, 1939) uses Bachofen's evolutionary stages to maintain a creationist, 'feminine' specificity as exclusively Eros. Descriptionist, functionalist and structuralist factions (Lowie, 1937; Boas, 1948; Lévi-Strauss, 1963, 1967; Radcliffe-Brown, 1965), marked anti-historicism, provides no scientific evolutionary basis to human development because their adaptive, descriptive analyses ignore the possibility of underlying dynamic principles or laws which would help illuminate their findings. Proceeding as if cultural superstructures (religion/family) developed apart from, or even in opposition to, technological and productive needs, they see no conflicting patterns that exist behind human progress (Reed, 1978, p. 195).

Structuralism (Levi-Strauss, 1963) confines itself to the creationist model, mixing anti-evolutionary Freudian psychoanalytic structures (Mead's emphasis on weaning and toilet training) with phallocentric anthropological perspectives as a basis for human development, allowing the creationist tenets of gender role specificity to remain unchallenged (Harris, 1968, pp. 422–448). When Levi-Strauss (1963, p. 142) differentiates between two distinct village structures amongst indigenous Indonesian Indians as 'sacred' and 'profane,' 'inner' and 'outer,' the sacred 'inner' structure is automatically designated the bachelor house, a meeting-place strictly for men. Although matrilineal descent and the formation of outer matrilocal residences are practised, Levi-Strauss labels the 'outer' structure as profane, with women, by definition, excluded and outcasted from religious ceremonies. Von Franz (1988, p. 9) rightly criticises such paradigms for artificially separating archetypal structures (sacred/profane) when they, in fact, overlap as conflictual yet complementary 'twin' phenomena (Eros/Thanatos) as I propose in this research.

Although twentieth-century neo-evolutionism (White, 1959, pp. 106–125; Parsons, 1971) and cultural materialism (Harris, 1968, 2001) explore the historical impact of productive and unproductive forces on socio-economic structures, adapting in part Morgan's original thesis, neither commit to evidence of earlier matrilineal kin clan communal structures. Harris (1968, pp. 217–249) emphasises the theoretical debt owed to both Morgan and Marx's evolutionary materialism, but in its diachronic rather than its Hegelian sense. Harris (ibid., pp. 186–189, pp. 386–387, pp. 502–505) mentions the existence of both matrilineal and patrilineal cultures with property laws but without evaluating their socio-economic impact, staying within a particularistic, descriptive, demographic framework. Hoebel (1984) argues that archaeological verification of matrilineal communal inherited social structures is too tenuous and cannot be extrapolated into the past, even though research evidence into medieval, early modern history and the present, show remarkably similar communal living and inheritance rules which cannot be ignored as mere coincidences.

Similarly, Smith, Kish and Crawford (1987) note that poorer indigenous cultures, past and present, favour female inheritance rights, wealthier decedents favour male inheritance, likewise linking surplus of capital to an original changeover of inheritance rules between the sexes, but attach no historical significance to it. By sidestepping any evidence of an earlier matrilineal system of exchange, a blind spot has formed. Speculative creationist ideas about gender roles remain unchallenged and the effects of primogeniture on both sexes are rarely cited.

Twenty-first-century anthropological paradigms, however, have made positive reassessments of Morgan's work, reprinted in 2000 with an introduction by Fox (1994, 1997, 2000, pp. xv–liii; 2011[2]). Marxist dialectic historicism, influenced by Morgan, has been resurrected into the forum of anthropological debate (Patterson, 2009). Morgan's resuscitation is significantly due first, to the reclamation of 1960s and 1970s radical feminists (Millett, 1971; Daly, 1978) of active/Thanatos feminine contributions to mythmaking by renaming and reinterpreting past and present one-sided patrilineal symbols of the sacred; second, 'hippie' communal experimentations of the 1960s and 1970s showed that communal does not necessarily mean authoritarian communist regimes; and third, the research findings of late twentieth- and twenty-first-century tenacious feminist archaeologists underline Morgan's findings of a non-binary gender specificity in earlier matrilineal communal structures where roles mixed and overlapped.

Although scepticism still exists about postulating the precise nature of earlier matrilineal communal structures, recent feminist archaeological research is reinterpreting archaeological data and offering valid descriptive evidence and analyses to support its existence and question the hitherto exclusive legitimacy of the creationist model of binary gender specificity. Examples are as follows:

> Gimbutas (1989, p. 318) extends Morgan's evolutionary classification of matrilineal communism in her exploratory work on mother goddess figurines of the Palaeolithic and Neolithic eras to include its influence into medieval times in areas on the North West European fringes, such as Wales, which remained relatively independent of Indo-European influence. Her differentiated work on goddess figurines resurrects the neglected 'first' sacred feminine rites of birth, death and regeneration, lost under monotheistic, patrilineal structures of control.

Joyce (2008, p. 10) in her examination of Palaeolithic figurines from Dolni Vestonice, now in the Czech Republic, however, refutes the homogenised cult of the mother goddess by observing that social life was not organised around sexual reproduction (Eros) as a primary identification. A re-evaluation reveals that making textiles was valued as a skill, just as much as the ability to hunt or bear children. Rather than treating figurines as evidence of female fertility, specific figurines with textiles across the chest or abdomen could indicate specific variations of skills among women, between women and men, or between animals. Joyce's reassessment of Palaeolithic burial objects found in Tlatilco, Mexico, puts age, individual skills and status as more important classifications of social agency between people than their sex. Kus (2006, pp. 108–111) similarly explores the trajectory of an active 'feminine' agency.

Likewise, Hollimon (2006, pp. 435–450) through mortuary analyses of the presence or absence of baskets between male and female burials of the Chumash tribe in California reveals the possibility of fluid third gender individuals not governed by heteronormativity. Davis-Kimball (2002) has excavated multiple forms of 'femininity,' including active aggression, from Iron Age burial sites, which include daggers, arrowheads and riding equipment. Such archaeological evidence re-affirms an original overlapping of twin functions between the sexes (Eros/Thanatos) before land became the fixed property of one sex under primogeniture.

Such overlapping creates the impression of third/fourth gender variations instead of a strict binary division of labour envisaged in Freud's creationist theory of sexuality. Such a four-gender variation corroborates my research (Brodersen, 2015, *Laws of Inheritance*, chapter 5) of same-sex, second born male twins who simultaneously display properties of their contra-sexual 'other' and, thereby, widen the collective acceptability of the 'other' as a normal gender variation.

The development of inheritance rules and the changeover to patrilineal inheritance

The development of patrilineal property began during the upper Neolithic period with the owning of livestock, the introduction of cattle breeding, metal working, weaving and field cultivation (Morgan, 1877; Engels, 1884; Hann, 1998). Such activity yielded noticeable surplus over subsistence with outsiders and 'marry-in' spouses from 'other' hordes/clans brought in to increase productivity from which emerged 'interlocal' exchange and sex-differentiated productivity (Leibowitz, 1986, pp. 61–64). Farming required groups stabilised around plots of land, tilling the soil and raising livestock within territorial boundaries. Such developments introduced a new kind of property and servitude. Although lands were still owned collectively, a possessory right to cultivated plots of land developed and was recognised by the individual or group. This right became a subject of inheritance. The old clan communal system began to break down, first into kin corporate clans, second, into separate farm families called extended families (pairing families), and finally into individual, nuclear families. During this process, families ruled by the father replaced the matrilineal communal system (Reed, 1975, pp. 401–507; Coontz and Henderson, 1986a, pp. 1–42).

Evolutionary anthropologists do not dispute the changeover from matrilineal to patrilineal inheritance but are divided about its roots and the form it took. Engels (1884, pp. 225–251) speculates that inheritance rules during the middle- to upper-Neolithic period based on matrilineal descent became increasingly cumbersome as the owner's own offspring could not inherit. According to mother right, his herd, weapons and right of land usage passed first to his brothers and sisters and to his sister's children or to the descendants of his mother's family. Matrilineal descent was, thus, overthrown as wealth correspondingly increased in favour of men and their need to protect their own property from disintegration within their own gens. The elegant solution was to exchange the egalitarian, diffuse, matrilineal structure of inherited entitlement with a hierarchical, first-born male preference, which consolidated property. Engels contends (ibid., p. 95) that the overthrow of mother right was the 'historic defeat of the female sex' and a decisive revolution:

> The reckoning of descent through the female line and the right of inheritance through the mother ... [was] overthrown and male lineage and the right of inheritance from the father instituted.

Feminist anthropologists, Coontz and Henderson (1986a, pp. 36–42) contend that no such decisive revolution occurred and that the takeover was a gradual development. They speculate that the development of surplus meant that a variety of residence and descent rules (matrilineal/matrilocal and patrilineal/patrilocal) intermingled, but the graduation from communal to kin corporate property led to a greater emphasis on unilineal as patrilineal descent (Coontz and Henderson, 1986b, p. 121) because patrilocal lineages exerted increasing control and reproductive power over in-marrying wives from other clans. Such wives lost their natal, lineage claims and became outsiders, subordinated producers within kin corporate groups where they were no longer owners and had less say over the allocation of consumption versus redistribution (ibid., p. 131).

Patrilocal/patrilineal corporate kin groups with a greater concentration of related males resulted in a mutual reinforcement of hierarchical frameworks between men and between men and women. Matrilocal/matrilineal had different structural, ideological characteristics with work carried out co-operatively among collaterally related kin. Coontz and Henderson (1986b, p. 133) argue that two types of inherited structures coexisted, which support this research argument: the earlier, matrilocal/matrilineal as inclusive and egalitarian, and patrilocal/patrilineal as conical (lineal, hierarchical). Patrilineal kin corporations were better placed to prosper and adapt economically through acquisitive incentives, such as polygamy, and to accumulate resources as male territory, which further elevated patrilineal inheritance as 'god'-given. Matrilineal clans, by contrast, consumed surplus rather than accumulated it hierarchically for exchange.

The changeover was probably more a complex, dialectical, intertwining of old, intermediary and new inheritance rules as old kinship, matrilineal loyalties could not be easily dissolved without appropriate compensations. Reed (1975, pp. 257–269) interprets first-born male sacrifice and bride price, past and present, as such compensatory structures to untie matrilineal kin inheritance claims and loyalties and avoid cannibalism. Despite the onset of primogeniture during the late Neolithic era, matrilineal and patrilineal systems of exchange coexisted as two opposing, overlapping twin entities rather than a peaceful coexistence. In the unresolved, dialectical interchange between the two inheritance models, such fractionation produced progressively richer and more complex inherited forms (Harris, 1968, pp. 66–71).

The changeover in property rules disadvantaged women. Formerly, all property was communally owned and handed down from mother-clans to daughter-clans; now, property was owned by individual men and handed down inter-generationally from father to first-born son. Women were supported by their fathers until their marriage when their husbands took over that responsibility. Men became the principal providers; women with children were relegated to the private realm (dwelling), robbed not only of their public, independent productivity but also of sexual freedom, first, through patrilocal residence and second, through monogamy which became irrefutably linked (Lerner, 1986, pp. 76–122). Under such property rules, only women's sexual attractiveness was valued in its dual function of sexual pleasuring and in the reproduction of legitimatised patrilineal progeny.

Briffault (1931, pp. 245–248) suggests that the patrilineal clan development is a specifically Middle Eastern model, arguing that European land, as horticulture, had been the province of women, which developed without the intervening pastoral stage. Europe never developed a fully pastoral society with men the chief owners of property through their ownership of livestock and harems. European land, broken up into relatively small patches of arable cultivation, remained owned by women (matrilineal) who tilled the land until as late as the twelfth century. The development of agriculture without any antecedent pastoral phase helped enhance the matrilineal position of women through their association with fertility rites. Such rites are missing in pastoral tribes (such as those that existed in the Middle East) that fostered monotheism and primogeniture.

Gimbutas (1989) attributes the spreading influence of patrilineal culture during the Neolithic era to the Kurgan tribes from the Volga basin, South Russia, with their domestication of horses, drive for land acquisition and the development of aggressive armament which opposed the Old European matrilineal, sedentary, peaceful, agricultural lifestyle. Divale and Harris (1976, pp. 521–581) also attribute the growth of warfare to the patrilineal 'male supremacist complex,' that is, from polygamy, bride price, sex restrictions and the elimination of property ownership for women, to demographic concerns about scarcity (land, food) which developed during the

Neolithic Revolution. Both these models, however, equate 'feminine' traits with sedentary fertility (Old Europe) as Eros, and 'masculinity' with invasive aggression (Indo-European) as Thanatos, a polarisation not shared by feminist anthropologists, such as Joyce, who correctly stress that non-binary specificity developed separately from any 'inherited' two-tier sexual specificity. Pre-Celtic British sources (Old Europe) reveal enough evidence of divisive, female, independent traits (Thanatos) without the need to speculatively allocate aggression exclusively to patrilineal cultures (Pokorny, 1908, pp. 66–69).

Likewise, Ardren (2002) has assembled enough evidence through studying signs on ancient codex of ceremonial sculptures to show that ancient Mayan civilisation may have traced their descent through matrilineal inheritance, not only as an occasional anomaly due to the lack of a male heir. Images of powerful women on ancient ceremonial edifices in Tikal, Guatemala, suggest a parallel system of inheritance with women both sharing power *and* passing it on to their sons.

One could argue that the existence and overlapping of dual systems of inheritance: communal under the matrilineal and hierarchical under patrilineal, represent two distinct 'twin' archetypal patterns of human interaction (Eros/Thanatos) which structure themselves in the laws of inheritance: horizontal and hierarchal. Both structures coexist: sometimes they fractionate in a revolutionary Marxist dialectical paradigm (Engels, 1884; Reed, 1975; Chevillard and Leconte, 1986); other times, they co-operate in progressive, parallel, complementary forms (Coontz and Henderson, 1986a). Neither paradigm need preclude the 'other.' The original structure of communal/egalitarian/horizontal elements (matrilineal) is one of fusion, participation mystique and identification with the land (Eros); the second form (patrilineal), based on a hierarchical structure, separates property into distributive surplus and hierarchical values to promote the classification and goals missing from the diffuse elements of the 'first.' Such a structure contains ascendant Thanatos qualities of separation/order/logos and independence. These creative 'twin' forces as inheritance laws behave as 'twins' as they overlap, influence and displace each other in a progressive mix still unresolved today.

The psychological effects of disinheritance: the position of women as 'other'

As we have observed in this chapter, the laws of inheritance, particularly the introduction of primogeniture, have played a major role in the socio-economic, psycho-sexual lives of women. From hypothesising women as equally creative beings with men during Palaeolithic, early Neolithic eras with mixed, interchangeable, twin archetypal characteristics of both Eros and Thanatos, their inherited role gradually diminished as fixed property became owned and controlled under new property rules during the onset of 'civilisation' ca. 3000–2000 BCE when lineage and property changed from matrilineal to patrilineal inheritance under primogeniture. Powerful church creationist doctrine dating back 2000 years played an increasingly potent, inculcating role in Britain in justifying this changeover.

In order to keep excluding women as 'other' from property ownership, creationist differences between the sexes were exacerbated to keep women as the 'lacking' often mad, monstrous twin 'other' (Ussher, 1991, 2006; Creed, 1993; Appignanesi, 2008) and, thus, incapable of owning property.[3] By the end of the nineteenth century, English wives could not administer their own property even if they had any, nor make a will disposing of it, without their husband's consent. The growth of nineteenth-century medical theories about madness, centred on women's inferior, pathological, profane physiology, expanded during the twentieth century to encompass her intellectual inferiority (Daly, 1973, 1978). Psychoanalytical discourse has done little to change the parameters of the *OT* creationist mindset.

The Freudian gender model still adheres to the fixed *OT* patrilineal god the father aggressively guarding his property, including livestock, wives and children, under a castration complex which he passes to his sons. Little attention has been given in psychoanalysis to earlier matrilineal/kin structures where co-operative systems of exchange existed. The active mother is still missing, presumed dead or buried alive as 'un-dead' (Mitchell, 1974; Kristeva, 1989, 1993, 2000; Wieland, 2000).

Labbie suggests (2006, p. 3) that the Lacanian model of gender roles adheres to the patrilineal Middle Ages image of courtly love whereby idle ladies, in masquerade, somehow inspire their troubadours to heroic feats of repetitive frustration in search for the missing grail. Butler (1999, p. 56) describes the Lacanian conundrum of positioning women as other: she explains, 'the masculine subject who "has" the Phallus requires this "Other" to confirm and hence "be" the Phallus in its "extended" sense.' Moving out of the symbolic into the real lives of working women, both past and present seems particularly challenging in psychoanalytical discourse due to its fixation with the phallus. The imaginary remains either a courtly masquerade of the 'feminine' or an extension of the phallus with little room for manoeuvre into the conscious/unconscious independent reality of women themselves.

Analytical psychology,[4] however, does attempt to resurrect an equally active matrilineal/Eros terrain to ego consciousness. Jung's preoccupation with the feminine (1911–1912/1952, paras. 300–418); its psychological influence as mother archetype and complex (1938, paras. 206–258); also as 'black anima' (1954a, paras. 646–648); and his personification of 'animus' and 'anima'[5] as mixed-sex twins, Artemis and Apollo, instead of a male sex twin dyad (1934, paras. 296–340; 1954b, para. 144; 1954a, para. 607), help restore the missing contra-sexual 'other' twin function and grapple with the problem of a single male sex creationist theory. Post-Jungian scholarship expands Jung's concept of 'anima' and 'animus' by offering a framework of flexible gender differentiation (Colman, 1998; Hammond, 2003; Schaverine, 2003; Scherer, 2003; Kast, 2006; McGrath, 2010).

As we have seen, women's real lives change with economic circumstances but their inherited, unconscious, hidden properties remain remarkably intact, ready to re-emerge when economic and social conditions are ripe figs.[6] After the experience of British women's competency during the Second World War, demands for equal job and educational opportunities were difficult to refute. In 1944, full-time education for both sexes was legally introduced and enforced in Britain. It took women about fifty years to catch up with two thousand years of missing higher education, which had been legally denied them under primogeniture (Robinson, 2009). The increasing use of multifaceted skills in modern technology has also promoted women's economic position. The contraceptive pill introduced in the 1960s finally legitimised women's socio-sexual freedom from monogamous contract. In marriage, women can now maintain their own surnames; outside marriage, women can legalise their own offspring, ending eons of untold suffering caused by punitive marital restraints under the legal auspices of primogeniture. This newfound freedom heralds a return to matrilineal kin clan structures at a more complex level, having integrated the focused goal-orientated function of hierarchical primogeniture in the process.

Conclusion

As I show, inheritance laws have exercised a profound influence historically on the psychological lives of both sexes because primogeniture legitimised the inherited position of the 'first-born' male over all 'other(s)' as the owner of property. Primogeniture was itself a response to changing economic conditions, and not just structural development, to justify an innate male superiority. Before such laws were introduced, varying in date, form and intensity, from the exclusive all male Middle East 3000 BCE model to the eleventh-century more mixed European model, men and women shared overlapping gender roles as evolutionary research into Palaeolithic and Neolithic epochs shows. These flexible roles continued longer in Britain and parts of Europe due to a different topography and climate until Christian creationist theories from the Middle East about property surplus became gradually enforced through the spread of monotheistic, ecclesiastical ideals about the 'first' and 'other(s).' The resurrection of the son *not* the daughter provided an easy transfer of land from matrilineal to patrilineal inheritance to increase church wealth and power.

I argue that this transfer required an appropriate, compelling creationist myth to justify it. Highly speculative and irrational in itself, the *OT* Genesis myth has, nevertheless, formed the basis of a 'civilised' mode of exchange because it justifies distribution in an orderly, hierarchical fashion. The earlier matrilineal concept of subsistence changed from fluid to fixed characteristics: women became earthbound and subjugated as 'second' (Eros/horizontal) with questionable intellect: only men, made in the ascended 'sacred' image of god, have the right to punish (Thanatos/logos).

In Britain, older common-law entitlements influenced primogeniture by loosening land as impartible assets through mortgage into fluid commercial, partible capital, which financed industry. The development of two classes in the eighteenth and nineteenth centuries, the middle class and working class, arose out of challenging the restrictive nature of primogeniture. This challenge intensified the twinning, overlapping, substituting relationship between earlier communal distributive structures and primogeniture in their fight for primacy. I argue that without the impulse towards centralising land and property ownership under primogeniture, however harsh, the 'others,' including working men and women, on land and in industry, may have remained diffused and fragmented in horizontal, small, cottage-based industries, powerless to enhance their own hierarchical/Thanatos position in the market place.

The movement from land created the trade union movement that demanded the collective recognition of workers' rights. The fight of women to join trade unions (1875), the right to vote (1918), strike for equal pay, all enhanced their status as a separate, viable, economic and political work force (Thanatos) which finally liberated them from their creationist, passive, contained, gender role (Eros) under male auspices. It heralded a return to more horizontal cultural and economic systems of sexual exchange at a higher level (Lewenhak, 1977; Miles, 1989).

By examining the laws of inheritance as 'twins' throughout history and speculating which twin (trait) came 'first,' one accesses the hidden, creative, overlapping, substituting, dialectical process as 'twins' at work. This model shows how each archetypal 'twin,' 'rationally' and 'irrationally' has structured, deconstructed and restructured itself, first, as matrilineal/Eros/communal; second, as patrilineal/Thanatos/hierarchical to reach a modern, 'twinning,' redistributive synthesis.

Notes

1 I suggest that misogyny developed out of ambivalent feelings towards the exploitation of feminine creativity, which could not be publicly acknowledged for fear of retribution and loss of profitability. This fear became displaced in the unconscious as hatred of the devalued aspects of the sexualised female form, in the shape of temptress, whore, vampire etc. The sexually safe, virginal, unploughed aspects of the feminine as fertile land untouched by agricultural exploitation became idealised, for example, as the *sacred* Virgin Mary, the embodiment of an immaculate conception, who gives birth without being touched by the exploitative, human hand. Lilith as vampire and Mary Magdalene as whore are her shadow *profane* twin counterparts. I interpret such splitting as an attempt to resolve the deep conflict of how to create new life without damaging the original, sacred quality of the

first. Sweet, chubby Eros and sharp, skeleton-faced Thanatos also reflect images of this split: both are equally powerful, ambivalent and overlapping forces, hence their twin-ship status.
2   Fox (2011, pp. 226–259), in particular, elucidates a strong evolutionary rhythmic connection between the pre-modern, primordial, tribal mores and the modern, 'civilised' mindset.
3   Nye (2004, p. 16) describes Kant's prudish, misogynist attitude to women as one of abstinence, the sexual act described as a source of degradation, a commonly held attitude by German ascetic philosophers.
4   I examine the in-depth contribution of Jungian psychology in disseminating inheritance laws, particularly in revitalising the matrilineal/Eros twin from the incestuous grip of the patrilineal/Thanatos twin in Brodersen (2016) chapter 7.
5   I expand Jung's concept of 'anima' and 'animus' as inherited images of 'feminine' and 'masculine' specificities by freeing each from her/his gendered perspective. Both sexes display 'anima' and 'animus' characteristics which I interpret as intrapsychic 'twins': Eros/anima/fusion; Thanatos/animus/separation. I expand upon this premise in Brodersen (2016) chapters 4, 5, 6 & 7.
6   The study of same-sex, second-born Thanatos girl twins in Brodersen (2016) chapter 5, section 2 twin research reveals the same preparedness.

References

Appignanesi, L. (2008). *Mad, Bad, Sad: A History of Women and the Mind Doctors from 1800 to the Present*, London: Virago Press.
Ardren, T. (ed.) (2002). *Ancient Maya Women*, Walnut Creek, CA: AltaMira Press.
Bachofen, J.J. (1871). *Myth, Religion and Mother Right*, Princeton, NJ: Princeton University Press, 1967.
The Bible (1989). *The Old Testament*. In *The Revised English Bible*, Oxford and Cambridge: Oxford University Press.
Boas, F. (1948). *Race, Language and Culture*, New York: Macmillan.
Briffault, R. (1931). *The Mothers: The Matrilineal Theory of Social Origins*, New York: Macmillan.
Brodersen, E. (2016). *Laws of Inheritance, A post-Jungian study of twins and the relationship between the first and other(s)*, Hove and New York: Routledge.
Butler, J. (1999). *Gender Trouble*, New York and London: Routledge.
Chevillard, N. & Leconte, S. (1986). 'The Dawn of Lineage Societies,' in S. Coontz & P. Henderson (eds.), *Women's Work, Men's Property, The Origins of Class and Gender*, London: Verso, pp. 76–107.
Colman, W. (1998). 'Contra-Sexuality and the Unknown Soul,' in I. Alister & C. Hauke (eds.), *Contemporary Jungian Analysis*, London and New York: Routledge, pp. 198–207.
Coontz, S. & Henderson, P. (1986a). 'Introduction: Explanations of Male Dominance,' in S. Coontz & P. Henderson (eds.), *Women's Work, Men's Property, The Origins of Class and Gender*, London: Verso, pp. 1–42.
Coontz, S. & Henderson, P. (1986b). 'Property Forms, Political Power and Female Labour in the Origins of Class and State Societies,' in S. Coontz & P. Henderson (eds.), *Women's Work, Men's Property: The Origins of Class and Gender*, London: Verso, pp. 108–155.

Creed, B. (1993). *The Monstrous-Feminine: Film, Feminism, Psychoanalysis*, London and New York: Routledge.
Daly, M. (1973). *Beyond God the Father*, London: The Women's Press, 1995.
Daly, M. (1978). *Gyn/Ecology, The Metaethics of Radical Feminism*. Boston: Beacon Press
Darwin, C. (1859). *The Origin of Species*, London and New York: Penguin, 1958.
Darwin, C. (1871). *The Descent of Man*. London: Penguin Classics, 2004.
Davis-Kimball, J. (2002). *Warrior Women, An Archaeologist's Search*, New York: Warner Books.
Divale, W. & Harris, M. (1976). 'Population, Warfare and the Male Supremacist Complex,' *American Anthropologist*, 78, pp. 521–538.
Engels, F. (1884). *The Origin of the Family, Private Property and The State*, London: Pathfinder, 1972.
Fox, R. (1994). *The Challenge of Anthropology: Old Encounters and New Excursions*, New Brunswick, NJ. Transaction Publishers.
Fox, R. (1997). *Conjectures and Confrontations: Science, Evolution, Social Concern*, New Brunswick, NJ. Transaction Publishers.
Fox, R. (2000) (Intro.) Morgan, L.H. (1871/2000). *Ancient Society*. New Brunswick, NJ: Transaction Publishers.
Fox, R. (2011). *The Tribal Imagination, Civilisation and the Savage Mind*, Cambridge, MA and London: Harvard University Press.
Freud, S. (1938) 'Application. In Moses and Monotheism (III),' in *Collected Works. Vol. 13, The Origins of Religion*, London and New York: Penguin, 2.
Gimbutas, A. (1989). *The Language of the Goddess*, London: Thames & Hudson.
Goldenweiser, A. (1937). *Anthropology: An Introduction of Primitive Culture*, New York: Appleton-Century-Crofts.
Hammond, M. (2003). 'The Elusive Elixir: Aspects of the Feminine in a Male Patient,' in E. Christopher & H. Solomon (eds.), *Contemporary Jungian Clinical Practice*, London: Karnac.
Hann, C. (ed.) (1998). *Property Relations: Reviewing the Anthropological Tradition*, Cambridge and New York: Cambridge University Press.
Harris, M. (1968). *The Rise of Anthropological Theory, A History of Theories of Culture*, updated edition, Walnut Creek, CA, Langham, New York and Oxford: AltaMira Press, 2001.
Harris, M. (2001). *Cultural Materialism*, Walnut Creek, CA and Oxford: AltaMira Press.
Hoebel, E.A. (1984). *Anthropology, Law and Genetic Inheritance*, London: Elsevier.
Hollimon, S. (2006). 'The Archeology of Nonbinary Genders in Native North America,' in S.M. Nelson (ed.), *Handbook of Gender in Archeology*, Walnut Creek, CA, and Oxford: AltaMira Press, pp. 435–450.
Joyce, R.A. (2006). 'Theories of Embodiment and Anthropological Imagination: Making Bodies Matter,' in P. Geller & M. Stockett, (eds.), *Feminist Anthropology: Past, Present and Future*, Philadelphia, PA: University of Pennsylvania Press.
Joyce, R.A. (2008). *Ancient Bodies, Ancient Lives*, London: Thames & Hudson.
Jung, C.G. (1911–12/1952). 'Symbols of the Mother and of Rebirth,' in *Collected Works, Vol. 5, Symbols of Transformation* (2nd ed.), London: Routledge and Kegan Paul, 1995.
Jung, C.G. (1934). 'Anima and Animus,' in *Collected Works, Vol. 7, Two Essays on Analytical Psychology* (2nd ed.), London: Routledge and Kegan Paul, 1990.

Jung, C.G. (1938). 'The Psychology of Rebirth,' in *Collected Works, Vol. 9i, The Archetypes of the Collective Unconscious* (2nd ed.) London: Routledge and Kegan Paul, 1991.
Jung, C.G. (1954a.) 'Adam and Eve,' in *Collected Works, Vol. 14, Mysterium Coniunctionis* (2nd ed.), London: Routledge and Kegan Paul, 1992.
Jung, C.G. (1954b.) 'The Personification of the Opposites,' in *Collected Works, Vol. 14, Mysterium Coniunctionis* (2nd ed.), London: Routledge and Kegan Paul, 1992.
Kast, V. (2006). 'Anima/Animus,' in R. Papadopoulos (ed.), *The Handbook of Jungian Psychology*, New York and London: Routledge, pp. 113–129.
Kristeva, J. (1989). *Black Sun*, New York and Chichester: Columbia University Press.
Kristeva, J. (1993). *New Maladies of the Soul*, New York and Chichester: Columbia University Press.
Kristeva, J. (2000). *The Sense and Non-sense of Revolt*, New York and Chichester: Columbia University Press.
Kuklick, H. (ed.) (2008). *A New Theory of Anthropology*, Malden, MA and Oxford: Blackwell Publishing.
Kus, S. (2006). 'The Midst of the Moving Waters,' in P. Geller & M. Stockett, (eds.), *Feminist Anthropology: Past, Present and Future*, Philadelphia, PA: University of Pennsylvania Press, pp. 105–114.
Labbie, E.F. (2006). *Lacan's Medievalism*, Minnesota, MN: Minnesota University Press.
Leach, E.R. (1961). *Rethinking Anthropology*, London: Athlone Press.
Leibowitz, L. (1986). 'In The Beginning...,' in S. Coontz & P. Henderson(eds.), *Women's Work, Men's Property, The Origins of Gender and Class*, London: Verso, pp. 43–75.
Lerner, G. (1986). *The Creation of Patriarchy*, New York and Oxford: Oxford University Press.
Levi-Strauss, C. (1963). *Structural Anthropology*, New York: Basic Books.
Levi-Strauss, C. (1967).*The Elementary Structure of Kinship*, New York: Beacon.
Lewenhak, S. (1977). *Women and Trade Unions*, New York: Ernest Benn Publishers.
Lowie, R. (1937). *History of Ethnological Theory*, New York: Farrar and Rinehart.
Malinowski, B. (1927). *Sex and Repression in Savage Societies*, New York: Meridian, 1960.
McGrath, S.J. (2010). 'Sexuation on Jung and Lacan,' *International Journal of Jungian Studies*, 2(1), pp. 1–20, March 2010.
Miles, R. (1989). *The Women's History of the World*, London: Harper Collins, 1993.
Millett, K. (1971). *Sexual Politics*, London: Sphere.
Mitchell, J. (1974). *Psychoanalysis and Feminism*, London and New York: Penguin, 2000.
Morgan, L.H. (1877). *Ancient Society*, New Brunswick, NJ: Transaction Publishers, 2000.
Nye, A. (2004). *Feminism and Modern Philosophy*, London and New York: Routledge.
Palmer, M. (1997). *Freud and Jung on Religion*, London and New York: Routledge.
Parsons, T. (1971). *The System of Modern Societies*. Englewood Cliffs, NJ: Prentice Hall.
Patterson, T.C.P. (2009). *Karl Marx, Anthropologist*, Oxford and New York: Berg.
Perry, W.J. (1923). *The Children of the Sun*, Cottonwood, AZ: Adventures Unlimited, 2004.
Pokorny, J. (1908). 'The Origin of Druidism,' from the *Celtic Review*, 5(17), pp. 60–73, in J. Matthews (ed.), *The Druid Source Book*, London: Blandford Press, 1997.

Radcliffe-Brown, A.R. (1965). *Structure and Function in Primitive Society*. New York: Free Press.
Reed, E. (1975). *Woman's Evolution*, London: Pathfinder.
Reed, E. (1978). *Sexism and Science*, London: Pathfinder.
Robinson, J. (2009). *Bluestockings*, London and New York: Penguin.
Sahlins, M. (1974). *Stone Age Economics*, London and New York: Routledge, 2004.
Schaverine, J. (2003). 'The Psychology of the Feminine and Contra-sexuality in Analytical Psychology,' in R. Withers (ed.), *Controversies in Analytical Psychology*, London and New York: Routledge, pp. 282–292.
Scherer, A. (2003). 'Jung and The Feminine,' in R. Withers (ed.), *Controversies in Analytical Psychology*, London and New York: Routledge, pp. 293–301.
Schmidt, W. (1935). 'The Position of Women with Regard to Property in Primitive Society,' *American Anthropologist*, 37, pp. 244–256.
Schmidt, W. (1939). *The Culture Historical Method of Ethnology*, S.A. Siber (Trans.), New York: Fortuny's.
Smith, E.C. (1928). *In The Beginning: The Origin of Civilisation*, New York: Morrow.
Smith, M.C., Kish, B.J., & Crawford, C.B. (1987). *Inheritance of Wealth as Human Kin Investment*, London: Elsevier.
Tylor, E.B. (1871). *Origins of Culture, Part 1 of Primitive Culture*, New York: Harper Collins, 1958.
Tylor, E.B. (1881). *Anthropology*, Ann Arbor, MI: University of Michigan Press, 1960.
Ussher, J. (1991). *Women's Madness, Misogyny or Mental Illness*, New York and London: Harvester.
Ussher, J. (2006). *Managing the Monstrous Feminine: Regulating the Reproductive Body*, London and New York: Routledge.
Von Franz, M.L. (1988). *Psyche and Matter*, Boston, MA and London: Shambhala, 1992.
White, L. (1959). 'The Concept of Evolution in Cultural Anthropology,' in B.J. Meggers (ed.), *Evolution and Anthropology, A Centennial Appraisal*, Washington, DC: The Anthropological Society of Washington, pp. 106–125.
Wieland, C. (2000). *The Undead Mother*, London: Karnac.

Chapter 4

From emancipation to liberation
A neo-Jungian critique of Theodor Adorno

Stefano Carpani

Adorno and Freud: an overview[1]

To provide a comprehensive and detailed view of Adorno's perspective on Freud is a task that would require a whole volume of its own. Here, therefore, I will simply examine Adorno's critique of Freud and psychoanalysis and its relationship with society.[2] Consequently, I will point out that traditional sociology has not been able to examine anyone other than Freud. To redress this, I will employ C.G. Jung and Mary Watkins as possible alternatives when examining society.

I propose that Adorno took Freud and his dogma as the only source from which to draw in the context of psychoanalytic investigation.[3] I propose that Adorno omitted any other view (e.g. Jung and Adler as well as the post-Freudians) and made of Freud and his dogma a model (paralleled by Marx's view of society) that afforded no space to pluralism or to other emerging views in line with the developments of society and within psychoanalytic theory's own development. Adorno paired Marx's theory with Freud's to build a theory of emancipation in the pursuit of happiness but failed to take into consideration that psychoanalysis does not simply equal Freud and does not lead to happiness. This view and approach have been the mainstream in sociology up to the present day. It is timely, therefore, for mainstream sociology to broaden its views of psychoanalysis.

Adorno studied and respected Freud's work, although he did not agree with Freud's viewpoints and conclusions. Adorno criticised psychoanalysis and Freud in *Minima Moralia* (1951/1975), which I have selected here as my main source of investigation[4] (and which I will parallel with Luigi Ceppa's introduction (1994) to Adorno's *Minima Moralia* and Jessica Benjamin's 'The End of Internalization: Adorno's Social Psychology' (1977)).

Adorno concentrated much of his work on the concepts of emancipation (within modern capitalist societies), pleasure and the dichotomy between instinct and reason. It could be said that he was obsessed with the working-class struggle towards emancipation and pretensions of happiness. In fact, for Adorno, emancipation meant reaching a state of *happiness*, which he saw as a forbidden state due to the oppression of the working class by the bourgeoisie. Therefore, Adorno's vast body of work focused on power relations, the dichotomy between emancipation and liberation in the pursuit of happiness. Emancipation, for Adorno, can only occur when authority is internalised and accepted.

According to Adorno, 'Freud's limitation lies in not having fully developed the most radical and dialectical aspects of his investigation'[5] (Ceppa, 1979/1994: XXXII), as if Freud had stopped halfway. In this regard, aphorism 37, titled 'The Side of the pleasure principle', is key. In this aphorism, Adorno initially discusses the concept of *transfer* and one's own annulment of oneself. He lashes out against this concept, in which he sees the perpetuation of oppression and dominance by society to the detriment of the oppressed individual. Thus, Adorno emphasises that the transference, which leads 'to the annulment of the self which was once brought about involuntarily and beneficially by erotic self-abandonment is already a pattern of the relax-dominated, follow-my-leader behavior which liquidates, together with all intellect, the analysts who have betrayed it'.

Adorno (again aphorism 37) attacks Freud in the context of the emancipation of the oppressed and the achievement – as the ultimate goal – of happiness and enjoyment. He (aphorism 37) emphasises that

> as a late opponent of hypocrisy, [Freud] stands ambivalently between desire for the open emancipation of the oppressed, an apology for open oppression. Reason is for him a mere superstructure [...] because he rejects the end, remote to meaning, impervious to reason, which alone could prove the means, reason, to be reasonable: pleasure.

In this regard, Jessica Benjamin (1977: 42) claims that at the core of 'critical theory's analysis of modern capitalism is a paradox about the nature of resistance to domination' and she highlights that there are aspects of 'consciousness where this resistance might be located – critical reason, individuation, integrity and ultimately resistance itself – [that] are tied to the process of internalising authority. As a result, the rejection of authority can only take place through its prior acceptance.' Hence, she continues, according to the Frankfurters, 'the only possible resistance to authority is located in the same process of internalization'. Therefore, emancipation can only occur if internalisation and acceptance of the authority/dominator have previously taken place.

Rather than examining internalisation and acceptance of authority, Benjamin (1977: 43) proposes examining mutuality and, to this end, she poses the following question: 'Could not the potential of emancipation be grounded in an intersubjective theory of personality, rather than an individual psychology of internalization?' Her response is that 'This possibility would call into question one of the major themes of critical theory's acceptance of Freudian theory: that ultimately it is our natural impulses, our "human nature" including love and desire, which betray us'.

I propose that today, emancipation from authority cannot occur due either to its internalisation and acceptance as proposed by Adorno or due to its mutuality, as proposed by Benjamin. Instead, the (inner) process of clarification and knowledge is key. I will explore this idea in more depth below, having first examined Adorno's views on instincts.

Adorno (aphorism 37) also confronted Freud on the concept of instinct:

> In the teeth of bourgeois ideology, he tracked down conscious actions materialistically to their unconscious instinctual basis, but at the same time concurred with the bourgeois contempt of instinct which is itself a product of precisely the rationalization that he dismantled.

Adorno continues (again aphorism 37): 'He [Freud] explicitly aligns himself, in the words of the *Introductory Lectures*, with "the general evaluation ... which places social goals higher than the fundamentally selfish sexual ones."' In this regard, aphorism 37 is again key. Ceppa (1979/1994: XXXII) underlines that, according to Adorno:

> Freud has not been able to fully control the weight of the mutual mediation between Es and I, pleasure and spirit. Thus, he blocked the formative process under the constellation (specifically bourgeois) of the drive sacrifice and renunciation, instead of illuminating it in the eschatological perspective of the drive satisfaction.[6]

Thus Adorno criticised Freud because he (Freud) 'concurred with the bourgeois contempt of instinct'. This is an interesting point when one considers the current age. Based on my sociological and clinical experience, I propose that today too (more than 100 years after Freud's theorisation and almost 70 years after Adorno's *Minima Moralia*), we can still recognise people's 'contempt for instinct and physical pleasure'. As was the case 100 years ago, this has nothing to do with the bourgeoisie; it has to do with human nature and how societies are built. And this is because, as emphasised by Philip Kime,[7] 'Freud mostly wrote about psychopathology and therefore by definition about situations where instinct caused a problem. Indeed, one could argue that it was repression of instinct that Freud was against, not instinct itself.'

Adorno claims that, for Freud, 'The instinctual sacrifice can develop for him in removal or sublimation' and from this 'the history of civilization coincides with the curse of Oedipus and with the threat of castration' (Ceppa, 1979/1994: XXXII). Adorno, instead, proposes 'a mediation of pleasure and spirit (*Lust* and *Geist*) that moves from the extreme – ideal – points of their archaic identity and their future reconciliation' (Ceppa, 1979/1994: XXXII). In aphorism 37, Adorno also states:

> Truth is abandoned to relativity and people to power. He alone who could situate utopia in blind somatic pleasure, which, satisfying the ultimate intention, is intentionless, has a stable and valid idea of truth. In Freud's work, however, the dual hostility toward mind and pleasure, whose common root psychoanalysis has given us the means for discovering, is unintentionally repressed.

In *King, Warrior, Magician, Lover*, Robert Moore and Doug Gillette (1991: 22) recognise that when Freud talked about the *Id*, 'he saw it as the "primitive" or "infantile" drives, amoral, forceful, and full of God-like pretensions'. They highlight that it comprises 'the underlying push of impersonal Nature itself, concerned only with satisfying the unlimited needs of the child'. Aligning with my proposal that the Frankfurters and sociology did not look beyond Freud's theory, they emphasise the need to examine Alfred Adler and his concept of 'the hidden "power drive" in each of us as the hidden superiority complex that covers our real sense of vulnerability, weakness, and inferiority'. They also examine Heinz Kohut who discussed '"the grandiose self-organization," which is demanding of ourselves and others in ways that can never be fulfilled'. Therefore, they both suggest investigating the most recent psychoanalytic theories as well as Jung's concept of the Divine Child as 'a vital aspect of the Archetypal Self' in order to approach things from a plural perspective.

In this spirit, I propose – as an alternative to Freud's and Adorno's views – examining Jung's approach in his essay 'Stages of life' (*CW* 8: 749/795) in which he proposes that instincts correspond to a primitive state, which he calls *natura primitiva* (when humans are unconscious). Jung (*CW* 8: 749) argues that 'If psychic life consisted only of self-evident matters of fact which on a primitive level is still the case, we could content ourselves with a sturdy empiricism'. Jung also claims – and this I believe is crucial when examining Adorno, Freud, instinct and sublimation – that 'It is just man's turning away from instinct – his opposing himself to instinct – that creates consciousness'. To explain this *turning away from instinct that creates consciousness*, Jung uses the Adam and Eve allegory of the tree of knowledge and claims that (*CW* 8: 749) 'Instinct is nature and seeks to perpetuate nature, whereas consciousness can only seek culture or its denial'. He then adds 'As long as we are still submerged in nature, we are unconscious, and we live in the security of instinct which knows no problems'. In the allegory of Adam and Eve, they are kicked out of the Garden of Eden because they cannot resist temptation (instinct). At the same time, this can be seen as a development from an unconscious state (parents' domination and control) to a conscious one where Adam and Eve need to become responsible for their actions (therefore, mature enough to live their lives, not under the protective control of parents or within their garden). Therefore, when leaving Paradise, they are confronted with the tasks of adulthood. In fact, ceding to temptation could also be seen as a type of emancipation.

In this regard, Jung (*CW* 8: 751) asserts that 'Every problem, therefore, brings the possibility of a widening of consciousness, but also the necessity of saying goodbye to childlike unconsciousness and trust in nature'. Jung claims that when humans are in a state of *natura primitiva* [when humans are unconscious], they cannot do much else than to follow their instincts. Only when they go through the (inner) process of clarification and knowledge, can they become conscious. However, this becoming conscious – I propose – does not exclusively mean sublimation as described by Freud.

In aphorism 38, Adorno turns his gaze towards psychoanalysis, writing that it 'prides itself on restoring the capacity for pleasure, which is impaired by neurotic illness'. He then adds in aphorism 40:

> Psychoanalysis itself is castrated by its conventionalization: sexual motives, partly disavowed and partly approved, are made totally harmless but also totally insignificant. With the fear they instil vanishes the joy they might procure. Thus, psychoanalysis falls victim to the very replacement of the appropriate super-ego by a stubbornly adopted, unrelated, external one, that it taught us itself to understand. The last grandly-conceived theorem of bourgeois self-criticism has become a means of making bourgeois self-alienation, in its final phase, absolute, and of rendering ineffectual the lingering awareness of the ancient wound, in which lies hope of a better future.

I propose that Adorno's vision is limited and that he does not contemplate the different psychoanalytic approaches, particularly those antagonistic to the Freudian approach (e.g. Jung and Adler, both driven to the liberation of the individual from a non-materialistic whole). Therefore, Adorno's problem is that, despite talking about transcendence, he remains imprisoned in the class struggle for emancipation in the pursuit of happiness.

Adorno's vision seems to me idealistic, because psychoanalysis is quite different from how he pictures it. I propose psychoanalysis as a process of *transformation* in which the analyst *accompanies* the patient (Watkins, 2003), helping the patient – as emphasised by Giegerich[8] – 'to get out of their own traps' and 'to understand who they are and what they want'. Thereby, living their own nature.

In this regard, Stefan Zweig (1931/2015: 23) writes that the 'reason and mission' of Freud's psychoanalysis 'was merely to clarify the extremes, not to reconcile it'. He also adds that 'Freud's combative absolutism always requires a decisive pro or con, a yes or a no, never a "one side or the other", never a "maybe" and a "meanwhile"'. Zweig then goes on to highlight that 'the half probable and approximate things have no value for him: only the full, one hundred percent truth attracts him'.[9] I wonder if this absolutistic vision is correct and up to speed with our current epoch or if it is, rather, a daughter of its time. I also wonder whether the Frankfurters are in line with Zweig's absolutistic proposal, namely of Freud and psychoanalysis as masters of the full truth. Marcuse's view, as I outlined elsewhere,[10] is going this way. As an alternative, I propose employing Jung's *I do not know* attitude, an approach that bridges the full truth and its opposite, where what counts is not the fixation of opposites but how to bridge these in the interests of the patient seeking clarification and knowledge. One could say, following Kime[11] again, that

> 'absolutism' in Freud isn't merely a methodological device rather than a real approach to truth. There is a use in stating clear, bold statements in empirical science so that they can be tested easily. Whether or not one thinks that psychoanalysis is 'scientific', that is certainly how Freud saw it.

I intentionally leave this question unanswered here.

Zweig (1931/2015: 17) emphasises that Freud's great achievement was to give to humanity the opportunity for clarification. Since Freud's focus was on clarifying and not on the pursuit of happiness, according to Zweig, Freud helped humanity to attain depth rather than happiness. For Zweig, Freud's work has given man the opportunity to clarify and deepen. Why, then, do the Frankfurters speak of emancipation and happiness? I propose that – basing my argument on insights derived from the clinical application of psychoanalysis – emancipation is not possible without the (inner) process of clarification and knowledge. Otherwise, it is merely compensation and leads to sublimation of the unconscious elements. Internalisation alone is not sufficient; it must also bring clarification and knowledge of unconscious contents. Only in this way can emancipation be achieved. In my paper titled *The Consequences of Freedom* (Carpani, 2020a), I proposed, following Jung, that clarification and knowledge are equal to inner meditation. In his essay, 'Self-knowledge', Jung (*CW* 14, paras. 707–708) claimed that 'what I call coming to terms with the unconscious the alchemists called "meditation"' and added, citing Ruland, that meditation is 'an Internal talk of one person with another who is invisible, as in the invocation of the Deity, or communion with one's self, or with one's good angel'.

Building on Adorno's internalisation and Jessica Benjamin's mutuality, I propose that, thanks to clarification and knowledge, one can know about the authority (consciously or unconsciously dominating), and on that basis build the premises for a dialectical relation which will eventually bring you to accept it (although not mandatorily internalising it) and – even more eventually – to mutuality. However, for a mutual relation to occur, there is a need for both parties to accept that mutuality.

In my view, emancipation equals *liberation*. Mary Watkins (2003: 3) suggests replacing the term 'development' with 'liberation', because 'with regard to economic and cultural progress, "development" of one group seems often to require an oppression of the other'. She adds that 'a dominant culture's idea of development is too often imposed on a culture, depriving it of undertaking its own path of development' (2003: 3).

In her discussion of ancient Hebraic tradition, Mary Watkins (2003: 2) noted that it is the capacity for dialogue, not reason, that distinguishes humankind from other living creatures. Such dialogue takes place with oneself, with one's neighbour, and with God (Niebuhr, 1955, cited in Watkins, 2003: 2) and 'the capacity for dialogue is a necessary precondition for human liberation' (2003: 2), particularly 'from rigid, stereotypic, and unidimensional narrowness' (2003: 2).

As one of the few psychoanalysts[12] to have worked on the concept of liberation, Watkins is undoubtedly useful to this research and her work is fundamental (when considering psychoanalysis as a political tool and when looking at emancipation) to examining current society and the social. Watkins claims that liberation opens one 'to the polyphony of thought, comprised of multiple voices and perspectives, best mediated by dialogue' (2003: 2). In this view, liberation is based 'on a paradigm of interdependence, where the liberation of one is intimately tied to the liberation of the other' (2003: 4). In this sense, 'the other' may comprise 'economic, political, sociocultural, spiritual, and psychological' entities (2003: 4). Thus, liberation – in my opinion – is the very thing that psychosocial studies seek to investigate.

Watkins also claimed that '"the other" – be it part of oneself, be it one's neighbour or enemy, nature – can be silenced, used, abused, destroyed' (2003: 4). Without liberation, there can be no development, and this is fundamental when viewing psychoanalysis as a 'relational dialogue' between two (or more) individuals, in the process of becoming oneself. Watkins (2003: 6) queries, however, whether it is 'likely for one to be able to achieve inner liberation while part of an oppressive cultural system? Does not liberation in one's daily context support liberation of thought?' The answer she provides is that one must 'maintain one's own voice amidst the fray of relationship' (Watkins, 2003: 23), since dialogue ultimately requires both 'the capacity to deeply receive the other and the capacity to receive oneself' (Watkins, 2003: 26).

> Dialogue – Watkins claims – "is both a fact of our givenness and a deep potentiality of our being. From our very beginning, we are 'thrown' into a multiplicity – ancestors, family, trees, rivers, earth, animals, neighbours. In the words of Jung (*CW* 7: 477), 'The self comprises infinitely more than the mere ego, as symbols have shown since time immemorial. It is just as much another or others as it is the ego. Individuation does not exclude the world but includes it.' Thus, we are always selves-in-relation or selves-in-dialogue. What is at stake is the kind of relationship we are in, and the paths from it to a manner of dialogical relationship that liberates being (Watkins, 2003: 10/11).

Suffice it for now, however, to note Watkins' (2003: 5) claim that 'in the most private of the dialogues in our dreams and fantasies, in the most intimate portions of our conversations with ourselves, we come upon the metabolization of culture, economics, and politics', which allows us 'to transcend culture' and become liberated. From this, it could be argued that Watkins – following Hillman – views liberation mystically, therefore cutting it off from the dayworld claims of ordinary people. I would, however, refute this notion: Watkins develops from Hillman's perspective in claiming that our thought process, our inner critic, is a mélange of voices from our past – mother, father, teacher – as well as the structural resonance of school and workplaces. Thus, she (2003: 6) says of the interior, the imaginal:

> It is a distillation of history, culture, religion, and nature. If we can hear how the intimate, so called interior, dialogues of thought and dream represent the public, the cultural and the economic, then can we continue to believe that these dialogues can deeply transform without attention to interpersonal, cultural, ecological, and economic life?

Adorno (aphorism 39), contrary to Watkins, emphasises that psychoanalysis 'expropriates the individual by allocating him its happiness'. He (aphorism 40) also claims that 'Instead of working to gain self-awareness, the initiates become adept at subsuming all instinctual conflicts as inferiority complex, mother-fixation, extroversion and introversion, to which they are in reality inaccessible'. This point is important for two reasons. First, because Adorno's view is opposite to that of Zweig. Second, because in his reference to the complex of inferiority, maternal bonds, extroverted and introverted, we may recognise his familiarity with some classical Jungian themes. But why did Adorno not look beyond Freud? Elsewhere, I have proposed that this could be related to his loyalty to Durkheim's[13] view of psychology and the Frankfurt school's inability to go beyond Freud's dogma and examine the irrational side of the psyche. Finally, making of Jung a persona non grata in twentieth-century sociology, the Frankfurters saw Jung's psychology – following Walter Benjamin (cited in Samuels, 1993: 295/296) – as 'the devil's work' and an 'auxiliary service to National Socialism'.

If Adorno had looked seriously beyond Freud (and possibly at Jung), he might have realised that psychoanalysis undoubtedly provides the work of reflection on oneself (particularly Jung's school). This would have allowed Adorno to grasp that the patient – contrary to his assertion – does not '[end] up being satisfied with an illusory recovery obtained through the integration of the patient into his perverse environment' (Ceppa, 1979/1994: XXXIV).

When examining psychoanalysis and society, Adorno (aphorism 39) writes with regard to psychology that 'in the bottomless frauds of mere inwardness [...] is reflected what bourgeois society has practiced for all time with outward property'. He then concludes that 'psychology repeats in the case of properties what was done to property. It expropriates the individual by allocating him its happiness'.

I claim that this is an incorrect view (albeit in line with critical theory's approach), and I propose instead substituting this view with that of Jung as well as relational psychoanalysis; they claim that patient and analyst are equal co-participants in the transformation of both, who mutually affect each other. Therefore, there is no top-down relation, as in Adorno's view. Instead, there is mutuality. Additionally, if Adorno had examined Jung, he might have realised that psychoanalysis does not merely help the patient to fit in with his/her own class and culture or society, but enables him/her to clarify who he/she is and what he/she wants, as suggested by Giegerich (2010: 233). Psychoanalysis investigates freedom and enables the individual to 'choose' to become free or not, although freedom is only for the courageous.

Ceppa (1979/1994: XXXIV) also stresses that, for Adorno, the 'psychology of the ego, runs the risk of betraying, in the name of social adaptation, the original anarchic, subversive, hedonistic inspiration of psychoanalysis'. However, psychoanalysis is not merely about social adaptation. Instead, following Jung (*CW* 8: 794), I propose that 'a life directed to an aim is in general better, richer, and healthier than an aimless one, and that it is better to go forwards with the stream of time than backwards against it'. This purpose is key to understanding why the wish for emancipation alone, without clarification and knowledge of one's own purpose, does not help to overcome oppression.

Moreover, following Shamdasani (Hillman and Shamdasani, 2013: 96), I wish to disrupt Adorno's vision of psychoanalysis and society (taking, here, individuation and psychoanalysis as synonyms): 'Individuation is an opening to the contemporary world, an opening to the dead and history.' Following Hillman (Hillman and Shamdasani, 2013: 96), 'It is an opening to the dead and the deeply personal. And the deeply personal is connecting back through history, it's connecting to all that's been left out and forgotten.' Therefore, Hillman (Hillman and Shamdasani, 2013: 96) claims that individuation is 'the process of connection or restoration or remembrance. The process of remembering. Recollecting the forms that animate us, the forms that are neglected, forgotten, mainly feared. Not ours.' Hillman (Hillman and Shamdasani, 2013: 92) also highlights that the purpose of individuation 'is to enable someone to envisage new possibilities, is to imagine new ways of consideration'. However, this view is antithetic to Adorno's view and truly speaks of the emancipation of the oppressed. It is about the individual and his/her being in the world in connection with his/her own individuality, ancestors and community, the collective and the environment (therefore, culture and society), and it is also finalistic! Thus, Adorno's vision of psychoanalysis (anarchic, subversive and hedonistic) is naive, and does not allow the individual to recognise and deal with his/her shadow; that is, one's dark (immature, undeveloped) side.

Leonardo Ceppa (1979/1994: XXIX) states that for Adorno, the human being (or *man* in the old-style gender-certain lexicon) cannot be other than in relation to his/her class and work. If we follow this view, however, we afford little space to the subject's own transformation and search for clarification and knowledge (where these are the only tools for transformation) and spirituality. By transformation, I do not mean the move from an original inferior state – e.g. working class – into something superior. This would merely be Adlerian compensation. Rather, by transformation (as a consequence of the process of clarification and knowledge), I mean an understanding of who one is and what one wants, beyond class, gender, religion, ethnicity, nationality and a Marxian predetermined 'objective' identity.

While I agree with Adorno that psychoanalysis must be emancipatory (Ceppa, 1979/1994: XXXIV), for me, it must be emancipatory – following Jung, Kast (1993) and Hillman (1996) – from one's own complexes. This emancipation leads to the discovery of one's own place in society. Therefore, psychoanalysis is emancipation only when it follows a process of clarification and knowledge gained about oneself (Hillman's concept of remembering is fundamental). Without this, there is no emancipation.

I also agree with Adorno (aphorism 34) that 'the almost insoluble task is to let neither the power of other, nor our own powerlessness, stupefy us'; however, for me – again – this is merely separation from one's own complexes and it might help to move away from a one-sided view of the world based on domination, on the idea of victim vs. perpetrator. Therefore, I claim that Adorno's view is *passé* in the twenty-first century's affluent societies. His view that the human being is objectively positioned by birth in *certainties* such as class, gender, religion, ethnicity and nation, was appropriate – as Beck and Beck-Gernsheim (2002) highlighted – within the constraints of modernity. However, in a second-modern (Beck and Beck-Gernsheim, 2002), twenty-first-century affluent and post-certain society, Adorno's view no longer works and for two reasons: First, because (as asserted by Beck), society has gone beyond the certainties of modernity; Second, because, it is time to go beyond the one dimensionality of the conscious world. Therefore, I propose a multidimensional and pluralistic view (Samuels, 1989), where conscious and unconscious are interwoven and mutually affect each other. This begs the question: is it correct to claim – following Adorno (see Ceppa, 1979/1994: XXIX) – that 'man is the social world'? Jung's concept of the collective unconscious is fundamental here because he proposes an approach that is multidimensional, historic and spiritual (as well as symbolic). It is not limited to the here and now (χρόνος/chronos) and modern – enlightened – certainties. Rather, Jung's collective unconscious is beyond-temporal (καιρός / kairos).

Leonardo Ceppa (1979/1994: XXIX) highlights that:

> Spiritualism [...] is for Adorno a sort of empiricism of interiority. It rightly poses the problem of the subject and of the meaning of life,

but errs when it moves unreflectively from the immediate data of consciousness, assuming that it originates from the sentimental experiences that are already the fruit of a complex historical-social mediation (or construction).

I find this interesting and I see a *fil rouge* from Nietzsche, Marx, Freud and Adorno. However, I propose challenging this view by examining Jung's collective unconscious and spirituality, to move beyond Adorno's historical-social mediation (or construction). Therefore, I propose that historical-social mediation (or construction) does not encapsulate one's own soul and now even the soul of a culture. I prefer employing Jung's (*CW* 8: 805) view on religion. He claims that, since the Age of Enlightenment, a peculiar point of view has developed, according to which:

> all religions are something like philosophical systems, and like them are concocted out of the head. At some time someone is supposed to have invented a God and sundry dogmas and to have led humanity around by the nose with this 'wish-fulfilling' fantasy. But this opinion is contradicted by the psychological fact that the head is a particularly inadequate organ when it comes to thinking up religious symbols. They do not come from the head at all, but from some other place, perhaps the heart; certainly from a deep psychic level very little resembling consciousness, which is always only the top layer.

Thus, Jung claims, 'this is why religious symbols have a distinctly "revelatory" character; they are usually spontaneous products of unconscious psychic activity' and adds that 'Anyone who cherishes a rationalistic opinion on this score has isolated himself psychologically and stands opposed to his own basic human nature' (*CW* 8: 807). This is another reason why Adorno went with Freud rather than Jung.

Ceppa (1979/1994: XXXIII) emphasises that:

> in the present circumstances every form of adaptation, integration, theoretical synthesis is for Adorno a figure of false consciousness. Psychic qualities can not be subordinated to social laws – as did Heinz Hartman's ego psychology or Talcott Parsons' sociology, integrally functionalizing the unconscious to control reality. We can not deduce social laws from psychic laws, explaining capitalism on the basis of the *auri sacra fames* and an *innate selfish instinct*.

This point is crucial in my PhD thesis. In Chapters 2 and 3, I proposed that psychic qualities and social laws can be merged – not in the sole understanding of explaining capitalism – but to explain what being in the world is for human beings, bridging inner and outer realms that are mutually influential.

Post-Freudian psychoanalysis has demonstrated that much of what we are derives from the kind of attachment we have to the mother (of whatever sex, of course!). However, the Jungians go beyond this, to examine the concept of *daimon*, fate and destiny. This view (antithetic to Calvinism and enlightenment) is where, I believe, sociology – which concentrated on the ways in which structure and agency are related – fails to accept the power of the unconscious and of God. Adorno mistakenly believes that psychoanalysis should bring emancipation and happiness, but I propose that neither psychoanalysis nor class struggle should lead to happiness; instead, both must lead to clarification and knowledge and the recognition of one's own daimon. To this, Adorno thinks that:

> if sociologism betrays, betrays the unconscious and its claims of happiness, in the name of existing society and instrumental rationality, therapeutic psychology eludes – by contrast – the objective dimension of autonomous social irrationality. Thus it ends up being satisfied with an illusory recovery obtained through integration.
>
> (Ceppa, 1979/1994: XXXIV)

In conclusion, Jessica Benjamin (1977: 42) is again helpful as a contrast to Adorno's view. She states:

> analytic psychology contains the realisation that human beings affect one another, particularly in the process of child rearing, and therefore that what appear to be innate or natural *properties* of a person are actually the result of social interaction and human agency.

She also (1977: 47) asserts that 'Horkheimer and Adorno see reason as a universal historical, ontologised process developing out of the opposition of nature' and that 'The impasse of authority grounded in the antinomy of reason and nature is central to critical theory's analysis of modern culture'. However, she also claims that 'while critical or emancipatory reason must be developed to counter instrumental or dominating reason, they both emerge out of a conflict with inner and outer nature' (Benjamin, 1977: 43). This is something the Frankfurters and mainstream sociology failed to acknowledge or to study in depth.

Notes

1 Extract from chapter 4 of my PhD.
2 This chapter is the first part of a trilogy on Adorno, Horkheimer and Marcuse. The second part (cropped in one paper only) is titled 'From Compensation to Purpose: A Neo- Jungian Critique of Horkheimer and Marcuse' (Ph.D. Thesis, University of Essex (unpublished).

3 One could also say, following Dr Eric Green, that 'Adorno used Freud, and not Jung for example, not entirely because he didn't think Jung's work was worthy, but really because he thought Jung was a fascist' (private conversation). Or one could say, with Dr Jon Mills, that

> Adorno had his own agenda, and his limited readings, as well as the other Frankfurt members, were more appropriate of that time when the field of psychoanalysis was restricted to Freud: recall they would not support Jung in Germany due to his perceived antisemitism, as no one there reads Heidegger either.
>
> (private conversation)

4 I have decided to take *Minima Moralia* as my source of reference – instead of, for example, *The Authoritarian Personality* (New York: Harper & Brothers, 1950) or *Dialectic of Enlightenment* (Stanford, CA: Stanford University Press, 2002) where Adorno and his co-authors heavily draw on psychoanalysis – because of the way these aphorisms are written, as a stream of consciousness.
5 This and all future quotes from Ceppa's introduction to Adorno's *Minima Moralia* are my translations from the Italian.
6 My translation from Italian.
7 Private conversation, 2019.
8 Private conversation during clinical supervision, 2018 and 2019.
9 My translation from Italian.
10 Carpani (2020b).
11 Private conversation.
12 As a post-Jungian, and close to archetypal psychology.
13 As I outlined in chapter 2 of my PhD thesis (unpublished), following Lukes' (1982) introduction to Durkheim's *The Rules of Sociological Method*, we understand that Durkheim sought to demarcate sociology from psychology, claiming sociology to be a 'special psychology, having its own subject-matter and a distinctive method' (Durkheim, 1982: 253), while psychology is 'the science of the individual mind' whose object or domain is as follows (Durkheim, 1982: 40): (1) states of individual consciousness; (2) explanation in terms of 'organico-psychic' factors, pre-social features of the individual organism, given at birth and independent of social influences; (3) explanation in terms of particular or 'individual' as opposed to general or 'social' conditions (focusing, say, on individuals' intentions or their particular circumstances); (4) explanation in terms of individual mental states or dispositions. However, if we look carefully into a psychosocial parallel between Durkheim and Jung, we might recognise that these four points can be linked respectively to Jung's concepts of (1) the personal unconscious, (2) archetypes and the collective unconscious, (3) the persona, and (4) Jung's theory of neurosis and psychodynamics (the Syzygy).

Bibliography

Adorno, T.W. (1951/1975). *Minima Moralia*. London and New York: Verso.
Adorno, T.W. (1951/1994). *Minima Moralia*. Torino: Einaudi.
Beck, U. and Beck-Gernsheim, E. (2002). *Individualization: Institutionalized Individualism and its Social and Political Consequences*. London: Sage.

Benjamin, J. (1977). 'The End of Internalization: Adorno's Social Psychology', in *Thelos*, 77(32), pp. 42–64.
Carpani, S. (2020a). 'The Consequences of Freedom', in E. Brodersen and P. Amezaga (Eds.), *Jungian Perspectives on Indeterminate States: 'Betwixt and Between' Borders*. London and New York: Routledge, pp. 221–239.
Carpani, S. (2020b). 'From Compensation to Purpose: A Neo-Jungian Critique of Horkheimer and Marcuse' (Ph.D. Thesis, University of Essex (unpublished).
Ceppa, L. (1979/1994). *Introduction to* Minima Moralia. Torino: Einaudi.
Durkheim, E. (1982). *The Rules of Sociological Method*. New York: The Free Press.
Freud, S. (1969). *Introduzione alla Psicoanalisi*. Torino: Boringhieri.
Freud, S. (1991). *Introductory Lectures on Psychoanalysis*. London: Penguin.
Freud, S. (2003). *Beyond the Pleasure Principle: And Other Writings*. London: Penguin.
Giegerich, W. (2010). *The Soul Always Thinks*. New Orleans, LA: Spring Journal Books.
Hillman, J. (1996) *The Soul's Code: In Search of Character and Calling*. London: Penguin Random House.
Hillman, J. and Shamdasani S. (2013). *Lament of the Dead: Psychology after Jung's Red Book*. London and New York: Norton & Company.
Horkheimer, M. (1979). *La Società di Transizione*. Torino: Einaudi.
Jung, C.G. (1992). *Collected Works*, Vol. 14. London: Routledge and Kegan Paul.
Jung, C.G. (1992). *Collected Works*, Vol. 7. London: Routledge and Kegan Paul.
Jung, C.G. (1992). *Collected Works*, Vol. 8. London: Routledge and Kegan Paul.
Kast, V. (1993). 'Animus and Anima: Spiritual Growth and Separation', in *Harvest*, 39, pp. 5–15.
Lukes, S., (1982) 'Introduction', in E. Durkheim, *The Rules of Sociological Method*. New York: The Free Press.
Moore R. and Gillette D. (1991). *King, Warrior, Magician, Lover*. San Francisco, CA: Harper Collins.
Niebuhr, R. (1955). *The Self and the Dramas of History*. New York: Scribner's.
Samuels, A. (1989). *The Plural Psyche*. London: Taylor & Francis.
Samuels, A. (1993). *The Political Psyche*. London: Routledge.
Watkins, M. (2003). 'Dialogue, Development, and Liberation', in I. Josephs (Ed.), *Dialogicality in Development*. Westport, CT: Greenwood.
Zweig, S. (1931/2015). *Freud*. Roma: Castelvecchi.

Chapter 5

A spatial rapprochement between Jung's technique of active imagination and Desoille's *Rêve éveillé dirigé*

Laner Cassar

In this chapter I will be focusing on the interior spatial metaphors used in Jung's technique of active imagination and in Desoille's *Rêve éveillé dirigé*. Both Jung and Desoille used specific internal spatial language and tropes when engaging in their waking-dream techniques. While sharing a common goal, that of a return to oneself, the path to wholeness led them down separate roads, which converge at times through their linguistic symbolism and spatial metaphors. In choosing spatiality as a comparative tool, I am following recent scholarship in several disciplines that have become increasingly spatial in their orientation. These include such fields as literary and cultural studies, sociology, political science, anthropology, history and religion (Nora, 1984; Soja, 1989, 1996; Bourdieu, 2000; Massey, 1994, 1995, 2005; Lefebvre, 1991; Bordwell and Thompson, 2008). The American Professor of Geography Denis Cosgrove refers to this shift as a "spatial turn" (Cosgrove, 1999, p.7) while the French philosopher Michel Foucault (1986a), in a lecture given in 1967, argues how the great obsession of the nineteenth century with history and its temporal stages of development have given way to "the epoch of space".

The notion of interiority has a long history in the Western world (Foucault, 1986b; Taylor, 1989; Cary, 2000). Transformation is often experienced and described as a process of turning inwards. Moreover, the language and metaphors of inwardness are built into our psychological and epistemological language so intimately that we have literally embodied them. According to Lakoff and Johnson (1980), conceptual understanding is, in fact, structured by metaphors. Lakoff and Johnson also argue that metaphorical concepts structure how we perceive the world and as such, create reality.

The idea of interiority is a precursor of the concept of the inner-self experience, which was eventually absorbed into psychology. Diaries of early Greek philosophers, along with autobiographies and biographies of religious people, which focus on conversion and inner life, (as we will be seeing in this chapter), are in fact the forerunners of modern psychological introspection and analysis. The particular interior dimension of both Jung's and

Desoille's psychological discourse helps to shape and distinguish their own waking-dream methods. Moreover, their emphasis offers a seemingly essential vantage point for deliberating over a remaking of their own lives. Both offer a theoretical paradigm, suggesting that inward movement from world to self is not to be understood merely as a regressive retreat into oneself, but as a movement that leads into deeper levels of relatedness to the world and other people. It is an inward movement of awareness that reaches into and through one's own core. This inward movement of awareness eventually leads towards an outward release of energy from that core. Both Jung and Desoille physically exteriorised psychic space into a public arena through their writings about their imaginative methods. In fact, both Jung's autobiographical account of his own active imagination in *The Red Book* and Desoille's biographical accounts of his patient's *rêves éveillés* resonate well with other classic personal accounts in devotional literature such as St. Augustine's *Confessions* and St. Teresa of Ávila's *The Interior Castle*, amongst others, which were the means of physically unfolding their private inscapes into a public arena.

In fact, in both methods there is a dialectical movement between interior and exterior, secrecy and revelation, image and word, aloneness and presence. However, at times, interiority has been idealised in the case of Jung's active imagination and literalised in the case of Desoille to the extent that it has limited the development of both techniques from further developing and updating with the times. Current psychological language is characterised by new contemporary discourse which has superseded the interior–exterior divide and which reflects changes in social, political, technological and economic issues. Hence, we would expect that the development of the waking-dream methods would also centre on a new "interior" trope.

The concept of interiority and its development in Western Europe

To begin with, I would like to explain the common understanding that exists when it comes to the meaning of the word "interior". It usually refers to an inner space or dimension, a place which contains the inner self, the true being of the person. The concept of a psychological interior is meant to refer to the idea that a person has within themselves a space, into which one may subjectively turn, and not a feature that can be examined from without or in any physical manner. The word interior connotes a localised centre of awareness bounded by the physical body and which is, in turn, surrounded by an unbounded field of extensional space. The notion of interiority is nowadays frequently associated with the discipline of psychology. However, it is also present in other disciplines such as philosophy[1] and spirituality[2] but maybe not to the extent of psychology. Jesus in the New Testament says: "It is from within, from the human heart, that evil intentions come" (Matt 7, 18).

Historical and philosophical studies in relation to the "interior" include those of Foucault (1986b), Taylor (1989), and Cary (2000). Michel Foucault (1986b) traces the development of modern identity to Augustine (354–430 AD) who he describes as the innovator of our modern sense of "inwardness" and the "interior" that is now embedded in modern reflexive language. Cary (2000) highlights the contribution of Plotinus (232 to 304 CE) on interiority. The "interior" that Plotinus describes is a medium between soul and God, and is quite different from our modern psychological "interior". The major insight of Taylor's (1989) *Sources of the Self* is that modern subjectivity has its roots in ideas of human good. Taylor shows that the modern turn inward is not disastrous but is in fact the result of our long efforts to define and reach the good.

In Western culture there is a long tradition about the ancient notion of the "cultivation of the self", a lifelong process of acquiring self-knowledge (Foucault, 1986b). St. Augustine's *Confessions* is a personal account of his own inner conversion to Christianity and can be considered as the first Western autobiography ever written, which became an influential model for Christian writers throughout the following 1000 years of the Middle Ages. Furthermore, the Christian monastic ascetic tradition of the Early Church, which started in Eastern Europe before moving to the West, focused on meditation on the Holy Scriptures so as to be able to climb up the ladder of perfection. In the High Middle Ages (1000–1300 CE), mystics such as Hildegard of Bingen, Bernard of Clairvaux and Bonaventure, and later the Beguine mystics and the mystics of the Rhineland such as Meister Eckhart, Johann Tauler, and Henry Suso in the Late Middle Ages (1300–1500 CE), contributed to a personal experience of faith in God through contemplative prayer, which led to many visions of union with God. Their inner fervour and practice of finding the heart, spread from the monk, the troubadour, and the saint, to the common person. The lay citizens were encouraged to look into their own hearts for their source of spirituality. All of this suggested a movement towards the humanistic, that is, a looking within oneself, rather than to an outside authority, for the source of knowing.

The spiritual landscape of the seventeenth century shifted from scholastic authority to more experiential spirituality, from the mind to the heart. Pascal's dictum "*le coeur a ses raisons que la raison ne connait point*/the heart has reasons which reason knows not", is perhaps the best-known expression of what at the time of the *Pensees*,[3] was becoming a devotional commonplace (Papasogli, 1991). Moreover, the idea of depth and interiority connoted not only the rhetoric of sin, but also the positive language of affective mysticism, which promised plenitude with every turn. The *Confessions* then emerged in the seventeenth century as a book with two interrelated concepts of interiority, namely the interior as dark centre of the secretive subject but also the interior as the burning, experiential heart visited by mystics. Mysticism was no longer for the few who had been schooled in the theology of Pseudo-Dionysius or

Tauler, but became an experience for those without knowledge of Christianity's great mystical works. The popularising of mysticism can be observed in the mutations of two key words in seventeenth-century spirituality, words that gradually lost their theological importance even as they were provoking more enthusiasm in devotional literature. These words were "*interieur*/interior" and "*coeur*/heart". Devotional literature moved away from the Augustinian distinction between exterior man, that is, the part of man also shared by animals, such as perception, and interior man, referring to faculties that animals do not have, such as reason. Instead, interior came to designate a vague psychological space to which logic, reason and even language were foreign, indeed exterior (Paige, 2001).

The Church's position started to include the role of human emotion in gaining an understanding of God. Following St. Teresa of Ávila's vision, the heart pierced by an arrow, which symbolised revelation through emotion, came into greater prominence. At this point, the interior disappeared from theological discourse, and became instead an essential part of devotional literature, literature intended for consumption by a wider audience. This was also seen in Protestantism, which is commonly viewed as stressing inner devotion over external ritual. The late seventeenth-century reform movement known as Pietism[4] represented an intensification of Lutheran inwardness that had long-lasting cultural effects, especially in Northern Germany. Pietism altered the religious and the linguistic landscape by transmitting its soul-searching vocabulary to the eighteenth century's culture of sensibility.

In literature, literary figures became increasingly enamoured with their innermost depths. Like Goethe's (2015) troubled protagonist Werther,[5] readers thrived on the relentless self-examination such characters undertook. By the turn of the century, metaphors of depth and inwardness saturated the prose of authors such as Novalis, Wackenroder, Tieck and Jean Paul (Draaisma, 2000; Watkins, 2011). The breadth of meanings that those metaphors evoked in the 1800s rivalled those of religious discourse circa 1675. Taking Pietism's emphasis on subjective experience to its limit, Romantic thinkers invested the self with qualities usually reserved for the divine; unknowability, unscrutability, even infinity. Watkins writes: "By merging the divine and human they transformed the inner realm from a private site of prayer and reflection into an unfathomable abyss" (Watkins, 2011, p.29). While Pietists believed that the inward journey ultimately reached the divine, their romantic counterparts tended to stray further and further into the fathomless depths of subjective interiority.

All the above philosophical, theological and literary traditions of interiority in the Western world were steeped in the works of both Jung and Desoille and can be identified if one looks closely at the metaphors chosen to describe the internal landscapes. A close look at Jung's *The Red Book* reveals the frequent citations of St. Paul, St. Augustine, Meister Eckhart, Thomas a Kempis, Jacob Boehme, Swedenborg, Joseph von Görres and Jeanne

Guyon, amongst others, while Desoille makes reference to St. Augustine, St. Denis the Areopagite, Blaise Pascal, St. Theresa of Ávila and St John of the Cross, and Therese Neuman in his 1938 book. Desoille also references the work of the psychoanalyst John Leuba (1925), "*Psychologie du Mysticisme Religieux*/Psychology of Religious Mysticism"; the book of the Jesuit Joseph Maréchal (1924), "*Études sur la Psychologie des Mystiques*/Studies on the Psychology of Mystics"; "*De l'Angoise à l'Ecstase*/From Angst to Ecstasy" of Pierre Janet (1927); and the work of William James (1906) "*Les Variétés de l'Expérience Religieuse*/The Varieties of Religious Experience", who were open to mystical experiences. Desoille's position, despite his strong scientific attitude, does not pathologise mystic experiences and values their creative and transformational aspects. Desoille also writes the preface of the book of the philosopher Genevieve Lanfranchi, "*De la vie interieure à la vie de relation*/From the interior life to the relational life", where he argues that psychology can see mystic states in a positive healthy way (Desoille, 1966). Desoille and Jung's respective ideas about the transpersonal seem to have been on the same lines.

Spatial metaphors on interiority in Jung's and Desoille's accounts of waking dreams

Aristotle tied down the notion of place in his *Physics* to that of a merely bounded space when he argued that place is the inner limit of a containing body. Space was robbed of substantive meaningfulness to become an ordered, uniform system of abstract linear co-ordinates. This was further reinforced by Newton and Galileo's claims of an infinite and infinitely open space. In their methods, space offered a means for measuring time; therefore space was subordinate to time, and the importance of place largely forgotten. The French philosopher Gaston Bachelard (1964), in his *Poetics of Space*, has produced an experiential account of our lived spaces. Bachelard renewed the mytho-poetic idea of inner place, when he posited that the invisible is revealed in the interiority of the human soul and, as such, it is intrinsically a place. Such an idea of psychological space makes up for the impoverished one of Euclidean and Newtonian space. Likewise, both Jung and Desoille claimed that the creative action of the poetic imagination provides an abode of intimate immensity that mirrors the external immensity of the cosmos, and provides a space capable of a marvellous transformation. However, it was Hillman who clearly deconstructed the notions of an interior space and place where somehow both Jung and Desoille are caught in. For Hillman, the sense of "in-ness" refers neither to location nor to physical containment: "[...] but an imaginal metaphor for the soul's non-visible and non-literal inherence, the imaginal psychic quality within all events" (Hillman, 1975, p.173).

However, in this chapter I will be keeping to Jung's and Desoille's "traditional topology" of inner space and place and will choose to focus more on their choice of tropes and on an inner spatio-analysis of the workings of their methods.

Altitudo: on spatial vertical dialectics

Jung and Desoille's methods encourage the patient to go inside and to imagine the inside as if it were an outside and to experience it. For both of them, the interior place is not just the closed small world of one's intimacies. It can also be an infinite challenging universe which man can chart. In fact, the theme of *"homo viator*/man on the way"[6] is an archetypal one and features considerably in classic authors such as Plotinus, Homer, Virgil, Valmiki and Dante (Papasogli, 1991; De Waal, 1993). Jung describes wandering as "a symbol for longing, of the restless urge which never finds its object, of nostalgia for the lost mother" (Jung, 1912/1967, p.205 [*CW* 5, para.299]). However, the preferred routes or road-maps for the peregrination are not the same. Several times, the adventures do not unfold horizontally but are played vertically. The vertical axis, in latin *altitudo*, extends between ultimate heights and ultimate depths and incorporates both. Gaping altitude or culminating depth, the extreme acuminal and the extreme abyssal meet and coincide.

In the alchemical tradition, the Sky and the Earth are the vertical alchemical couple and *axis mundi* corresponding to the horizontal Brother–Sister couple. The accent can be put on one or the other. In our Western literary tradition, there has been emphasis on "anabasis", that is, ascents. Since Plato's *Phaedrus*, where he describes the loss of wings of the soul and its subsequent fall, further echoed in the myths of Icarus and Bellorophon, there remains a yearning and nostalgia for unity with that which is above. In the Platonic tradition, the above *logos* outside the cave is the sole truth and below is the murky shadow. Bachelard's book *L'Air et les Songes* (1943) further idealised the aerial heights and later the fire of the imagination. Man carries in himself an inclination, something like a tropism towards his eternal origin.

The above concepts have been challenged by postmodernism.[7] Derrida speaks about plunging into "the horizontality of a pure surface" (Derrida, 1978, p.28) and that for deconstructionists everything is surface, appearance, horizontality. Not only do deconstructionists deny absolute transcendence, but even relative height or depth. For Fredric Jameson, our contemporary era has abandoned the "depth models" of modernism in favour of "multiple surfaces" (Jameson, 1991, p.12). Both utilise concepts of flatness and surface as primary metaphors. Jameson in *Postmodernism* describes the supreme feature of postmodernism as "a new kind of flatness or depthlessness, a new kind of superficiality in the most literal sense" (ibid., p.9), which took the place of modernism's dualistic models of depth and surface, essence and appearance, latent and manifest, authenticity and inauthenticity, signified and signifier (ibid., p.12). While surface is essential for both Jung and Desoille in order to bring back the images that are met in the depths and heights, the unconscious remains central to both practitioners.

Interior wetsuits and interior spacesuits
Jung's precipitating depths and Desoille's soaring heights

Following a Kantian epistemology, Jung holds that one cannot tell what the psyche is, one can only say how it appears to us without concluding that it is how it is in itself. Jung's psychology is based on soul and a being in soul (*esse in anima*). For Jung, all we know about the world is in images, since that is how psyche presents itself directly. Jung chooses to represent the psyche's depths, which he himself has chosen to face. Like a Surrealist *flâneur*, Jung inserts himself into the anonymous figures and landscape of the depths. He thus exemplifies the historical shift from *Gemeinschaft* to *Gesellschaft* by trying his best to feel at home in the crowd of strangers of the unconscious. For Jung, in *The Red Book*: "the inner is as infinite as the world of the outer [...] and is no way poorer than the outer one" (Jung, 2009, p.264). Jung moves from the external sensitive faculties to the fine bottom of the heart, from top downwards and from outside towards the interior: "He whose desires turn away from outer things reaches the place of the soul" (ibid., p.232). From the periphery towards the centre, towards this mysterious depth called "desert", "abyss", "Hell" – (from latin *locus infernos* meaning the place beneath), "bottommost", "immeasurable depths". Jung describes how one's being "pulls you to the bottom like lead" (ibid., p.266).

Consequently Jung demolishes and reverses a European tradition that idealises ascents and is resistant to the fall, towards an embracing of descents: "Let fall what wants to fall; if you stop it, it will sweep you away" (Jung, 2009, p.244). Jung describes how the spirit of the depths approached him and said: "Climb down into your depths, sink" (ibid., p.240), since he has been too much in the summits. In the 1925 seminar, Jung (1925/1989, p.63) recounted how the first time he practised active imagination, he had reached a depth of about one thousand feet and later when he tried it again he went much deeper. Jung subverses the principles that have governed the space of intimacy before him. In order for this to be achieved Jung had to descend to the very lowest of himself and embrace all that was inferior in himself.

In *The Red Book*, Jung peregrinates through various underground caves as well as horizontal places, such as deserts in which he finds fertile fields, gardens, libraries and lodges. The dryness and light of the desert, to which we are introduced in *The Red Book*, contrasts sharply with the darkness of the sea. Jung uses the metaphor of the sea and the night to describe the inner depths. Jung attributes the term "night sea-journey" to Frobenius, to whose extensive study of myths Jung refers in the *Collected Works* (Jung, 1912/1967, p.210 [*CW* 5, para.308]). The night sea journey or *Nekyia* is a recurring cross-cultural ancient mythical theme, which reappears, relatively more recently, again and again in the fairy tales and legends of the dragon-slaying heroes. Moreover, darkness and night time should not always be associated with the shadows of evil, for they provide the opportunity for the most intense contemplation. It can be a time of sorrow, as it was for Job; however, the anguish led to deliverance. Moreover, it was during the night that Christ came into the world, and it is at night that salvation can be attained. These themes of the nocturnal sea appear again and again in the *Collected Works*, from *Symbols of Transformation* (1912/1967) through to *Mysterium Coniunctionis* (1955/1970).

In *The Red Book*, Jung describes man as a "drop in the ocean" who "wander [s] vast distances in blurred currents and [...] mount[s] the billows of huge storms and [is] swept back into the depths" (Jung, 2009, p.266). Jung's references to the night sea journey also parallel those of French seventeenth-century moralist and devotional literature for whom the sea trope with its rough seas and forceful winds was a metaphor of man's search and journey towards God. These sea metaphors reflect the vastness of the outer world, which also belongs inside. These metaphors are inspired by the geographical discoveries of the new worlds by the European powers (Papasogli, 1991; Gross and Gross, 1993). Furthermore, the image of man lost at sea connotes man's alienation from God. The passions are also associated with rough seas which man has to try to sail through without drowning in them (Papasogli, 1991).

Jung uses the images of the *Nekyia* (the night sea journey) and of *Katabasis* (descent into the lower world) almost interchangeably. In the *Visions Seminars* (1930–1934), Jung explains how in ancient times, people would go down to the "oracular cave", or to "a hidden spring", since the secret place of initiation was below (Jung, 1998, p.92). James Hillman, however, made some clear distinctions between *Nekyia* and *Katabasis*:

> The descent of the underworld can be distinguished from the night sea-journey of the hero in many ways [...] the hero returns from the night sea-journey in better shape for the tasks of life, whereas the nekyia takes the soul into a depth for its own sake so that there is no "return".
> (Hillman, 1979, p.88)

In the case of Desoille, the vertical line determines the anthropological structure of the human being. Both Jung and Desoille agree that the structures of above and below were not made up but both believe in their archetypal basis. Jung even says that Dante intuited this when he wrote his opus of the *Divine Comedy*. For Desoille (1938), the heights are almost always connected with good feelings while the depths evoke fear and primitive anxiety. Desoille makes use of the symbol of the descent, but puts greater emphasis on that of the ascent. Eventually the descent to the cave becomes one of his main initial stimuli when Desoille tried to give more structure to his approach. The experience of going down many times becomes a maritime one. The patients face the dark depths of the sea and they undergo several underwater explorations. Desoille encourages his patients to wear wetsuits and to face the dangerous sea monsters that hinder them from exploring further. He even provides his patients with magical solutions of how to overwhelm the menacing figures. In Desoille's case studies, he mentions several times how his patients are afraid of going down and how he has to encourage them to explore the space above by jumping on a rainbow or a ray of light or a cloud, which transports them on higher planes where many times they find fields of gold, rich palaces, saintly and angelic figures and dazzling light.

Desoille (1938) gives more descriptions of the heights rather than the depths and after the patient experiences the heights more frequently, the figures encountered usually shift to an experience of being enveloped by light. Desoille's bias towards the heights has been fuelled by the five writings on the "material imagination" of his close friend, philosopher Gaston Bachelard (1943), who used the Empedocles' doctrine of the Four elements as the roots and "*hormone*/hormones" of the psyche. One can appreciate how networking can lead to the sharing and influencing of ideas. Bachelard writes about the material, movement, will and intimacy of imagination in his five books on the imagination. He dedicates the fourth chapter of *L'Air et les Songes* to Desoille where he equates imagination with "*mouvement*/movement". Bachelard was heavily influenced by Jung's text *Psychology and Alchemy* and by the French psychoanalytic pioneer Rene Allendy (1889–1942) who was very much interested in alchemy and in Jung's work. Bachelard makes a close link between poetry and alchemy. Novalis is more the poet of fire, Edgar Allan Poe of water, Nietzsche of the air, while Goethe is the poet of the earth (Chiore, 2004). Jung also seems to be following Goethe in his metaphorical descriptions on the inner depths. In his *Pilgrim's Progress*, Jung says that it consisted of having to go down a "thousand ladders" to reach out to the "little clod of earth that I am" (Jung, 1973, p.19). In *Memories, Dreams, Reflections* (1963/1995) Jung is quoted by Jaffé as saying that he needed to materialise the images of his waking dreams in stone by building his tower in Bollingen. Here Jung seems to be echoing the lyrical writings of the French philosopher Roger Callois (1970) "*L'Ecriture des Pierres*/The Writing of Stones". Jung's ideas of having to use one's will to face the images so that ultimately one can find some rest are also elaborated in Bachelard's (1948) works, namely "*La Terre et les Reveries de la Volonte: Essai sur l'Imagination des Forces*/Earth and Reveries of Will: An Essay on the Imagination of Strength". For Bachelard, the will to "hammer" the earth into new forms brings energy to what is seemingly inert. Working wilfully with the hands on matter energises the imagination to create something new and enliven that substance.

If we use the interpretation given by the post-Jungian James Hillman (1979) on the difference between soul and spirit we can maybe position both waking-dream approaches better. Hillman distinguishes between soul and spirit since soul is the lost dimension in the tripartite structure of human nature, namely spirit, soul and body. So while peaks are associated with the search for spirit or the drive of the spirit in search of itself, vales are connected to depressive moods. Hillman emphasises the fact, not to try to liberate the soul from the vale so as to reach transcendence, and neither to reduce the spirit to a complex. To the contrary one must aim for a marriage, a *coniunctio* between the high-driving spirit and the soul, between Eros and Psyche. Hillman argues how the soul can contain, nourish, and elaborate and deepen in fantasy the *puer* impulse, while the soul's reflections need to be seen through in terms of higher and deeper perspectives. In this context Desoille's directed waking dream emphasises more the spiritual element. Desoille's emphasis on light imagery connotes the last stages of the *via mystica*, namely the *via illuminativa* and the *via contemplativa* where there is union with God. Furthermore, some of his initial stimuli, such as the road, the mountain, the stairway and the ladder, are all metaphors which mystics mention in their progress of union with the Divine being. The ascent, directed by the therapist, becomes a reward for an *ascesis* (discipline), not in the sense of asceticism but in the Greek psychagogic sense of psycho-spiritual development.

Jung chooses to keep both the two poles. In *The Red Book*, Jung's (2009) ka-soul came from below, out of the earth, slightly demonic, while the almost God-like spirit Philemon appeared from above in the sky, as if both soul and spirit were inspired by the image of a bird. Moreover, *The Red Book* has several references to the ascetic spiritual practices of the Desert fathers or anchorites although it gives considerable importance to the earthly horizontal journey and peregrinations to the bowels of the earth. For Jung in individuation one aims for the attainment of full knowledge of the heights and depths of one's character.

Confronting the depths directly or facing them gradually?

Jung and Desoille both agree to face one's inferior parts, however they differ in the approach used. For Jung, the psyche's odyssey to reconquer its unity is very tortuous and the right way to wholeness is a *longissima via* a painful experience of the union of opposites. It is a *discensus ad inferos*. At one point in *The Red Book* in the *Liber Primus*, Jung describes how "Elijah climbs before me into the heights to a very high summit, I follow him" (Jung, 2009, p.251). Jung explains this move as his resistance to go down. His stronger tendency was to go up since: "on the heights, [...] you are your best, and you become aware only of your best..." (ibid., p.266). Jung further adds that: "Your values want to draw you away from what you presently are, to get you ahead and beyond yourself" (ibid.).

So, for Jung, one cannot arrive to the heights prematurely since it would be an escape into becoming before one fully immerses into his depth of being which is the "bath of rebirth" (ibid., p.266). However, one can move from experiencing the depths (being) to soaring to the heights (becoming), since both are possible. He writes: "your way leads you from mountain to valley and from valley to mountain" (ibid., p.266).

Desoille finds very little difficulty in stopping the descents and offers the patient shelter in the waking dream by encouraging him to ascend to a higher place. While in Jung's *Red Book*, we can almost hear him shiver with fear of looking inwards, nonetheless, he soldiers on alone. In *Memories, Dreams, Reflections* and in Shamdasani's (1996) introduction to *The Psychology of Kundalini Yoga*, Jung does describe how, when faced with terrifying moments, he would stop to do some actual breathing exercises before returning again to the depths. In fact, in *The Red Book*, he faces the Red One as well as the terrifying Izdubar on his own. Even though Jung recommends active imagination after going through a process of analysis, and therefore after having strengthened one's ego, he still warns against the dangers of being overwhelmed by the unconscious. The unsuccessful descent to Hades by Pirithous is a case in point. Moreover, the allegory of the Sorcerer's Apprentice contains a warning of how easy it is to make the waters gush out, but how difficult it then is to control them and command them back. Desoille is very aware of this and he goes about it in a very supportive manner. Jung's waking dreams are very much non-directive while Desoille takes a more directive approach. Moreover, the presence of the therapist seems to provide holding for the patient in moments of distress and the voicing of the oneirodrama to the therapist serves as an anchor when charting rough seas.

Conclusion

For the American playwright Tennessee Williams, the writers in the "long-weekend" between the wars tried to compensate for the malaise of place-loss by throwing themselves into motion. In the words of the protagonist Tom in Williams' *Glass Menagerie*, they attempted "to find in motion what was lost in space" (Williams, 1945, p.75). In a similar fashion, in resorting to their own internal fantasy world, both Jung and Desoille tried to work on their own issues and personal losses as well as to address the moral deficit in the Western world's balance sheet.

In describing the different spatial metaphors of interiority in both Jung and Desoille's waking dreams, it is clear that Jung and Desoille favour different poles of the vertical axis and describe different ways of reaching them. Jung believes that one must face the depths first in order to enjoy the heights while Desoille emphasises the importance of reaching the heights in order to sublimate one's problems. While Jung's descent into the unconscious is a difficult, dangerous and long process, for Desoille, facing the heights provides a means of strengthening oneself so as to be able to face the darker depths. Moreover, while Jung has to bear the accompanying fear and trepidation in his *descensus ad inferos*, Desoille offers his patients support and ways to emerge unharmed from the precipitous depths with its perilous environment.

Notes

1 Amongst philosophers for example, the phenomenologists such as Husserl, Heidegger and Sartre, look for philosophical truth in the human interiority just as Descartes did before them, although most of them do not accept Cartesian rationalism (Pivcevic, 1970).
2 A spirituality of interiority can be found in the Catholic *Devotio moderna* of Thomas à Kempis, the "Spiritual Exercises" of St. Ignatius of Loyola and the devotional practices of apostolic religious orders. In modern times, the Catholic retreat house became the central Catholic place of spirituality of interiority (Griffin, Beardslee and Holland, 1989).
3 The *Pensées*, which means "thoughts" is a collection of fragments on theology and philosophy written by seventeenth-century French philosopher and mathematician Blaise Pascal. Pascal's religious conversion led him into a life of asceticism and the *Pensées* was in many ways his life's work (Copleston, 1958).
4 Pietism refers to an influential religious reform movement that began among German Lutherans in the seventeenth century. It emphasised personal faith against the main Lutheran church's perceived stress on doctrine and theology over Christian living. Pietism quickly spread and later became concerned with social and educational matters. As a phenomenon of personal religious renewal, its indirect influence has persisted in Germany and other parts of Europe into the twenty-first century. Two important scholarly books on the subject are F. Ernest Stoeffler's 1965 book *The Rise of Evangelical Pietism* and Douglas H. Shantz's 2013 work entitled *An Introduction to German Pietism: Protestant Renewal at the Dawn of Modern Europe*.
5 Werther is a fictional character in Johann Wolfgang von Goethe's epistolary, loosely autobiographical novel, *The Sorrows of Young Werther*, first published in 1774.
6 The journey theme is one of the great archetypal themes of world literature. Great epics such as *The Odyssey*, *The Aeneid* and *The Ramayana* present the adventures of a hero who sets out on a journey. The collective journey of the Hebrew people in the exodus constitutes the central spiritual experience of the Judaic tradition. The journey of the soul to the Good is the central theme of Plotinus's *Enneads*. The inner spiritual journey of Dante in the *Divine Comedy* stands as one of the greatest poetic and religious expressions of Western civilisation. From Gilgamesh to Frodo of The Lord of the Rings, the quest and search is a fundamental theme of humanity. To be human is to be homo viator. The outer quest may be more Western, the inner quest more Eastern.
7 Postmodernism is a philosophical movement that is largely a reaction against the philosophical assumptions and values of the modern period of Western (specifically European) history, that is, the period from about the time of the scientific revolution of the sixteenth and seventeenth centuries to the mid-twentieth century. Indeed, many of the doctrines characteristically associated with postmodernism can fairly be described as the straightforward denial of general philosophical viewpoints or metanarratives that were taken for granted during the modern period. For a critical study of postmodernism, see *Post-modern Theory: Critical Interrogations* by S. Best and D. Kellner (1991) and *Postmodernism: A Very Short Introduction* by C. Butler (2003).

References

Bachelard, G. (1943). *L'air et les songes: essai sur l'imagination du movement [Air and dreams: Essay on the imagination of movement]*. Paris: Librairie Jose Corti.

Bachelard, G. (1948). *La terre et les rêveries de la volonté: essai sur l'imagination des forces [The earth and the reveries of will: Essay on the imagination of forces]*. Paris: Librairie Jose Corti.

Bachelard, G. (1964). *The poetics of space*. New York: Orion Press.

Best, S. and Kellner, D. (1991). *Postmodern theory: Critical interrogations*. London and New York: Macmillan and Guilford Press.

Bordwell, D. and Thompson, K. (2008). *Film art: An introduction* (8th Ed.). Boston, MA and London: McGraw Hill.

Bourdieu, P. (2000). *Esquisse d'une théorie de la pratique [Outline of a theory of practice]*. Paris: Seuil. (Originally published in 1972).

Butler, C. (2003). *Postmodernism: A very short introduction*. Oxford: Oxford University Press.

Callois, R. (1970). *L'ecriture des pierres. [The writing stones]*. Genève: Editions d'Art Albert Skira.

Cary, P. (2000). *Augustine's invention of the inner self*. Oxford: Oxford University Press.

Chiore, V. (2004). *Il poeta, l'alchimista, il demone [The poet, the alchemist and the devil]*. Genova: Il Melangolo.

Copleston, F. C. (1958). *A history of philosophy: From Descartes to Leibniz*. Glen Rock, NJ: Paulist Press.

Cosgrove, D. (1999). Introduction. In D. Cosgrove (Ed.), *Mappings*. London: Reaktion Books.

Derrida, J. (1978). *Writing and difference* (A. Bass, Trans.). Chicago, IL: University of Chicago Press.

Desoille, R. (1938). *Exploration de l'affectivité subconsciente par la méthode du rêve éveillé: sublimation et acquisitions psychologiques [An exploration of the subconscious emotions through the waking dream method: Sublimation and psychological acquisitions]*. Paris: J. L. L. D'Artrey.

Desoille, R. (1966). Preface. In G. Lanfranchi (Ed.), *"De la vie intérieure à la vie de relation" [Preface to the "Interior life and the life of relating"]* (pp.17–19). Paris: Editions sociales françaises.

De Waal, E. (1993). *The spiritual journey: Word & spirit – a monastic review*. Petersham, MA: St. Bede's Publications.

Draaisma, D. (2000). *Metaphors of memory: A history of ideas about the mind*. Cambridge: Cambridge University Press.

Foucault, M. (1986a). Of other spaces (J. Miskowiec, Trans.). *Diacritics*, 16, Spring, 22. (Originally published as *Des espace autres* in 1967).

Foucault, M. (1986b). *The care of the self: The history of sexuality, Vol. 3*. London: Penguin Books.

Goethe, J. W. (2015). *The sorrows of young Werther* (B. Quincy-Morgan, Trans.). London: Alma Books. (Originally published in German as Die lieden des jungen Werthers in 1774).

Griffin, D. R., Beardslee, W. A., and Holland, J. (1989). *Varieties of post-modern theology*. Albany, NY: State University of New York Press.

Gross, F. L. and Gross, T. P. (1993). *The making of a mystic: Seasons in the life of Teresa of Avila.* Albany, NY: State University of New York Press.
Hillman, J. (1975). *Re-visioning psychology.* New York. Harper Colophon Books.
Hillman, J. (1979). *The dream and the underworld.* New York: Harper & Row.
James, W. (1906). *L'experience religieuse. Essai de psychologie descriptive [The religious experience. An essay on descriptive psychology]* (F. Abauzit, Trans.). Paris: Alcan/ Geneve: Kundig.
Jameson, F. (1991). *Postmodernism or the cultural logic of late capitalism.* Durham, NC: Duke University Press.
Janet, P. (1927). *De l'angoise a l'extase [From anguish to ecstasy].* Paris: Alcan.
Jung, C. G. (1912/1967). *Collected Works, volume 5: Symbols of transformation* (W. McGuire, Exec. Ed., Sir H. Read, M. Fordham, and G. Adler, Eds., and R. F. C. Hull, Trans.). Princeton, NJ: Princeton University Press.
Jung, C. G. (1955/1970). *Collected Works, volume 14: Mysterium coniunctionis* (W. McGuire, Exec. Ed., Sir H. Read, M. Fordham, and G. Adler, Eds., and R. F. C. Hull, Trans.).
Jung, C. G. (1973). *Letters, vol, 1 (1906–50).* Princeton, NJ: Princeton University Press.
Jung. C. G. (1925/1989). *Analytical psychology: Notes on the seminar given in 1925* (W. McGuire, Ed.). Princeton, NJ: Princeton University Press.
Jung, C. G. (1963/1995). *Memories, dreams, reflections.* London: Fontana Press.
Jung, C. G. (1998). *Visions. Notes of the seminar given in 1930–1934, Vol. 1* (C. Douglas, Ed.). London: Routledge.
Jung, C. G. (2009). *The red book, liber novus* (S. Shamdasani, Ed., M. Kyburz, J. Peck, and S. Shamdasani, Trans.). New York: W.W. Norton & Company.
Lakoff, G. and Johnson, M. (1980). *Metaphors we live by.* Chicago, IL: University of Chicago Press.
Lefebvre, H. (1991). *The production of space* (D. Nicholson-Smith, Trans.). Oxford: Blackwell.
Leuba, H. J. (1925). *Psycholsssogie du mysticisme religieux [The psychology of religious mysticism]* (L. Herr, Trans.). Paris: Alcan.
Maréchal, J. (1924). *Études sur la psychologie des mystiques [Studies on the psychology of mystics].* Paris: Alcan.
Massey, D. (1994). *Space, place, and gender.* Minneapolis, MN: University of Minnesota Press.
Massey, D. (1995). *Spatial divisions of labor: Social structures and the geography of production.* New York: Routledge.
Massey, D. (2005). *For space.* London: Sage.
Nora, P. (1984). *Les lieux des memoires. [Places of memory].* Paris: Gallimard.
Paige, N. (2001). *Being interior: Autobiography and the contradictions of modernity in seventeenth century France.* Philadelphia, PA: University of Pennsylvania Press.
Papasogli, B. (1991). *Il "fondo del cuore". Figure dello spazio interiore nel Seicento francese ["The bottom of the heart". Figures of interior space in sixteenth century France].* Pisa: Goliardica.
Pivcevic, E. (1970). *Husserl and phenomenology.* New York: Hutchinson University Library.
Shamdasani, S. (1996). Introduction to C. G. Jung, *The psychology of Kundalini Yoga: Notes of the seminar given in 1932 by C. G. Jung,* Princeton, NJ: Princeton University Press/London: Routledge.

Shantz, D. H. (2013). *An introduction to German pietism: Protestant renewal at the dawn of modern Europe.* Baltimore, MD: Johns Hopkins University Press.
Soja, E. (1989). *Postmodern human geographies: The reassertion of space in critical social theory.* London: Verso.
Soja, E. (1996). *Thirdspace: A journey into Los Angeles and other real-and-imagined places.* Oxford: Blackwell.
Stoeffler, E. F. (1965). *The rise of evangelical pietism.* Leiden: Brill.
Taylor, C. (1989). *Sources of the self.* Cambridge: Cambridge University Press.
Watkins, H. (2011). *Metaphors of depth in German musical thought: From E.T.A. Hoffmann Arnold Shoenberg.* Cambridge: Cambridge University Press.
Williams, T. (1945). *The glass menagerie.* New York: Random House.

Chapter 6

A critique of containing space in therapeutic work

Martyna Chrzescijanska

Introduction to 'Critical analysis of the model of containing space'

'Critical analysis of the model of containing space' is a chapter that offers a critical analysis of some of its aspects, focusing on its origins, discourses, functions and shadow forms. The critical analysis presented aims to demonstrate the inadequacies and flaws of the existing and dominant model of space in depth psychology. The critical analysis will deploy discourse analysis and philosophical and psychotherapeutic tools of analysis. It will discuss: (1) the political and social contexts of understanding boundaries and borders; (2) the philosophical understanding of categories of thinking as containers and a critique of the geometrisation and rationalisation of the experience of space; (3) a feminist critique of the involvement of depth psychology in maintaining traditional, societal discourses; (4) a psychotherapeutic analysis of the defensiveness of psychotherapy as a discipline; and (5) the shadows of the containing space that reveal some of its negative aspects or possible implications.

Boundaries and borders

First, we need to consider the concept of boundaries and borders, including the history and social and political meanings thereof. Again, no psychotherapeutic concept develops in a void – psychotherapy is part of a discursive construct and all psychotherapeutic concepts are embedded in social, cultural and political contexts. Although borders are defined and practised differently in politics and psychotherapy, a number of similarities between these disciplines will be discussed here, to reveal certain aspects of the containing space that stem from social and political contexts.

In depth psychology, the boundaries of containing space are about the creation of space for the integration of (unconscious) elements. However, this is not exclusive to psychotherapeutic boundaries. In the case of any boundary/border, what is inside is meant to be integrated, implying that there is something that is kept out and that, hence, cannot be integrated. Outside of the psychotherapeutic perspective, integration is not necessarily seen in a positive light. Although we may speak generally of intercultural integration, most anthropologists distinguish its different types, such as acculturation and assimilation. In anthropological studies, a distinction is made between borders and boundaries depending on whether they can be defined as territorial limits constituting political entities (borders) or socially constructed identities through symbolical differences between classes, ethnicities, etc. (Fassin, 2011). Delimitation can either be imposed structurally or appear (more or less) naturally as an expression of social distinction between different groups.

It is no coincidence that psychotherapy uses spatial metaphors in at least three instances: to describe (1) the self or the mind, (2) the setting, and (3) containment. These three elements are interrelated and refer to the idea of a closed, unified and coherent identity. A very similar idea appears in politics and the concept of nations. The idea of borders occurs primarily in terms of the delimitation of territory and the construction of national identity. Borders serve to distinguish between 'us' and 'not us'; what is clean and unclean; the sacred and profane (Douglas, 1966; Kristeva, 1982; Eliade, 1959).

Borders might be an expression of an urge to introduce order. They not only protect but are also used as part of a colonising practice of dominating and structuring the land, as in the case of arbitrarily drawn borders in Africa. Borders are both a social and psychological category that appear in particular situations. For instance, in his theory of uncertainty-identity, Hogg (2014) makes a connection between the sense of uncertainty and groups searching for distinctive and clearly defined boundaries. In other words, a psychological state of uncertainty leads to the reinforcement of social boundaries.

Indeed, on a social scale, the need for borders occurs particularly at moments of uncertainty and fear. We have seen that, in the case of the 'refugee crisis', European nations returned to a very old idea of borders in their most physical form – the building of fences and walls (Rheindorf & Wodak, 2018; Gerrard, 2016). The phantasy of 'uncontrolled migration' and a 'surge of refugees' thus triggered very basic and primitive defence mechanisms.

In some cases, borders become walls (as in the case of the US–Mexico border and Trump's fantasy about an even more literal and concrete protection from a projected danger). First, this stems from a denial of the fact that if a danger exists, it is within not outside, and, as a result, it becomes projected onto 'the other' – 'the other' from whom we can protect ourselves by creating borders:

> Here, despite bringing in the suffering and pain into 'our' lounge rooms, boundaries and borders of feeling and politics are created in the apparent distance, strangeness, violence or danger of the Other.
> (Gerrard, 2016, p. 5)

Second, this physical and literal understanding of self-containment in the form of the wall or fence is a spatial enactment of mental boundaries. In other words, it is a social defence mechanism stemming from a psychological insecurity and a sense of danger, which takes a geographical, political and physical form. As such, it represents a shadow of boundaries that were meant to protect a process. This may be why in most theories of space in psychotherapy, there is a recurring tendency to picture mental space in a three-dimensional form – the same tendency that occurs in politics and social practice. As a rule, when there is uncertainty and fear, there is a wall or border.

In fact, if we pay attention to the psychotherapeutic explanation of therapists, boundaries are about fear: as the psychotherapeutic process evokes and reveals painful and strong emotions, it must be bounded and protected. Even if the danger is not projected, it is introjected; according to a psychoanalytic dictum, unconscious contents must be integrated. The psychotherapeutic containing space is put in place in situations of mental distress experienced as a psychological danger. It is established and safeguarded to create a safe space, which is a demarcation from the therapist's personal life and other types of relations that both the patient and therapist may have (Temperley, 1984). As such, it protects the 'psychotherapeutic identity' of the relationship within the boundaries, and gives it a distinctive status. It does involve otherness, while at the same time being separated from it by the boundaries (just as in the model of the vessel).

Here, I propose thinking about the wall or borders as the shadow of containment. If the main role of containing boundaries is to protect the process that leads to growth, the wall serves a slightly other purpose: to separate, hide and self-protect. The main difference is the lack of integration in the case of building walls and fences. On the other hand, walls are raised in order to constitute a coherent (social) identity. It must be borne in mind that whatever is integrated *inside*, there is always something that remains *outside*. The fantasy of the 'integrative pot' gives us an almost omnipotent illusion that things might be integrated inside, in the safe space, while what is outside will be kept away. The main issue here is that the concept of containment cannot abolish the distinction between inside/outside, and psychotherapy is entrapped in a spatial way of thinking about psychic life that largely stems from the Western way of thinking about identity and space (as external and internal; subjective and objective). We suggest here that one of the possible origins of thinking about containing space as a model of an integrated self may stem from a political and social formulation of identity in spatial, national or group terms, defined by borders and the outside/inside distinction.

Another important aspect to consider is the distinction between how people imagine or establish borders (usually as a political practice) and how people actually practice such borders in daily life. Borders are either reinforced or (legally or not) crossed. The image of a perfectly contained and closed space is a fantasy that societies and individuals maintain as a construction or scaffolding of their identities. Just as in the case of cities and buildings built on the plan of sacred geometry, in practice, it is very often an illusion that is impossible to realise. Groups have been mixed for centuries and in reality there is nothing like a pure nation or national identity. Why, then, do we dream about perfect borders? On the other hand, there is a complementary fantasy about a complete lack of boundaries, or global citizenship.

Self-contained and autonomous identity

In this section, the model of identity promoted by depth psychology will be critically discussed, particularly its origins in the Western tradition. In order to understand how depth psychology reproduces patterns of thinking about identity, we need to understand the broader context of emergence of the concept of the subject in Western societies. There is no agreement between scholars about the origins of the Western concept of autonomous individuality. Possible origins, such as Epicureanism (Lindsay), primitive Christianity (Troeltsch), Italian Renaissance (Burkhardt), Protestantism (Weber), the industrial revolution, modern nationalism and human rights are usually listed in the context of the emergence of individualism (Lukes, 1973). Whether the individual and autonomous self exists as a thing in itself we cannot know; nevertheless, there is definitely a powerful narrative in this regard, which involves concepts such as privacy, dignity, self-development, autonomy and rationality. As a rule, it is a chronological narrative that is dominant in the discourse of the autonomous self: it evolved from the more 'primitive' form of self, associated with social groups, particularly the family, into a modern individualised sense of 'I'. As with any narrative, however, doubts may arise. The narrative usually does not focus on the spatial dimension, but rather on the temporality of experience.

Many researchers concede that Christianity played an important role in constituting the concept of individuality. Siedentop (2015) proposes that we think about Western individualism in terms of the secularisation of the Christian concept of soul in the discourse of humanistic liberalism that 'preserves Christian ontology without the metaphysics of salvation'. The concept of the soul as individualised and separate from the body returns in some ideas about psyche in-depth psychology, which, as it can be argued, also preserves some Christian ontology in a secular way (as is particularly visible in Jungian readings of 'the Self' that tend to omit or downplay the body).

The second important source of the concept of the autonomous self is the emergence of individual narratives in the Renaissance. However, many scholars argue, in contradiction to Burkhardt's classic idea that the Renaissance was the era when individualism began, that the sense of self in the Renaissance was neither firm nor as autonomous and wilful as we are accustomed to thinking (Davis, 1986; Martin, 2006). For the purpose of this thesis, it must be recalled that the ideas of Theatre of Memory, geometrisation and the use of perspective in art were distinctive to Renaissance culture. Therefore, there might be a link between the Renaissance concept of interior space (for instance, memory as a 'storage container'), which can be represented and understood geometrically, and the emergence of the concept of the individual. Even if, as some scholars claim, the Renaissance self can be seen 'rather as the harbinger of the postmodern ego, fragmented, divided and fictitious' (Martin, 2006, p. 5), it developed a narrative of the self-contained subject. A vital connection might be supposed between representations of space in the Renaissance and the emergence of the concept of the autonomous individual. Such a concept would entail understanding the self as an 'inner theatre' and subjectivity as opposed to objectivity. Both traits are distinctive to the Western concept of identity.

In general, the concept of the self in Western society is based on the notions of coherence and continuity; the 'essence' persisting through change. Although some elements constituting an entity do change, the essence is unchangeable. Significantly, even in the ancient world, identity was pictured as the vessel in which parts are replaced but the vessel itself does not lose its identity. As we can read in Plutarch's *Theseus*:

> They took away the old timbers from time to time, and put new and sound ones in their places, so that the vessel became a standing illustration for the philosophers in the mooted question of growth, some declaring that it remained the same, others that it was not the same vessel.
>
> (as cited in Thiel, 2011, p. 24)

The concept of the vessel, understood as both a process of transformation and a form of individuality, is also present in Jungian psychology. It can be suggested that it is preserved in a form of idea of the essence, understood as the unchangeable part that constitutes the self. Similarly, in order to protect or even enable a process of transformation, the alchemical vessel must itself remain unchanged. Analogously, the identity understood as a container is a form containing changing aspects of personality (an idea that may stem from Aristotle's theory of form and matter, in which the soul is identified with a form).

The subjective sense of one's identity can be distinguished from the concept or narrative of the self. In some cases, we might have access to the narrative of subjective experience of the self (although always mediated by social and cultural concepts and discourses). However, what we usually have access to are social and cultural representations of the self. The idea of the self-contained identity must be distinguished from the subject being a product of power and social relations. Most cultures and societies produce phantasies about identity, but does the phantasy of an autonomous subject protect against the fearful vision of a fragmented self? Is this what depth psychology does, when it demonises impingements in the contained state, while simultaneously idealising the primal infant–mother relationship and the maternal space? In other words, is the vessel/container not so much about integration as it is about maintaining a comforting phantasy of, all in all, the unchanged self?

Traditional psychotherapy has reproduced this model – embedded in Western cultural history – of the individual as autonomous, the subject as wilful and the psyche as reducible to the 'inner world'. But how is this model expressed in depth psychology? First, from the perspective of depth psychology, the idea of the individual is based on the concept of separateness, particularly from the mother, which is a condition for further development. As Kristeva says: 'For man and for woman the loss of the mother is a biological and psychic necessity, the first step on the way to autonomy. Matricide is our vital necessity, the *sine qua non* of our individuation' (Kristeva, 1989, p. 27). Similarly, the model of individuation requires the hero to kill the mother-dragon in order to grow as an individual (Jung, 1956/1911–1912, *CW* 5). It is crucial to observe that Jung was using the figure of a, typically male, 'hero' to describe the psychological journey of the individual. Paradoxically, the 'killed' mother, as a psychological condition for growth, is restored in the concept of maternal space in depth psychology. It returns as a ghost – the indestructible 'maternal space'.

Second, in depth psychology, the psyche is understood as the 'inner world' or 'inner space'. This idea might stem from the religious concept of the indestructible part of oneself that is essential, as opposed to the material and temporary body, which was preserved and developed by the Western philosophy of dualism. The inner space is sometimes called the 'Cartesian theatre' (Dennett, 1991). Again, let us bear in mind here the Renaissance concept of Theatre of Memory and representations of interiority as a predominating space in culture and art. It is probably no coincidence that depth psychology uses the concept of container or *temenos* as a 'stage' for integrative processes forging the modern subject. The idea of a 'theatrical self', most likely stemming from Renaissance culture, had its less-known version of Theatre of Memory. Theatre of Memory is also a spatial metaphor of memory, where memory is understood as a storage for memories of past events. It also uses sacred geometry, the same concept that was used by C.G. Jung, to extend the idea of the self onto the Self. In that sense, we may suppose, the Renaissance concept of Theatre of Memory preceded the concept of individual and psychotherapeutic space in depth psychology. For instance, the contained self (the mind), understood as a container for memories that might be transformed into coherent narratives, gives the self meaning, as it becomes understood as a structured wholeness. Similarly, Theatre of Memory was designed to give meaning to universal knowledge by structuring it using the concept of cosmological order and sacred geometry. Therefore, Ps ←→ D (which describes the process of meaning-making from a fragmented state of impressions) can be a description of not only the concept of the contained–container by Bion, but also the Theatre of Memory.

Paradoxically, classical Freudian psychoanalysis began with a challenge to the notion of the autonomous self. Freud, in his famous essay, announces a great and hurting blow to the humanistic notion of individuality:

> But human megalomania will have suffered its third and most wounding blow from the psychological research of the present time which seeks to prove to the ego that it is not even master in its own house, but must content itself with scanty information of what is going on unconscious in its mind.
>
> (1917, S.E., 15, p. 284)

Freud, as a modern thinker, was not particularly content with this 'scanty information'; thus, he devoted his work to the restoration of control in the 'house'. In other words, although Freud discovered the 'uncontained' self, he later began to reproduce the old schema of thinking about the self-contained self as a telos of human individuation and growth. In this way, psychoanalysis, although originating in a discovery of the 'fragmented self', became a part of the discourse promoting a 'self-contained' self, based on the ideas of wholeness and functionality. These are also the origins of the concept of containing space.

The discovery that the ego itself is not the whole house did not change the concept of the individual as the house that must be explored, taken under control and, we might say, 'colonised'. The psyche-house as described by psychoanalysis has a structure, including the walls and layers. The individual came to be seen as possibly spatially 'containable', and this was established as the main aim of psychotherapeutic work. Similarly, the concept of the Self in Jungian psychology does not change the general model of thinking about individuality, but merely shifts the ego into a less privileged position. Consequently, psychoanalytic thinking about the spatial mind can be seen as a project to restore wholeness. This is probably the idea that most psychoanalytic theories share (such as the model of contained–container, the Self, the ecopsychological concept of nature as the eco-self or Freud's house model): longing for the lost paradise of the whole Self, centralised, meaningful and contained.[1] The idea of restoration can be understood in terms of the colonising tendency of psychoanalysis: it promotes a single model of the subject and well-being as the aim of therapy.

But can depth psychology, with its colonising tendencies, withdraw from the project to restore the autonomy of human agency? One possible answer is to start by changing the concept of space. This is where the psychogeographical practice of space may be introduced. A psychogeographical interpretation of psychotherapeutic space will challenge the classical thinking by questioning its principles: what if there is no 'house' and no boundaries or centre?

The concept of the autonomous individual is based on an idealised and unrealistic situation. Similarly, in depth psychology, the idea of the autonomous self is based on the premise that there is (in a perfect situation) a contained relation between the mother and infant that is later introjected by the infant as 'a psychic apparatus'. Let us now reimagine this situation and consider that there is never any original exclusive contained state that involves only the mother and infant – as there are many other elements present from the beginning, including the father, the environment and other carers of the infant. What, then, is introjected by the infant to later create its sense of identity?

Bion distinguishes the subjectivity that is constructed at the stage of formulation of α-elements (dream work α) from the identity itself as a final 'product' of maturation achieved through containment. If the dream thoughts processed as alpha elements already constitute subjectivity (for instance, forming the emotional memory), it is through containment that the coherent narrative may occur. In Bion's model, the identity is associated with boundaries (as a result of being contained) and coherence (impressions and protothoughts constituting a narrative).

Indeed, what we usually mean by 'identity' is the 'product' of containment, usually associated with thought and coherence. We rarely think of the subjective experience of α-elements as a possible type of identity or subjectivity (which could be called 'dreaming identity'). Behind thinking about the mind in a topographic or archaeological way, there is a project of representing something intangible in a more representative form. A spatial subject is a subject that can be understood, an idea that stems from the Enlightenment project of the rationalised subjectivity.

We suggest here that the shadow of the concept of spatial psyche originates from the fact that it is an ego-construct, a phantasy of contained, safe psychic organisation. Just like the use of borders, it not only keeps something in, it also keeps something out. For instance, in a topographic or archaeological model, the id is already integrated into the structure. However, can the id-space or any non-ego space be represented in the form of an enclosed system? What if there are topographies of the mind of which psychotherapists are not fully aware or do not want to be aware, as they promote the therapeutic space as a space organised exclusively by the principle of integration? What would topographies of uncontained states of mind be?

Uncontained states of mind and defensiveness

How do we, as a society, tolerate what is uncontained and unthinkable? How do we deal with the unbearable pain, suffering and tragedies that are a constant part of our reality? One possible way is to create a phantasy that we are capable of managing. The idea that we can avoid impingements in the process of therapy is an illusion. Similarly, the concept of the psychotherapeutic container might be an idealisation as we are in a state of continuous becoming.

While the containing space is undoubtedly an important part of psychotherapeutic thinking, it is not the only way in which the psychotherapeutic space can be considered. Furthermore, thinking about therapeutic space in terms of boundaries and the setting is in many ways reductive. It completely misses the point of exploration, non-linearity of experience, and what cannot be contained. It is claimed that the containing creates the space for exploration, as Cartwright describes: 'Once these "constraints" are in place the analyst is able to use preconscious and unconscious areas of mind to probe, explore and generate new experiences' (Cartwright, 2010, p. 49). Are containing boundaries set in order to create a space for exploration, or are they merely protective? What would exploration beyond these boundaries comprise?

The psychotherapeutic space, understood as geometrical, contained and safe, is just one aspect of psychotherapy. The other aspect is mourning the loss of this idealised model of space (Cartwright, 2010). For Jungian psychology, this would mean embracing what is beyond the temenos/mandala without reducing it to the sacred space in the totalising and universalising concept of integration.

Depth psychology seems to suffer from a fear of failure of the 'maternal uterus' and, as a result, it creates an idealised image of the therapeutic womb. It needs to accept that therapy cannot provide the patient with perfect conditions and the idealised image thus needs to be mourned – not only by the patient but also by psychotherapy itself. Otherwise, the image of the containing space becomes a symptom of the 'saviour complex', the idealisation of the therapeutic situation or the therapists themselves. In this case, moving away from this idealised image and mourning the containing space is a more important task of the therapeutic process than creating a containing space. Accepting what is uncontained and cannot be integrated, and moving away from the privileged and superior status of the therapeutic space, is a necessary step to allow psychotherapy to move beyond its delusional state.

In fact, in psychotherapeutic practice, the setting is very often altered or breached. Despite an enormous number of publications regarding the essentiality of the setting (such as Brown & Stobart, 2008; Gray, 2013), the psychoanalytic literature also provides some self-reflective and good examples of breaking or altering the setting (Akhtar, 2011; Luca, 2004). For successful and effective psychotherapeutic work, impingements may be as important as boundaries. For instance, some unplanned changes and unexpected events may bring surprisingly good results for the treatment. Once we realise that boundaries and the setting are idealistic illusions, both psychotherapists and patients may feel more comfortable with what is uncontained and is not meant to be contained. Would psychotherapy lose its power by loosening or even withdrawing from the concept of the setting? Does psychotherapy exercise its power by using concepts, such as the containing space, that protect its exclusive and superior position?

Although the practice may differ from the theory, in the psychotherapeutic literature, the therapeutic frame is defined in a rigid way. For instance, according to Langs:

> The ideal therapeutic frame is composed of ground rules that include: (1) total confidentiality; (2) privacy; (3) predictability and consistency manifested in a set fee, location, time and length for all sessions; (4) therapist neutrality; and (5) therapist anonymity.
> (Quoted in Cheifetz, 1984, p. 216)

On the other hand, the boundaries as a key element of psychotherapy have been criticised within psychotherapy itself. The setting can easily become a neurotic and defensive space if flexibility is not allowed and many of the fears of both patient and therapist can be projected and maintained in the so-called containing space. The containing space can easily become its own shadow. Cartwright, writing about patients living in the 'claustrum', observed that:

> These apparently neurotic anxieties (being on time, obsessive interest in the beginnings and ends of sessions, preoccupation with payment, ritualized ways of starting sessions, and so forth) often have an autistic edge to them that block the processing of experience that is jointly constructed as the session unfolds.
> (2010, p. 154)

Something similar can be said about psychotherapy becoming too obsessive about the containing space, understood as the sole permissible kind of setting. What, in theory, is supposed to protect the client, can unconsciously serve as a defensive function not only of the therapist but also of psychotherapy in general. Although psychotherapy is in great need of the ethical regulation of practice, it has a shadow in the form of moralism, normative categories and defence. As Samuels writes:

> First, then, I propose that psychotherapy and counselling have overdone the stress on providing a secure container within which a therapy relationship can thrive [...] This leads to behavioural conformism and a corresponding moralism. What are the disadvantages of the current stress on the frame, on boundaries, on the container? Doesn't this lose the element of surprise, the risk inherent to psychotherapy [...], the exposure to danger that is involved in any process of self-understanding and/or growth?
> (Samuels, 2014, p. 185)

In a similar manner, Totton says:

> The developing concept of appropriate boundaries increasingly forces therapists into defensive practice and to work in ways that are based not on giving the client the therapeutic environment best suited to them, but on avoiding vulnerability to misconduct hearings.
>
> (2010, p. 13)

Psychotherapy needs to question the way it uses the concept of containment, as boundaries may serve not only to protect the therapeutic space, but also protect from engagement with another human being or to protect one's own therapeutic practice. This is how boundaries are sometimes used as part of the setting – not only protecting the patient but also the therapist – from both ethical responsibility and being overloaded. The setting may mean that psychotherapists are protected in the space of the consulting room. As a result, they turn a blind eye to social, cultural and political practice, focusing solely on the inner and relational process. To keep something in, something must be kept out. The setting, just as the concept of the mind as the 'inner world' or the private and autonomous self, produces an abstract metaphor of social and therapeutic conditions that has little to do with reality.

Another issue is the universalising (hence, colonising) character of the setting. The setting implies that, as Totton puts it, 'all clients at all times should be treated within the same set of boundaries' (2010, p. 13). This may, as a result, overlook what is individual and unique. It ignores the unique nature of the psychotherapeutic process and replaces experiences with thinking in terms of boundaries.

We should ask in the first place: why does psychotherapy need the setting and boundaries? It needs them because this is the only aspect that distinguishes it from any other 'human encounter'. Psychotherapy has branded the concepts of containment and boundaries that allow it to protect its privileged position. In other words, the concept of boundary-setting ensures that a psychotherapeutic meeting is special because it is protected. The analytical relationship wants to distinguish and exclude itself from any other form of social relationship. In theory, the setting protects the relationship and therapeutic process 'from contamination' (Brown & Stobart, 2008, p. 3).[2] On a functional level, boundaries distinguish the analytic relationship and make it unique – while, in ordinary life, unexpected and uncontrollable changes happen all the time, the therapeutic setting proceeds with regularity and stability. It creates a simulacrum that is false and out of touch with reality. The psychoanalytic theory is very clear about what type of phantasy it maintains – it is a simulacrum of the uterus, the illusion of the safe womb in the dangerous, post-natal world.

Most clinicians are aware, although the theory very often denies it, that the containing space protecting from impingements is merely an illusion, an idealised image that was created in the psychoanalytic theory. The setting and boundaries cannot be maintained as absolute in clinical practice – delays occur; depending on where the consulting room is, a stranger may knock or even enter a room (which quite often occurs in hospitals); noises come from outside the window or from other rooms; and plenty of unexpected things may occur to either the patient or therapist. Similarly, although confidentiality is a key principle of the setting and containing space, in practice, therapists share the details of their patients' lives with their supervisors and during supervision groups. When a patient gives permission, their life story can also be shared as 'a case' and used at conferences or published. Moreover, the setting as a space cannot be excluded from social and power relations. On the contrary, the psychotherapeutic setting is exactly where social practice is focused and condensed. Even the concept of boundaries, as demonstrated above, is an example of how a societal discourse becomes part of the psychotherapeutic setting and co-constructs its key categories, such as the setting itself.

The setting of a perfectly well-sealed container exists only in the imagination, as a psychoanalytic phantasy. Much has been written about the ideal conditions for psychotherapy, but as Maria Luca observes 'little is written on therapeutic technique that is outside the remit of these idealisations or on therapeutic failures, therapeutic mistakes and transgressions that prove valuable' (2004, p. 9).

Ecopsychology argues against this reductive and detached model of the therapeutic space, claiming that the broader surroundings need to be taken into account in a psychotherapeutic process. However, as argued above, it cannot be merely about the enlargement of the containing space. Rather, we need to think of a completely new therapeutic space. Similarly, crossing the boundaries and altering the setting in psychotherapeutic practice does not change the model itself, which, as has been shown in this chapter, is embedded in the Western tradition of thinking and traditional societal discourses. There is a need to change the model itself and imagine alternative ways of thinking about space in depth psychology that would correspond more to the changing times and society.

Notes

1 The restored wholeness has very different meanings in Freud's and Jung's theories. If the wholeness of the Self in Jung's case comes from religious and spiritual concepts and is represented by geometrised spaces, Freud's project stems from utilitarianism: the restored house has a functional meaning. The functionality can be described according to several rules such as: (1) self-contained system of energy; (2) connected parts working together mechanically; (3) conversion of energy into a higher level of consciousness ('Where there was id, there shall be ego').
2 The term 'contamination' used in the context of the setting is, in many ways, fascinating. The setting protecting the psychotherapeutic relation from 'contamination' corresponds with the division between sacred and profane space (Eliade, 1959) and is visible in Jung's models of therapeutic space inspired by the temenos, mandala, *vas bene clausum* and sacred geometry.

References

Akhtar, S. (2011). *Unusual interventions: Alterations of the frame, method, and relationship in psychotherapy and psychoanalysis*. London: Karnac Books.

Brown, R., & Stobart, K. (2008). *Understanding boundaries and containment in clinical practice*. London: Karnac Books.

Cartwright, D. (2010). *Containing states of mind: Exploring Bion's 'container model' in psychoanalytic psychotherapy*. London: Routledge.

Cheifetz, L.G. (1984). Framework violations in psychotherapy with clinic patients. In J. Raney (Ed.), *Listening and interpreting: The challenge of the work of Robert Langs* (pp. 215–253). New York: Aronson.

Davis, N.Z. (1986). Boundaries and the sense of self in sixteenth-century France. In T.C. Heller, D.E. Wellberg, & M. Sosna (Eds.), *Reconstructing individualism: Autonomy, individuality, and the self in Western thought* (pp. 53–63). Stanford, CA: Stanford University Press.

Dennett, D.C. (1991). *Consciousness explained*. Boston, MA: Little, Brown & Co.

Douglas, M. (1966). *Purity and danger: An analysis of concepts of pollution and taboo*. New York: Frederick A. Praeger.

Eliade, M. (1959). *The Sacred and the profane: The nature of religion* (Willard R. Trask, Trans.). New York: Harcourt Brace.

Fassin, D. (2011). Policing borders, producing boundaries. The governmentality of immigration in dark times. *Annual Review of Anthropology*, 40, 213–226.

Freud, S. (1917). Introductory lectures on psycho-analysis. 1916–1917. In J. Strachey (Ed. and Trans.), *The standard edition of the complete psychological works of Sigmund Freud* (S.E.) pp. 15–16. London: Hoghart.

Gerrard, J. (2016). The refugee crisis, non-citizens, border politics and education. *Discourse: Studies in the Cultural Politics of Education*, 38(6), 1–12.

Gray, A. (2013). *An introduction to the therapeutic frame*. Routledge.

Hogg, M.A. (2014). From uncertainty to extremism: Social categorization and identity processes. *Current Directions in Psychological Science*, 23(5), 338–342.

Jung, C.G. (1956/1911–12). Symbols of transformation. In H. Read, M. Fordham, & G. Adler (Eds.), *The collected works (CW 5)*. (R.F.C. Hull, Trans.). London: Routledge & Kegan Paul.

Kristeva, J. (1982). *Powers of horror: An essay on abjection*. New York: Columbia University Press.

Kristeva, J. (1989). *Black sun: Depression and melancholia*. New York: Columbia University Press.

Luca, M. (2004). Boundary issues in psychotherapy: From the literal to the figurative frame. In M. Luca (Ed.), *The therapeutic frame in the clinical context: Integrative perspectives* (pp. 8–35). London: Routledge.

Lukes, S. (1973). *Individualism*. Oxford: Basil Blackwell.

Martin, J.J. (2006). *Myth of renaissance individualism*. Basingstoke: Palgrave Macmillan.

Rheindorf, M., & Wodak, R. (2018). Borders, fences, and limits – Protecting Austria from refugees: Metadiscursive negotiation of meaning in the current refugee crisis. *Journal of Immigrant & Refugee Studies*, 16(1–2), 15–38.

Samuels, A. (2014), Shadows of the therapy relationship. In D. Loewenthal, & A. Samuels (Eds.), *Relational psychotherapy, psychoanalysis and counselling: Appraisals and reappraisals* (pp. 184–192). London: Routledge.

Siedentop, L. (2015). *Inventing the individual: The origins of Western liberalism*. London: Penguin.
Temperley, J. (1984). Settings for psychotherapy. *British Journal of Psychotherapy*, 1(2), 101–111.
Thiel, U. (2011). *The early modern subject: Self-consciousness and personal identity from Descartes to Hume*. Oxford: Oxford University Press.
Totton, N. (2010). Boundaries and boundlessness. *Therapy Today*, 21(8), 10–15.

Chapter 7
Alchemy and individuation
Clare Crellin

Introduction

Jung's work on alchemy is often regarded as a deviation from his psychological purpose. In fact, Jung's fifty-year fascination with alchemy lies at the heart of his thinking. I propose that a full understanding of the subtleties of meaning of the main concepts and theoretical constructs in his theory of personality is impossible without understanding the alchemical ideas that helped to shape these concepts.

Any attempt to encapsulate Jung's theory by enumerating his main concepts leaves half of the story untold. Its unique aspect is the fusion of Jung's psychological concepts with his knowledge of religious and cultural history. The typology is often thought of as 'Jung's theory of personality', but it is not the core of his personality theory. The core is individuation, a position of balance and unity.

The chapter extract introduces alchemy and cosmology and shows the specific ways in which alchemical ideas and images shaped Jung's approach to therapy and his concept of the collective unconscious with its intimations of immortality.

Alchemy

Alchemy has been described variously as an art and a science (Holmyard, 1957), as a sacred science (Eliade, 1978), as a science of the cosmos, and as a royal art (ars regia; Burckhardt, 1997). Its practice was concerned with transforming metals and distilling elixirs for medical purposes. However, Holmyard distinguishes between alchemy's exoteric practice and its hidden esoteric and symbolic aspect. Its outward (exoteric) practice was primarily concerned with the making of gold. This was to be achieved through attempts to prepare a substance, the Philosopher's Stone or Lapis, which would have power to transform base metals into precious metals (Holmyard, 1957: 16). Even this practical goal carried symbolic significance. Holmyard reminds us that gold had been regarded as a sacred metal long before it was used as a measure of commercial transactions. Burckhardt (1997: 11) notes that gold and silver were regarded as earthly reflections of sun and moon and of spirit and soul and that preparation of ores was the prerogative of priests in ancient Egypt. Alchemy's hidden (esoteric) nature had arisen from the belief that the Stone could only be obtained through divine grace. This led to the development of a devotional system in which the transmutation of metals became the symbol for the transformation of a human into a perfect being through prayer and submission to the will of God (Holmyard, 1957: 15–16).

The several strands of alchemy are linked with different geographical cultures. These are: Egyptian alchemy (through metallurgy and embalming practices to ensure the immortality of the soul), pre-Islamic alchemy (emphasising the soul's development in its quest to become closer to God), Chinese alchemy (linking the idea of immortality with the untarnishability of gold), and Indian alchemy (linked with the practice of yoga). Historians of alchemy have had difficulty in tracing exactly which texts came into Europe, when, and from where. Some Hermetic ideas were incorporated into Islam and reached Europe via Moorish Spain. A flood of texts, in Latin translations, came to Western Europe in the Renaissance of the fifteenth and sixteenth centuries. The alchemical texts known to Jung were from the late Middle Ages (Arnaldus of Villanova, Ramon Llull), the Renaissance and late-Renaissance periods (Paracelsus, Pico della Mirandola, Marsilio Ficino, Michael Maier), and the seventeenth and eighteenth centuries (Nicholas Flamel and Isaac Newton). In addition to European alchemy, Jewish, Arabic, Chinese, and Indian traditions are represented in the collections to which Jung had access. Alchemy also incorporated ideas from cosmology – speculations on the nature of the universe that reach as far back in time as the earliest origins of thought itself. It is these cosmological ideas that are in the background of Jung's thinking, with ideas about the immortality of the soul being most relevant in relation to his own conception of the soul.

Cosmology

Cosmologies were attempts to describe topographically and theologically the entire Divine Grand Design of Creation. Cosmologists were concerned with questions like: What is God? How did God create the universe? What might have been the process? What has God as Divine Intelligence to do with creation? Preclassical and medieval cosmology answered these in the following way: The world is the result of God's imagination. Matter reflects and embodies God's imagination, although it is not wholly contained in matter. The sun's energy and light enliven matter, changing and transforming it. This transformation is the direct result of God's energy, which is an aspect of God's intelligence and imagination. The spark or scintilla, the tiny bit of light in every creature, is the result of the sun's (therefore God's) action on matter. Matter is not inert but receives light and then actively participates in the transformation. This active principle of matter relates to deeply held ideas about the male/female principle. The female (earth/mother) is acted upon but participates equally in the transformative process, bringing her own nature to the field of change.

All cosmologies start with the principle of undivided unity (oneness) and move through many levels of division from binary (such as the polarities of male/female) through further subdivision to multiplicity and the entire diversity of Creation.

Jung's alchemical sources

The index of the *Collected Works* reveals that Jung consulted a number of Renaissance collections of alchemical tracts, mainly in Latin versions. Through these collections, Jung had access to most classical alchemical authors in translation (from original Arabic and Greek mainly into Latin). For example, he had access to the visions of Zosimos of Panopolis, Maria Prophetissa, the Egyptian Magus, Hermes Trismegistus, and many famous illustrated texts such as the Rosarium philosophorum and the Chymical Wedding. The most striking features of alchemical texts are their coded illustrations and their rich visual and literary symbolism. Alchemists describe their theories, operations, and materials in 'language efflorescent with allegory, metaphor, allusion and analogy' (Holmyard, 1957: 16). Modern textual exegesis relies on the comparative study of different texts. The meaning contexts in which terms occur are compared for illumination and amplification. According to Marie-Louise von Franz, the Jungian writer and researcher into alchemy, this was also Jung's method (von Franz, 1977: 21). Common themes in alchemical texts are transformation, healing, spiritual openness, individual life in relation to the cosmos, the oneness or unity of the self, and the male and female principle.

Jung's psychological interpretation of alchemy

In 1942, Jung gave lectures to the Swiss Society for the History of Medicine on Paracelsus, the sixteenth-century Swiss healer-alchemist. Paracelsus believed that healing assists God because it assists nature. Because it is God's work: 'You must be of an honest, sincere, strong, true faith in God, with all your soul, heart, mind and thought, in all love and trust' (Paracelsus, Paragranum, cited in *CW* 13 1942 §146). Distillations of minerals and organic matter were used to restore balance and assist nature's healing powers in the body, thus helping God's purpose by accelerating nature's task. To heal a body was to heal nature itself, but more than healing was involved. Jung tells us that, for Paracelsus, the alchemist's task was 'bringing to perfection the divine will implanted in nature' (*CW* 13 1942 §236).

Jung's psychological interpretation was to suggest that alchemists' activities could be understood as a projection which 'results in the activation and development of a psychic centre, a concept that coincides psychologically with that of the self' (*CW* 13 1942 §189). The unconscious psychological process consisted firstly of a confrontation with inner darkness, then dissolution, and finally a transformative resolution. For this reason, Jung claimed that alchemy was the forerunner of the psychotherapy of the unconscious (*CW* 13 1942 §237). At the same time, the alchemist was concerned with transforming and perfecting the self so as to achieve sufficient closeness to God for 'the work' to succeed. The alchemical adept sought connection with the Divine in attempting to create Nature's perfect metal (gold). The intensity of spiritual openness required a guide if the adept was to avoid what might now be termed depression and psychosis. Similarly Jung emphasised the dangers of the psychic journey towards individuation and the protective function of the psychic guide (psychotherapist).

Jung used alchemy as a veil to draw attention away from the highly subjective origins of his ideas. He could say through alchemy what he could not say directly: 'Alchemy ... has performed for me the great and invaluable service of providing material in which my experience could find sufficient room, and has thereby made it possible for me to describe the individuation process' (*CW* 14 1955–1956 §792). This is why it is essential to look closely at his work on alchemy to understand the meaning connotations for his key theoretical terms.

The very early years: 1896 to 1918

In these early years, Jung was preoccupied with the problem of opposites and the existence of inherent 'primordial ideas' in the unconscious, which he later called the archetypes. He was interested in Gnostic ideas, especially the duality or ambivalence of God.

Symbols of Transformation (*CW* 5 1911–1912/1952) was Jung's first attempt to demonstrate his method of dream interpretation based on a systematic amplification of dream images by comparison with myths. The book contains a wealth of mythological and symbolic material, some of which is alchemical. At that time Jung used alchemical texts primarily as sources of literary allusions, whose purpose was to support his concept of the 'collective unconscious' and its hypothesised autonomous contents, the primordial images.

Jung had not yet fully worked out an alchemical theory of individuation or the elaborate alchemical metaphor for psychotherapy. However, during this early period, other evidence suggests that he is developing a cosmological view of humankind that is very much in resonance with the alchemical model. His first published mandala picture, the systema munditotius, which dates from about 1916, expresses his cosmological worldview, showing opposites in relation to unity and a dual-natured God-image (Jeromson, 2006). Thus, although there is evidence before 1918 that Jung was aware of alchemical ideas, which were perhaps working in him, he was not yet drawing on them in the formation of his main theoretical concepts.

The midlife years: 1918 to 1935

Jung's serious study of alchemy began in the late 1920s. Jung is reported (in Jung & Jaffé, 1963) to have said that he took a more active interest in studying alchemy after 1928 when he read a translation of the Chinese text The Secret of the Golden Flower and that he recalled commissioning a Munich bookseller to notify him of any alchemical texts that came into his hands. Subsequently, over a period of ten years from around 1930, he made a lexicon of key phrases 'as if I were trying to solve the riddle of an unknown language' (Jung & Jaffé, 1963: 231).

In the period 1918 to 1935, Jung began to express psychological processes in alchemical terms. By 1928, he was moving away from using dreams to support his concept of the collective unconscious and towards seeing dreams as bringing about the transformations that he observed in himself and his patients. Alchemy was helping him to understand psychotherapy in terms of moving through stages, like the steps of an alchemical process. In his subsequent discussions of the stages of psychotherapy and its techniques, Jung used alchemical imagery as a direct means of expression of its stages and processes. In 'The technique of differentiation between the ego and the figures of the unconscious' (*CW* 7 1928 Pt 2 chapter III), Jung compares differentiation as a change of personality that involves a transformation of general attitude (*CW* 7 1928 §360) with the concept of Tao, the 'middle way' of Lao-Tzu (*CW* 7 1928 §365), in which the creative centre and equilibrium of all things is achieved by a transformation brought about by a transcendent function. Jung gives a twentieth-century case example in which transformation of personality is brought about by the patient's active participation, merging herself in the unconscious processes and gaining possession of them 'by allowing them to possess her' and consequently opening her consciousness to unconscious contents. Jung expressed this psychological process as 'transmutation in the alchemical heat, the genesis of the "subtle spirit" that is the transcendent function born of the opposites' (*CW* 7 1928 §368).

Part IV of 'The technique of differentiation between the ego and the figures of the unconscious' (*CW* 7 1928) has two long quotations from Goethe's Faust, reminding the reader of Jung's early fascination with Faust's description of personal transformation. In Part V, Jung expresses the idea that imagination is the creative source of all that has made progress possible to human life (*CW* 7 1916 §492). The route to individuation is 'hermeneutic treatment of imaginative ideas' (*CW* 7 1916 §497). Development of individuality is a divine pathway, a duty, a moral task, just as the alchemical adept had a divine duty to prepare spiritually for the sacred task. Individuation of the personality is presented here as a moral aim whose outcome is to take both oneself and the outside world equally seriously 'with a sound sense of the general good' (*CW* 7 1916 §502).

Alchemy and psychotherapy

Jung first presented his idea that psychotherapy fosters individuation in 'Problems of Modern Psychology' (1929), translated by Baynes and Dell for publication in *Modern Man in Search of a Soul* (Jung, 1933/1981). In 'The practical use of dream analysis' (1934), he explains the process of Jungian psychotherapy in the 'Tavistock Lectures' (1935), introducing his concept of dynamic unconscious archetypes and the technique of amplification. In lecture IV, he says people feel less isolated if they see that the archetypes of their dream images are not merely particular and personal but are universally human (*CW* 18 1935 §232–233).

Through alchemy, Jung began to understand psychotherapy as a cycle of separation, regeneration, and transformation. He described the stages in detail. The first stage was to see the subjective value of the images that create difficulties for patients and to encourage the patient to try to 'find out why they are a part of himself' (*CW* 18 1935 §367), then to assimilate the contents of the neurosis. The second stage, when this has been achieved, leaves projections that 'belong to the structural elements of the psyche' and are important protective features (*CW* 18 1935 §368). These projections feel as if they are located outside one's ego and do not belong to one. Jung is differentiating here between the personal and the collective unconscious. He reminds us that archetypes, although irrational, have a tremendous fascination and are powerful enough to change history:

> The powerful factor, the factor which changes our whole life, which changes the surface of our known world, which makes history, is collective psychology, and collective psychology moves according to laws entirely different from those of our consciousness. The archetypes are the great decisive forces, they bring about real events, and not our personal reasoning and practical intellect. Before the Great War all intelligent people said 'We shall not have any more war, we are too reasonable to let it happen' … and now look at reality! … Man's unconscious psychology decides, and not what we think and talk in the brain-chamber up in the attic.
>
> (*CW* 18 1935 §371)

The patient had to have a full recognition of the importance of his or her archetypal images. Jung thought that alchemy, religion, and therapy seek the same treasure and that this treasure is the self. When describing the technique by which the patient objectifies collective (nonpersonal) images from the unconscious, he expresses the healing and transformative process through the language and imagery of alchemy, behind which is the language and imagery of religion. First, he said, the patient has to 'secure the treasure in the unconscious', since in the unconscious which is nature, 'there is gold, there is the treasure and the great value' (*CW* 18 1935 §375). The person no longer places the guarantee of his happiness outside of himself but 'comes to realise that everything depends on whether he holds the treasure or not. If the possession of that gold is realized, then the centre of gravity is in the individual and no longer in an object on which he depends' (*CW* 18 1935 §377). Healing, he tells us, has to do with detachment, acceptance and transformation, as in 'Eastern practices of detachment and … all the teachings of the Church' (*CW* 18 1935 §377). If the individual could be helped to relate to the images that have taken on form and are living their own characteristic life in him, 'he is in touch with that vital function which from the dawn of time has been taken care of by religion' (*CW* 18 1935 §378).

The mature years: 1936 to 1944

We have seen how, in midlife, Jung's conviction that alchemy had a psychological as well as a spiritual meaning led him to think about the healing process of psychotherapy in terms of a stage-process. He developed his technique of 'hermeneutical treatment of imaginative ideas' through a series of steps that resembled the stages of the alchemical process. During this period, he began to differentiate between a personal and a suprapersonal collective unconscious, and he speaks of psychotherapy as enabling the patient to detach from outer objects so as to realise possession of the treasure within, later expressed as the God-self or the God-within.

During the years 1936 to 1944, alchemy became the main focus of Jung's writings. In his lectures of 1935 to 1936, alchemical symbols and dream symbols signified a parallel process (*CW* 12 1944 p. x; *CW* 14 1955–1956 §705, §711). The step-by-step alchemical process worked in matter to release the world-creating spirit, and the same processes work in the individual psyche to bring about the unified self (*CW* 14 1955–1956 §759–760).

Jung's most substantial published work on alchemy can be found in Volume 12 of the *Collected Works*, which is based on two lectures given at the Eranos conferences of 1935 and 1936. The lectures were 'Traumsymbole des Individuations-prozesses' Eranos-Jahrbuch 1935 and 'Die Erlösungsvorstellungen in der Alchemie' Eranos-Jahrbuch 1936 (see *CW* 12 1944 p. vii). The substance is a comparative analysis of a series of dreams recorded by a colleague (unnamed in the text, but now known to have been the physicist Wolfgang Pauli; see Brown, 2011: 198–199). Here Jung states his view that alchemy's redemptive work releasing Christ in the individual is both spiritual and psychological (*CW* 12 1944 §557). He saw this as an age-old, pre-rational process that uses an intuitive and pragmatic form of thinking (see the next section) which senses what does and does not benefit the psyche. At a simple level, such pragmatic judgements are essential for survival; at a more developed level, they are essential for the human psyche to develop itself.

Pragmatic logic

The third of his collection of three essays (1902–1932), 'Phénomènes occultes', deals with the question of the soul's existence after death. Jung proposed the existence of an intuitive and feeling-based pragmatic logic that he believed must have existed before reason and before any kind of philosophical thinking. The significance for investigating Jung's use of alchemy to articulate his personality theory is his proposition that this kind of logical 'test' is what makes humans able to make use of symbols as an inner guide. In speaking about the usefulness of unverifiable ideas like immortality, Jung says:

> We know that salt is indispensable for our physiological health. We do not eat salt for this reason, however, but food with salt in it tastes better. We can easily imagine that long before there was any philosophy, human beings had instinctively found out what ideas were necessary for the normal functioning of the psyche.
> (*CW* 18 1938 §743)

The later years: 1945 to 1961

The main development in relation to his personality theory was his articulation of his concept of the archetype and the presentation of further alchemical research. It was a period in which Jung repeated, explained, and clarified the psychological vision that alchemy helped him to develop.

There were several publications during this period. The first major one was Psychology of the Transference: interpreted in conjunction with a set of alchemical illustrations (*CW* 16 1946). This complex work gives a detailed comparison of similarities Jung perceived between the alchemical processes depicted in the allegorical illustrations to the text Rosarium philosophorum (1550) and transference phenomena he observed in psychotherapy. In 1946, Jung also published a foreword to a Yale University Library catalogue of books and manuscripts from the collection of Paul and Mary Mellon in which he asserted his projection theory of alchemy. On this occasion, Jung reflected that alchemical language is perhaps intended to reveal rather than conceal: 'Alchemical language ... does not disguise a known content but suggests an unknown one, or rather, this unknown content suggests itself' (*CW* 18 1946/1968 §1691). I think that exactly this is true of Jung's own use of an alchemical language, to enable an 'unknown' content to suggest and reveal itself to him and to his readers.

Mandala symbols and the self

An important group of studies published in 1950 brought Jung's alchemical and religious ideas together and emphasised the central concept of individuation in his personality theory. The first is a 'thoroughly revised and enlarged' version of an earlier (1934) Eranos lecture entitled 'A study on the process of individuation'. It is a study of the paintings (mostly in the mandala form) made by a woman who had studied with Jung in the late 1920s. In his detailed analysis of the 24 paintings, Jung identified symbols whose significance for alchemists pointed to a process of transformation towards wholeness and unity. His concluding remarks voiced his growing confidence in making the inner process of the mandala 'more intelligible': 'They are ... self delineations of dimly sensed changes going on in the background, which are perceived by the "reversed eye" and rendered visible with pencil and brush, just as they are, uncomprehended and unknown' (*CW* 9.1 1934/1950 §622).

His subsequent essay 'Concerning mandala symbolism' (1950) recounts the history of mandalas in Indian religious rituals and in Tibetan Buddhism and analyses 54 illustrations painted by different people, some of whom were patients of his. Jung's conclusion was that:

> Their basic motif is the premonition of a centre of personality, a kind of central point within the psyche, to which everything is related, by which everything is arranged, and which is itself a source of energy. The energy of the central point is manifested in the almost irresistible compulsion and urge to become what one is.
> (*CW* 9.1 1950 §634)

Alchemy and the collective unconscious

Jung's last book, *Mysterium Coniunctionis*: an enquiry into the separation and synthesis of psychic opposites, written between 1941 and 1954, examined a number of alchemical texts in detail (*CW* 14 1955–1956). The most striking and salient fact from the point of view of this enquiry is that Jung sought to finish his life's work with a clear statement about the wider canvas that alchemy offered for the study of the collective unconscious. Jung needed a multitude of comparative examples to demonstrate that the core of the human psyche is the same for all.

Jung completed 'Symbols and the interpretation of dreams' (*CW* 18 1961) in the year of his death. His final words returned to the problem of opposites, the importance of symbols, and the unifying potency of the unconscious:

> Our actual knowledge of the unconscious shows it to be a natural phenomenon, and that, like nature itself, is at least neutral. It contains all aspects of human nature – light and dark, beautiful and ugly, good and

evil, profound and silly. The study of individual as well as collective symbolism is an enormous task, and one that has not yet been mastered. But ... a beginning has been made.

(*CW* 18 1961 §607)

Conclusion

It was no coincidence that Jung became interested in alchemy, in which immortality was a central concern. Jung's 'collective' unconscious is immortal in an unusual sense of the word. Jung's conception of immortality is not of the person as he or she has been in life. He drew on Paracelsus's vision, which affords immortality both to the Astrum (the Divine spark) and, to a degree, the Iliaster (the autonomous dynamic individualising principle). The Paracelsian way of envisioning a human form of immortality gave Jung an important new perspective, the 'third idea' that allowed him to answer his questions about opposites, about how to reconcile infinite diversity with oneness and death with immortality. He concluded that the unconscious represents the borderline between psyche and soma, mind and instinct, humanity and nature. This both precedes and continues beyond individual life, because it is the matrix, the *materia prima*, from which individual life is formed. Viewed from this perspective, the unconscious includes an aspect that is part of the world-soul, part of the universe. In it, humanity and nature meet and melt into one another. Furthermore, Jung's collective unconscious, as nature, has generative power that individuals can access. By bringing this into conscious awareness, individuals can tap a creative source of which they are also a part. The individual participates in its own genesis, having inside itself the source of its own being. It is both creature and creator. It may be said to mirror the Divine imagination as expressed in the idea 'as above, so below' in the alchemical vision. Through borrowing from alchemy's philosophy, Jung felt able to give an account of the collective unconscious that satisfied him, as well as of the dynamic, autonomous process of individuation. No other imagery or philosophy could have achieved this for him.

Discussion

The historical accuracy of Jung's picture of alchemy

Jung's understanding of alchemy accords with recent scholarship that recognises the dual significance of alchemy both as an early practice of medical chemistry and as a philosophical religious practice. Historians of alchemy (such as Holmyard, Corbin, and Ball) have emphasised this point. We can regard Jung as one of the serious scholars of alchemy of his time. He carried out extensive researches into primary sources and acquired a vast knowledge of alchemical symbols. Whilst there are critical voices, his ideas on alchemy are treated with respect by historians of alchemy today, for example, by contributors to Encyclopaedia Britannica. There is, however, a significant problem with reflexivity of influence. Historians writing in the latter part of the twentieth century are themselves likely to have been influenced, directly or indirectly, by Jung's work on alchemy and his psychological interpretation of alchemical practice. Many acknowledge this. For example, Henry Corbin, a philosopher who sought to expound and explain pre-Islamic religious thought (Sufism) to Western readers, met and conversed with Jung, as both men contributed regularly to the Eranos lectures from 1949. In the resulting cross-fertilisation, it is difficult to disentangle who influenced whom. Corbin uses the discourse of depth psychology and the concept of individuation to articulate mysticism, while Jung recasts the yearning towards the divine into a psychological discourse, as individuation.

Titus Burckhardt, a publisher of ancient manuscripts, many of which he translated from Arabic, and a prolific writer on Sufi doctrine, alchemy, and Middle Eastern culture, objected to Jung's approach to alchemy on the grounds of reductionism, saying that: 'The alchemical work is not a treatment for mental illness' (Burckhardt, 1997: 101). Burckhardt felt that Jung reduced the profound mystical and religious philosophy of alchemy to a kind of practical psychotherapy. In this, he does Jung an injustice. Jung does not reduce alchemy to a psychological projection of the alchemist's mind. Rather, he says that there is a psychological facet buried in the alchemical philosophical system, which, if understood, can expand the arcane and esoteric symbolism in a new way and opens the field of psychology to a totally new vision of personality.

Jung's alchemical project led to major developments in his theory of personality and provided a rich metaphor for the psyche's potential for self-transformation and for the stages of psychotherapy. Alchemy provided Jung with evidence for the existence of dynamic archetypes. In the alchemical literature, Jung found that others had expressed in pictorial form the transformational processes that he had expressed both verbally and in images in Liber novus. His alchemical studies were a kind of meditation on ideas and images that Jung allowed to 'react on him' and affect him so as to enable his own ideas to form and to emerge. He used alchemy and its rich imagery rather like a complex mandala symbol as a source of meditation and amplification that helped his own vision to crystallise in his mind and in his writing. This vision centred on personality, the individual self.

Alchemy continues to hold value for many psychotherapists as an important metaphor for the transformative processes in psychotherapy and has ongoing potential as a metaphor for the interpersonal, intra-psychic, and productive aspects of the therapy relationship. It may be suggested that all psychotherapists use a nonspecific alchemical 'theory' to understand transformative processes in psychotherapy, whether these are understood as social, interpersonal, educational, or biological processes, when they emphasise transformation from a kind of 'base material' to the fully developed person.

Jung shows how far it is possible for a personality theory to go. Its value is its vision. If Jung had not been part of psychology's history and a part of the early history of personality theory, there would have been a loss of a visionary conceptualisation of psychology itself. That Jung failed to leave an adequate legacy of empirical or other alternative research methods that would further his own ideas may not be negative, as it does not constrain the freedom to use modern research methods for those with a sympathetic understanding of his theory. What Jung did leave was his own method of active imagination, which may be why he offered no other methods, since he saw that as having almost infinite potential. This was his method of thinking and, from it, most of his theory emerged. Perhaps it should be ours.

References

Brown, R P (2011) 'The origins and development of Carl Jung's relationship with Wolfgang Pauli', *Spring*, 86: 193–222.
Burckhardt, T (1997) *Alchemy: Science of the Cosmos, Science of the Soul*, Louisville, KY: Fons Vitae.
Eliade, M (1978) *The Forge and the Crucible: The Origins and Structures of Alchemy*, trans. S Corrin, 2nd edn, Chicago, IL: University of Chicago Press.
Holmyard, E J (1957) *Alchemy*, Harmondsworth: Penguin.
Jeromson, B (2006) 'Systema Munditotius and Seven Sermons: symbolic collaborators in Jung's confrontation with the dead', *Jung History*, 1.2: 6–10.
Jung, C G (1911–1912/1952) *Collected Works, Vol. 5, Symbols of Transformation*, London: Routledge & Kegan Paul, 1956.
Jung, C G (1916) 'The structure of the unconscious', in *Collected Works, Vol. 7, Two Essays on Analytical Psychology*, London: Routledge & Kegan Paul, 1953.
Jung, C G (1928) 'The relations between the ego and the unconscious', in *Collected Works, Vol. 7, Two Essays on Analytical Psychology*, London: Routledge & Kegan Paul, 1953.
Jung, C G (1933) *Modern Man in Search of a Soul*, trans. W S Dell & C F Baynes, London: Routledge & Kegan Paul, 1981.
Jung, C G (1934/1950) 'A study in the process of individuation', in *Collected Works, Vol. 9, Part 1, The Archetypes and the Collective Unconscious*, London: Routledge & Kegan Paul, 1959.
Jung, C G (1934) 'The practical use of dream analysis', in *Collected Works, Vol. 16, The Practice of Psychotherapy*, London: Routledge & Kegan Paul, 1954.
Jung, C G (1935) 'The Tavistock Lectures', in *Collected Works, Vol. 18, The Symbolic Life*, London: Routledge, 1977.
Jung, C G (1938) 'Foreword to Jung: "Phénomènes Occultes"', in *Collected Works, Vol. 18, The Symbolic Life*, London: Routledge, 1977.
Jung, C G (1942) 'Paracelsus as a spiritual phenomenon', in *Collected Works, Vol. 13, Alchemical Studies*, London: Routledge & Kegan Paul.

Jung, C G (1944) *Psychology and Alchemy, Collected Works, Vol. 12, Bollingen Series*, 2nd edn, Princeton, NJ: Princeton University Press.

Jung, C G (1946) 'The psychology of the transference', in *Collected Works, Vol. 16, The Practice of Psychotherapy*, London: Routledge & Kegan Paul, 1954.

Jung, C G (1946/1968) 'Foreword to A Catalogue on Alchemy', in *Collected Works, Vol. 18, The Symbolic Life*, London: Routledge, 1977.

Jung, C G (1950) 'Concerning mandala symbolism', in *Collected Works, Vol. 9, Part 1, The Archetypes and the Collective Unconscious*, London: Routledge & Kegan Paul, 1959.

Jung, C G (1955–1956) *Mysterium Coniunctionis: An Inquiry into the Separation and Synthesis of Psychic Opposites in Alchemy, Collected Works, Vol. 14*, London: Routledge & Kegan Paul, 1963.

Jung, C G (1961) 'Symbols and the interpretation of dreams', in *Collected Works, Vol. 18, The Symbolic Life*, London: Routledge, 1977.

Jung, C G & Jaffé, A (1963) *Memories, Dreams, Reflections*, London: Fontana, 1977.

von Franz, M L (1977) *Alchemical Active Imagination*, Boston, MA: Shambhala, 1979.

Chapter 8

Pan stalks America
Contemporary American anxieties and cultural complex theory

Sukey Fontelieu

Introduction

Any theoretical position, such as a depth perspective, when employed to study a subject will necessarily limit the findings, because any method in and of itself serves to focus a search. Albert Einstein wrote "It is nonsense even if I said so ... in principle it is quite wrong to try to found a theory on observables alone ... It is the theory which decides what is observable" (as cited in Singh, 2007, p. 184). Many theories have studied violence and subsequent anxieties in American culture, but as Jungian analyst Andrew Samuels (1991) pointed out, a depth psychological attitude toward matters of culture and the body politic is a response that endeavors to reflect what is already there, rather than imposing a countertransferential-like, moral judgment on it: "You could say that the problem starts to resist a solution that does not arise from itself—its history, its distinguishing features, its needs, its goals and so forth" (p. 36).

A depth approach attempts to hear or see the underlying meanings, often ambiguous ones, in what is here, whether for a person or a culture. These underlying meanings have a weight that if not consciously carried by a person or the culture, act as an anchor and eventually impede progress (Luke, 1987, p. 109).

Rather than attempting to articulate a homogeneous American psychology, this writing aims to shed light on certain facets of America's *dominant culture*. The term "dominant culture" refers to behaviors, values, and social customs first established in American society by the early white settlers – norms in contemporary America which have tended to be controlled by social institutions such as public education, the media, and the political process.

This writing proposes that a *cultural complex* (Singer & Kimbles, 2004), anxious in nature, has been triggered by recent events in American history and endeavors to elucidate the effects of such an underlying cultural complex. It also maintains that a better understanding of the underlying meaning in the tendency to panic as a reaction to violence in the United States can be gained through the application of two of Swiss psychiatrist C. G. Jung's theories: the psychological functions of myth (Jung, 1951/1959a [*CW* 9I]) and the formation of complexes in the psyche (1948/1960 [*CW* 8]).

According to Jung, in an individual, a complex consists of an accumulation of affect-laden opinions, images, ideas, and associations (1948/1960 [*CW* 8]). Jung also theorized that a complex always has an archetypal component sheltered in its core (1948/1960 [*CW* 8]). Jungian analysts Samuel Kimbles and Thomas Singer (2004) first applied this theory to cultures recently, as the new millennium began. This thesis applies this theory to current crises in America and suggests that a cultural anxiety complex has congealed around an archetypal core, which was articulated earlier as an archetype in the myths of the Greek god Pan and the nymphs with whom he is associated. *Archetypes*, as defined by Jung, are "mythological associations, the motifs and images that can spring up anew anytime anywhere, independently of historical tradition or migration" (1921/1977, p. 485 [*CW* 6, para. 842]). In Jung's theory, archetypes function in a reciprocal relationship with consciousness.

Jung theorized that wounded and rejected aspects of the psyche cluster into *complexes* in the unconscious (1948/1960 [*CW* 8]). He observed that the origin of a complex was frequently traumatic and often due to an irresolvable moral conflict. He contended emotional shocks cause a disturbance in the unity of the psyche and therefore "every constellation of a complex postulates a disturbed state of consciousness" (1948/1960, p. 96 [*CW* 8, para. 200]).

This thesis suggests a pre-existing cultural complex has been activated in the collective American psyche by various forms of violence in the recent past. Two iconic events will serve as primary examples. These are the attacks on the World Trade Center and the Pentagon in 2001 and the 1999 school shootings at Columbine High School in Littleton, Colorado. In addition, the epidemic-like numbers of rape in the military are evaluated as evidence of an ongoing and intense emotional reactivity to violence in the culture, veering between the extremes of panic and torpor. This thesis will debate whether the panic-stricken reactions in America are part of a psychological cycle that desires an end to violence but is actually engendering further violence.

Relevance of Jung's theories of complexes and the psychological functions of myth for cultural problems

> Generalizations about national character and psychology, from all manner of sources, can be interpreted as a form of mythmaking crucial to a sense of Gemeinschaft (community). National characteristics, or rather what are claimed as national characteristics, are revealed as metaphors and as part of the contemporary quest for Gemeinschaft.
> (Samuels, 1992)

By listening for the symbolic meanings in the iconic stories of a people, and in the stories about the stories, intangible aspects of the psychological state of a culture come more clearly into view.

In depth psychological theory, unintegrated intrapersonal anxiety is understood to be unconsciously projected out, onto other members of one's society or onto other cultures (Jung, 1940/1973 [*CW* 11]). *Projection* of internal mechanisms in the human psyche is a foundational tenet in depth psychology and refers to the all too human tendency to blame one's unconscious, irascible feelings on others (Jung, 1940/1973 [*CW* 11]). Projection is understood as a form of defense against the aspects of oneself that feel unbearable and seemingly irresolveable (Young-Eisendrath & Dawson, 1999). This psychic material hovers just outside of consciousness and therefore is accessible to change. Jung named this part of the unconscious the shadow (1946/1977, p. 262 [*CW* 16, para. 470]). Jung also observed in his patients that dreams bring up scraps of myths and archetypal encounters. He noted that this happened even in people with no previous knowledge of the myths from which these images derived (1951/1959a [*CW* 9I]). "Such conclusions forced us to assume that we must be dealing with 'autochthonous' revivals independent of all tradition, and, consequently, that 'myth-forming' structural elements must be present in the unconscious psyche" (Jung, 1951/1959a, p. 152 [*CW* 9I, para. 259]). He concluded that the "whole of mythology could be taken as a sort of projection of the collective unconscious" (Jung, 1931/1981, p. 152 [*CW* 8, para. 325]). This would then include shadow aspects buried in the collective unconscious and so this thesis explores aspects of the cultural shadow and the unconscious, archetypal position from which it emerges.

Jung found evidence of archetypes in dreams, visions, and fantasies, both his own and in his patients' histories (1951/1959a [*CW* 9I]). Jung found that common experiences of an archetype include feeling they are autonomous and represent something numinous for the observer (Samuels et al., 2005). In Jung's view, an "archetype does not proceed from physical facts, but describes how the psyche experiences the physical fact" (1951/1959a, p. 154 [*CW* 9I, para. 260]). Also, he deduced that archetypes exist in a state of readiness and manifest in times of suffering (Jung, 1921/1977, pp. 120–121 [*CW* 6, paras. 193–194]).

A myth, as Jung understood one, is a "shimmering symbol" (1942/1967, p. 162 [*CW* 13, para. 199]) and thus invites both the meaning and the feeling it expresses to be experienced by the observer (1942/1967 [*CW* 13]). For Jung, myths symbolize the psyche most accurately for two reasons. Myths express the unconscious contents of the psyche visually and through a re-experiencing of an inner state in the listener. Jung viewed mythic structures as reflective of the entirety of the psyche and suggested, "it is possible to describe this [unconscious] content in rational, scientific language, but in this way one entirely fails to express its living character" (1951/1959a, p. 13 [*CW* 9I, para. 25]). He proposed, "what we are to our inward vision, and what man appears to be *sub specie aeternitatis* [eternally], can only be expressed by way of myth" (1961/1965, p. 3).

Jung cautioned against any definitive interpretations of myths or archetypes (Segal, 1998). He pointed out that "in the last analysis ... it is impossible to say what they refer to. Every interpretation necessarily remains an 'as-if.' The ultimate core of meaning may be circumscribed, but not described" (1951/1959a, p. 156 [*CW* 9I, para. 265]).

Jung's complex theory

Jung analyzes the origin and nature of complexes in his essay "A Review of the Complex Theory" (1948/1960 [*CW* 8]). He proposed that the origin of a complex is frequently traumatic and due to an irresolvable moral conflict (1948/1960 [*CW* 8]). He argued that complexes are initiated by an emotional shock, which causes a disturbance in the unity of the psyche (1948/1960, p. 96 [*CW* 8, para. 200]).

In the same essay, Jung (1948/1960 [*CW* 8]) made five main points to clarify the effects of a complex on a person. He stated that, within the personality, (1) a complex is a splintered off part of the psyche and (2) has an inner coherence, a wholeness to it. He found that (3) when strong enough a complex can take over the ego without the individual's conscious awareness. (4) Complexes can be recognized by the intense feelings they stir up. Jung understood this to mean a complex acts as a disruption and retriggers a past traumatic state in a person (1948/1960 [*CW* 8]). (5) Jung did not think complexes were always negative. He saw them as an expression of a characteristic state of the psyche and suggested complexes arise in all people and that they always serve a function (1948/1960 [*CW* 8]).

Jung proposed that the wounded and rejected aspects of the psyche cluster into complexes, psychic islands, in the unconscious (1948/1960 [*CW* 8]). When a complex is triggered it surfaces and the distress causes repetitious, avoidant patterns of behaviors (1948/1960 [*CW* 8]). Complexes also tend to isolate people, can cause panic and anxiety, and can lead to violent behaviors (1948/1960 [*CW* 8]).

[...]

Post-Jungian theory of cultural complexes

Jungian analysts Samuel Kimbles and Thomas Singer first advanced the idea of a cultural unconscious as a metaphorical scaffolding within the greater unconscious (Kimbles, 2000; Singer, 2004). Singer proposed the rationale that "cultural complexes structure emotional experience and operate in the personal and collective psyche in much the same way as individual complexes, although their content might be quite different" (2004, p. 6). He also emphasized "the premise that the psychology of cultural complexes operates both in the collective psychology of the group and in the individual members of the group" (p. 2). Kimbles (2000) suggested cultural complexes surface within individuals as a part of group functioning. Kimbles saw cultures as having the opportunity to consciously struggle with its complexes or unconsciously ignore them. Kimbles and Singer agree that that struggle takes place on an individual basis, within the members of that culture.

In Jungian theory, over-identification with one's *persona*, the face one shows the world (Jung, 1945/1953, p. 192 [*CW* 7, para. 307–308]), and the subsequent projection of shadow material (Jung, 1951/1959b [*CW* 9II]), are signals of a personal complex. Cultural complex theory attempts to articulate how these same types of symptoms tend to constellate around both conflicts in a group's need to form an identity and when a group struggles to find meaning for itself (Singer, 2004; Kimbles, 2000). Insecure cultures become rigidly polarized into an in-group/out-group pattern and this promotes stereotypical thinking about cultural behavior, which then leads to the beginning of mutual negative projections (Kimbles, 2000). Cultural complexes often become visible in the context of conflicts due to "ethnic, racial, class, religious, and gender differences" (p. 155) and tend to engender repetitious patterns of rage and violent behaviors (2000). In 2003, Kimbles refined his theoretical position stating that there are two dynamics that tend to activate a cultural complex: "(1) the constellation of repressed aspects of group identity and (2) the projection onto some group of reviled 'others' of disowned aspects of the group's identity" (p. 219).

Michael Vannoy Adams (2006), a Jungian analyst, concurred with other Jungians that a cultural complex circles around "especially emotionally sensitive" (p. 32) issues, though he understood the cultural unconscious to be filled with stereotypical rather than archetypal factors (2006, p. 32). Adams is critical of what he considers Jung's insufficient focus on the extent to "which the contents of the collective unconscious are *acquired by the individual through the culture*" (1996, p. 165; original emphasis).

Samuels (1993) weighed in early to this discussion, suggesting that "the characteristic of late modernity to try to make use of knowledge about itself can be recast as a struggle within our culture to become self-conscious; *our culture struggles to become psychological*" (p. 8; original emphasis). Kimbles (2003) expressed the same sentiment, concerning the need for ways for cultures to grow psychologically, concluding that awareness of cultural complexes might allow for "the creation of a narrating third, a space for symbolization, and the possibility of reflection ... The existence of cultural complexes opens the possibility that as a collective we might be able to do a therapeutic type of cultural analysis" (p. 232).

America

In the United States, certain beliefs about itself are proposed here as factors causing the formation of an unseen, anxiety-based, cultural complex. The complex can be observed in contemporary America in intense collective emotional reactions to threats to its security. This thesis proposes that the dominant culture in the US is still unconsciously functioning within the doctrines of exceptionalism (Lewis, 2012; Lifton, 2003) and manifest destiny (de Tocqueville, 1840). This has allowed the US to unconsciously act as if it has a divine right to lead (David & Grondin, 2006). One example is the story of how in 2002 the US government believed it had the right to defy the UN's leadership and attacked Iraq (World Press Review, 2012).

But before this, the turn of the millennium was bookended in the US by the school shootings at Columbine High in 1999 and the bombings of the Pentagon and the World Trade Center in 2001. The Y2K scare scarred the moment of the actual turn with intense media coverage transmitting numerous possible disasters (Quigley, 2005). The media cautioned that banks could close down, and that air traffic, emergency systems, and food supplies might be interrupted. The *Wall Street Journal* alone covered the upcoming event 262 times (Quigley, 2005, pp. 262–263). Meanwhile, aiming to ease bond traders' fears, the "Federal Reserve Bank of New York auctioned Y2K options to primary dealers" (Sundaresan & Wang, 2009, p. 1022). The contrast to the turn of the nineteenth century when "a millennial hope was in the air, yoked to the expectation of massive technological, political, and social change" (Aronson, 1999) helps to contextualize this new chapter in American history. In the United States, instead of millennial hope, the event was tinged with millennial anxiety and fear (Mueller, 2005, 2006; Richey & Feldmann, 2003; Furedi, 2007).

An insecure fixation on remaining the strongest and richest country in the world is causing anxiety and friction within the country and between the US and other nations (Lifton, 2003). These beliefs are being challenged by recent upheavals in the world today (Stein, 2004) and are understood here to have triggered a latent cultural complex. This complex is causing problems in certain areas: insecurity about one's power, bullying and being bullied, loud fanfare for all things military and having to do with warfare (such as the private use of AK-47s), abuse of women and any other group not feeding the autoerotic nature of this power complex. These are also the repeating motifs in Pan's myths. A few iconic events will be explored in depth to illuminate this basic point.

Columbine

"In its more abstract sense, *Columbine* has become a keyword for a complex set of emotions surrounding youth, risk, fear, and delinquency in early 21st Century United States" (Muschert, 2007, p. 365). The school shootings have left a reverberating question mark for Americans. How could those boys have done it? The narrative constructions advanced in media and popular print, such as alienated youth influenced by films, music, and video games (a so-called Trench Coat Mafia), narcissistic parenting and the community's "benign neglect," or psychopathic (natural-born) killers (Frymer, 2009) have not put traumatized concerns to rest. Nor have efforts to punish those responsible for school shootings stopped them from recurring.

Rather, it will be argued, the discourses themselves projected imagined simulacra onto the perpetrators. Manic leaps were generated by the media coverage as it followed the real-time action and an overnight metamorphosis froze the two shooters into veritable monsters (Cullen, 2009). The viewing public accepted an oversimplification of the factors that drove Eric Harris and Dylan Klebold to homicide/suicide. This attitude has not been influenced by the methodical study of the actual events in the years that followed – though much of what was first thought to be fact was later found to be erroneous (Cullen, 2009). The reportage was compelling to a horrified and fascinated public, driving the profit-driven news industry to exploit the victims and create instant heroes (Moore, 2002). Eric Harris and Dylan Klebold were immediately split off from the community. They were banished as aberrations of nightmarish proportions and viewed as symbolic of evil in a modern passion play in which the slain students became the martyred heroes (Spencer & Muschert, 2009). The tragedy came to be narrated as a hero myth.

The massacre at Columbine High School on April 20, 1999 really began years earlier (Harris, 1998–1999; Klebold, 1997–1999). As only a handful in the ever-growing numbers of school shooters, Eric Harris and Dylan Klebold have left behind a record venting their wounded, lonely feelings in their journals, basement tapes, and school projects. They had filmed revenge fantasies for school projects in which they played out their angry desire to murder the student body (Kurtis, 2008). The two boys' animosity was an open secret or as filmmaker Gus van Sant's (2003) *Elephant* implies, the elephant in the room. Klebold and Harris, "the two uncoolest kids at school" (*Politicrato*, 2008), were so alienated that they planned out on paper a fully orchestrated revenge, down to the minute.

Home-town pride in championship sports teams allowed a system to ignore harassment, effectively handing the team players power over the rest of the student body (Kurtis, 2008). The star athletes "ruled" the halls because they could. "Pranks," such as throwing a cup of fecal matter at Eric Harris, were reported to school officials but the bullies were left unpunished (Vanderau, 2013).

The question authorities focused on is why did *they*, Eric and Dylan, do this rather than what is wrong systemically (Kurtis, 2008; *Politicrato*, 2008). But if a definitive psychiatric diagnosis of Eric Harris and Dylan Klebold settled the affair, then why have school shootings proliferated since Columbine (Newman & Fox, 2009)?

The initial emotional responses to the shootings engendered constructive containment in all too familiar patterns, with rallies and prayer circles in the community (Cullen, 2009), but quickly led to mounting rage and the desire for revenge toward the shooters and their families. The negativity is encapsulated in the history of the crosses put up in the night for the lost children (including Eric and Dylan). The crosses were secretly erected at the school. But the two for the shooters were defaced and destroyed by the visitors to the makeshift shrine (Spencer & Muschert, 2009). Over the next few years the anger in the Columbine area congealed into lawsuits against the parents, the school, and the Jefferson County Sheriff's department. Better weapon containment through any significant revisions in gun control law atrophied at the state and federal level (Cullen, 2009; Larkin, 2007).

A number of motifs in the myths of Pan (Borgeaud, 1979/1988) resemble the sad story of Eric Harris and Dylan Klebold. Pan was a *hypermasculine* aggressor and a lonely isolate, as were they. Hypermasculinity is used here to describe a psychological state fixated on certain areas: self-absorption, the need for power over others, physical prowess, dangerous activities for excitement, and cut off from feelings of empathy (Klein, 2012). Pan's animal nature related to his virility, survival skills, and self-absorption, but his divinity denotes genuine sensitivity. Pan was quick to violence to get what he wants, as were they. He did not honor the sexual rights of the feminine figures in his myths, even as Eric wrote disrespectfully about women's sexual choices. At times in myth Pan shared their role as a bully, at other times he shared their role as a scapegoat. These characteristics match Dylan's and Eric's internal states as well as their outer objective to do what they wanted and disregard the norms of their cultures (Harris, 1998–1999; Klebold, 1997–1999).

When Pan was scapegoated, his cult performed a ritual to contain the anxiety this provoked (Borgeaud, 1979/1988), whereas Eric and Dylan were not contained by their family, school, or community while alive and believed their future was hopeless. So they planned and executed a violent revenge. Their uncontained anxiety and fears were violently projected. As will be shown, they targeted the entire American culture (Harris, 1998–1999; Klebold, 1997–1999). If this was an aberrant occurrence in the history of the US it would be a sad memory and perhaps one could conclude the monstrous boys theory is right. But it is so much more worrisome because these revenge plots continue to be enacted onto the "enemy" by alienated children in the American public school system and, like an epidemic, the numbers continue to increase (Larkin, 2007).

This thesis hopes to convey that the lack of containment of anxiety in modern American society is causing repetitive dramas of chaos and innocent fatalities. Efforts to fix blame and create lockdown systems are an inadequate solution because they do not address the cycle of anger, fear, and despair that school shootings provoke (Barak, 2005). From a depth psychological perspective, this suggests that an unconscious layer encompassing the entire culture drives the recurring horror of school rampages. This thesis endeavors to make connections between the faulty beliefs (called myths!) of exceptionalism and manifest destiny and the violence in the culture. The anxiety of a culture insisting it knows what is best and a vision that sees governance of the globe as hierarchal is unconsciously focusing attention away from areas such as the struggle of youths to feel connected to the culture. There is a high price for a complex being allowed to remain unconsciously projected onto the disenfranchised youth who protest about its state.

Nine eleven

Two and a half years later, 9/11 followed Columbine. American perceptions about safety and the stability of communities, shaken by Columbine and the Y2K scare, were now exponentially altered. One outcome of the tragedy is that freedoms once unchallenged for Americans became more costly and elusive. Safety, it could be said, trumped freedom.

Following the trauma of the terrorist attacks, mainstream American reactions solidified into two ways: panicked compulsive activity see-sawed with emotional states of torpor. The first was promoted by a swift call to action, an attempt to "shock and awe" the perpetrators fueled by then President George W. Bush's rhetorical "crusade" (Maddox, 2003). This was followed by a sluggish avoidance to relate to the painful experience at all, which reflects the naïveté in the culture. Bush's public recommendations encouraged a return to consumerism and to passively leave the terrorists to the experts (Pyszczynski et al., 2003).

Panic, derived from the Greek *panikos*, means "literally, of Pan" (*Webster's Unabridged Dictionary*, 1983, p. 1293). This projection of panic and subsequent torpor mirrors the outcome that followed the attacks.

> The intolerable affects of the terrorists are projected into the recipients of terror ... The victims experience a transformation of their subjectivity, as they are now possessed by terror. They now feel powerlessness, frustration, grief and terror previously carried by the terrorist.
> (Perlman, 2002, p. 32)

A recurring motif in Pan's myths reflects his tendency toward self-absorption and how his uncontained sexual arousal prompts him to chase young, innocent nymphs. These encounters were always unfulfilled for Pan! He was not effectual. But he did force the nymphs, overwhelmed by panic, to make their escape, as did many Americans, through metamorphoses into torpid, vegetative states. They escape by devolving (Larson, 2001) and Americans escaped into consumerism, opioids, and patriotism, leaving the problem to the "experts" in the government.

In other myths, where Pan is a general in one or another army, he used panic strategically in a similar way to the US and radical Islamists: by hurting the few it is possible to frighten the many. Al-Qaeda's admitted strategy to surprise and create panic was remarkably effective given the US military advantage. The Bush administration opportunistically retaliated by becoming the aggressor, using a pandean "shock and awe" campaign slogan against Saddam Hussein's Iraq (Clarke, 2004). The cultures mirror each other (Adams, 1996). Both sides appear driven to use aggression rather than communication to protect themselves. Both are in denial about these similarities and the unconscious projections onto each other.

Panicky anxieties and apathetic retreats into escapism are understandable knee-jerk reactions to Columbine and 9/11 (Pyszczynski et al., 2003). Cultural complex theory can help understand these choices as unhealthy reactions that can be transformed through the development of more reasoned and compassionate responses (Kimbles, 2003). Panic and torpor are part of the emotional landscape of Pan's mythic borderline territories where instinctive desire ignores the needs of the disenfranchised. If panic and torpor are emotional overreactions indicating the existence of an unconscious complex, then making it more conscious should lead to less reactivity.

Rape in the military

Women in the US military who are sexually assaulted by their fellow servicemen comprise an estimated 23 percent of their totals (Hankin et al., 1999). The numbers of sexual assaults and rapes are rising (Steinhauer, 2013, p. A1). The Department of Defense acknowledges the problem, yet it remains resistant to changing the methods for prosecuting rape charges. The reactions to the problem by the general public are apathetic. This thesis will consider whether an overly inflated attitude in the psyche of the American soldier, "The Few, The Proud ... The Marines" (usmilitary.about.com) shapes an ethos that allows sexual assault to go nearly unnoticed.

The best and the worst in the necessary evil of soldiering is also amplified in the Greek god Pan. Pan went to battle with many armies (Kerenyi, 1998; *Lucian*, 1913/1961, p. 53 [Dionysus. 4]; *Pausanias*, 1959, p. 149 [xxviii.4]). He also hunted down nymphs to satisfy his own lustings. The panic the soldiers inject in their victims and the apathy in the American public reflect the same pattern as the reactions to Columbine and 9/11 and is considered here as further evidence of an unconscious anxiety-based cultural complex.

Archetypal motifs of the Greek god Pan

Though Pan's unconscious influence can be thought about in relationship to the West as a whole, this essay limits itself to an understanding of contemporary American anxieties only. When the most brilliant strands of the dominant American culture are separated out from those of the West in general, it is this chapter's contention that one sees more of Pan in the US. The Wild West, the frontiers of space, vast utilizations of natural resources, and freedom for individuals crown American contributions, while stellar works of art, philosophy, literature, and architecture could be said to better epitomize

European culture. Pan's dominion over the natural world and his life as a separate and independent god, his freedom from the restraints of civilization and, above all, the sense of space that separates him from others in his own territory, parallel that which, by degree, differentiates the *zeitgeist* of the dominant culture in America from its European forbearers. The best and the worst in Pan meet in America. There is a bit of the rustic in both. Feelings of inferiority underlie the problems and lead to grandiose solutions.

Beyond an interesting comparison of Pan to America, can the myths and rites of Pan's cult help an understanding of how America can move to a less self-absorbed and one-sided vision in its future? Perhaps the question is better put, can the United States culture individuate?

This thesis will use the myths of Pan to "clothe" the archetypal core of the proposed cultural complex. Pan is most associated with panic and all its legion of psychological burdens (Boardman, 1997). Panic is with him from the moment of his birth when his mother abandoned him (Athanassakis, 1976) and it continues to dog him throughout his stories in the panics his unbridled sexuality created in the objects of his desire (*Apollodorus*, 1997). The goat god Pan tracked alone through the wilderness, hunting down quarry, mostly deer, or compulsively chasing after sex, uncorking dread and panic in those he pursued, who either froze or fled away (*Nonnos*, 1940/1962). Yet panic is also a tool that Pan wields skillfully in his role in battle, where he found victory without the aid of his keen-eyed marksmanship, but rather by instilling fear and confusion in the hearts of the enemies of his friends (*Polyaenus*, 1994). Pan did not instigate wars or fight for his own gain; rather, he was enlisted to come to the defense of Dionysus, Zeus, and the people of Athens, which, to the ancients, signified humankind (1994).

Today Pan is remembered for his insensitivity, violence, attempted rapes, and selfish, self-absorbed behaviors. These are all elements of the habitual nature of Pan as relayed to us through the myths and legends of the early Greeks and Romans (Borgeaud, 1979/1988). Pan embodied more than these best-remembered qualities. A god, half divine and half animal (Farnell, 1909/1971), he charmed the Olympians with his laughter (Athanassakis, 1976), played the pipes for the nymphs' night-long, labyrinthine dances (*Philostratus*, 1931/1960), provided sustenance from the herds and cheered the lonely hunts (*Pausanias*, 1935/1961), suffered the whip on his back for the good of those for whom he cared (*Theocritus*, 1999), opened portals to the divine through overwhelming a person with *panolepsy* (Borgeaud, 1979/1988), was a loyal ally to his friends (1979/1988), was named *All* by Zeus (Athanassakis, 1976), and provided the cipher of being a god who was proclaimed to be dead and yet was immortal (Borgeaud, 1983). Such is Pan's paradoxical history and nature.

Pan reflects American grandiosity in how he sees the world as his to use for his purposes. This one-sided inflation brings him to grief, even as the pursued are broken, made voiceless, and pine away (Borgeaud, 1979/1988). When his cult's hunt was unsuccessful, a rite to "right" the situation involved young boys leaping in a circle dance around his statue, whipping him to help them. In the Pan myths, one-sided grandiosity and inflation are humbled and fear and panic are quieted through a redemptive process of healing. Pan embodies the conjoined spirit of the animal and the divine within one body. Surely this is a hint of a direction in which things could go if this unconscious anxiety is laid plain and enough individuals decide to work with their own parts of the shadow.

Panic, as the Greeks would have it, is not a pathology, it is divine madness (*Plato*, 1914/1966, p. 467). This thesis proposes that Pan's compulsion into life, is a symbolic expression of what was once alive in the bold spirit of the European settlers of America, but has rusted in paralysis and avoidance of initiative towards contemporary problems. Where the US once unconsciously identified with the most courageous and expansive in the Pan archetype, now the archetype of panic stalks America.

References

Adams, M. Vannoy (1996). *The multicultural imagination: "Race," color, and the unconscious.* London: Routledge.

Adams, M. Vannoy (2006). The Islamic cultural unconscious in the dreams of a contemporary Muslim man. *Journal of Jungian Theory and Practice*, 8(1), 31–40. Retrieved from http://web.ebscohost.com.pgi.idm.oclc.org/ehost

Apollodorus (1997). *The library of Greek mythology* (R. Hard, Trans.). Oxford: Oxford University Press.

Aronson, R. (1999, Summer). Hope after hope? *Social Research*, 66(2), 471–494. Retrieved from www.jstor.org/stable/40971333 .

Athanassakis, A. (Trans.) (1976). *The Homeric hymns.* Baltimore, MD: John Hopkins University Press.

Barak, G. (2005). A reciprocal approach to peacemaking criminology: Between adversarialism and mutualism. *American Behavioral Scientist*, 9(2), 131–152. doi: 10.1177/1362480605051640.

Boardman, J. (1997). *The great god Pan: The survival of an image.* New York: Thames and Hudson.

Borgeaud, P. (1983). The death of great Pan: The problem of interpretation. *History of Religions*, 22(3), 254–283.

Borgeaud, P. (1979/1988). *The cult of Pan* (K. Atlass & J. Redfield, Trans.). Chicago, IL: University of Chicago Press.

Clarke, R. (2004). *Against all enemies: Inside America's war on terror.* New York: Free Press.

Cullen, D. (2009). *Columbine.* New York: Grand Central Publishing.

David, C.-G., & Grondin, D. (2006). *Hegemony or empire: The redefinition of US power under George W. Bush.* Basingstoke: Ashgate Publishing.

de Tocqueville, A. (1840). *Democracy in America. Volume II: The social influence of democracy.* New York: J. & H. G. Langley.

Farnell, L. R. (1909/1971). *The cults of the Greek states* (Vol. 5). Chicago, IL: Aegean Press.

Frymer, B. (2009, June). The media spectacle of Columbine: Alienated youth as an object of fear. *American Behavioral Scientist*, 52(10), 1387–1404. doi:10.1177/0002764209332554.

Furedi, F. (2007). *Invitation to terror: The expanding empire of the unknown.* London: Continuum.

Hankin, C., Skinner, K., Sullivan, L., Miller, D., Frayne, S., & Tripp, T. (1999). Prevalence of depressive and alcohol abuse symptoms among women VA outpatients who report experiencing sexual assault while in the military. *Journal of Traumatic Stress*, 12(4). Retrieved from: http://web.b.ebscohost.com.pgi.idm.oclc.org/ehost.

Harris, E. (1998–1999). Unpublished journal of Eric Harris. Retrieved from http://acolumbinesite.com/eric/writing/journal/jindex.html.

Jung, C. G. (1945/1953). Individuation. In H. Read, M. Fordham, and G. Adler (Eds.), *The collected works of C. G. Jung* (R. F. C. Hull, Trans.) (Vol. 7, pp. 171–239). Princeton, NJ: Princeton University Press.

Jung, C. G. (1959a). The psychology of the child archetype. In H. Read et al. (Eds.), *The collected works of C. G. Jung* (R. F. C. Hull, Trans.) (Vol. 9, Pt. 1, pp. 150–181).

Jung, C. G. (1951/1959b). The shadow. In H. Read et al. (Eds.), *The collected works of C. G. Jung* (R. F. C. Hull, Trans.) (Vol. 9, Pt. II, pp. 8–10). Princeton, NJ: Princeton University Press.

Jung, C. G. (1948/1960). A review of the complex theory. In H. Read et al. (Eds.), *The collected works of C. G. Jung* (R. F. C. Hull, Trans.) (Vol. 8, pp. 92–106). Princeton, NJ: Princeton University Press.

Jung, C. G. (1961/1965). *Memories, dreams, reflections* (A. Jaffe, Ed.) (R. Winston & C. Winston, Trans.). New York: Random House.

Jung, C. G. (1942/1967). Paracelsus as a spiritual phenomenon. In H. Read et al. (Eds.), *The collected works of C. G. Jung* (R. F. C. Hull, Trans.). Vol. 13, pp. 109–188 Princeton, NJ: Princeton University Press.

Jung, C. G. (1940/1973). Psychology and religion. In H. Read et al. (Eds.), *The collected works of C. G. Jung* (R. F. C. Hull, Trans.) (Vol. 11, pp. 3–105). Princeton, NJ: Princeton University Press.

Jung, C. G. (1921/1977). Definitions. In H. Read et al. (Eds.), *The collected works of C. G. Jung* (R. F. C. Hull, Trans.) (Vol. 6, pp. 408–486). Princeton, NJ: Princeton University Press.

Jung, C. G. (1946/1977). The psychology of the transference. In H. Read et al. (Eds.), *The collected works of C. G. Jung* (R. F. C. Hull, Trans.) (Vol. 16, pp. 163–320). Princeton, NJ: Princeton University Press.

Jung, C. G. (1931/1981). The structure of the psyche. In H. Read et al. (Eds.), *The collected works of C. G. Jung* (R. F. C. Hull, Trans.) (Vol. 8, pp. 139–158). Princeton, NJ: Princeton University Press.

Kerenyi, C. (1998). *The gods of the Greeks.* London: Thames and Hudson.

Kimbles, S. (2000). The cultural complex and the myth of invisibility. In *The vision thing: Myth, politics and psyche in the world* (pp. 155–169). London: Routledge.

Kimbles, S. (2003). Cultural complexes and the collective shadow process. In J. Beebe (Ed.), *Terror, violence and the impulse to destroy: Perspectives from analytical psychology* (pp. 211–234). Einsiedeln, Switzerland: Daimon Verlag.

Klebold, D. (1997–1999). Unpublished journal of Dylan Klebold. Retrieved from http://acolumbinesite.com/dylan/jindex.html

Klein, J. (2012). *The bully society: School shootings and the crisis of bullying in America's schools.* New York: New York University Press.

Kurtis, B. (Director) (2008). *Columbine: Understanding why.* [Documentary Film]. New York: A & E Home Entertainment.

Larkin, R. (2007). *Comprehending Columbine.* Philadelphia, PA: Temple University Press.

Larson, B. J. (2001). *Greek nymphs: Myth, cult, lore.* Oxford: Oxford University Press.

Lewis, D. (2012). Exceptionalism's exceptions: The changing American narrative. *Daedalus,* 141(1), 101–117. doi:10.1162/DAED_a_00132

Lifton, R. J. (2003). *Super power syndrome: America's apocalyptic confrontation with the world.* New York: Thunder's Mouth Press/ Nation Books.

Lucian (1913/1961). *Lucian* (M. D. MacLeod, Trans.) (Vol. I). London: William Heinemann.

Luke, H. (1987). *Old Age: Journey into simplicity.* Barrington, MA: Lindisfarne Books.

Maddox, G. (2003, September). The "crusade" against evil: Bush's fundamentalism. *Australian Journal of Politics & History,* 49(3), 398–411. doi: 10.1111/1467-8497.00294.

Moore, M. (2002). *Bowling for Columbine.* K. Glynn, J. Czarnecki et al., Producers [Motion Picture] MGM.

Mueller, J. (2005). Simplicity and spook: Terrorism and the dynamics of threat exaggeration. *International Studies Perspectives,* 6(2), 208–234. doi: 10.1111/j1528-3577.2005.00203x.

Mueller, J. (2006, September/October). Is there still a terrorist threat? *Foreign Affairs,* 85(5), 2–8. Retrieved from http://web.ebscohost.com.pgi.idm.oclc.org/ehost/detail.

Muschert, G. (2007). The Columbine victims and the myth of the juvenile superpredator. *Youth Violence and Juvenile Justice,* 5(4), 351–366. doi: 10.1177/1541204006296173.

Newman, K., & Fox, C. (2009). Repeat tragedy: Rampage shootings in American high school and college settings. *American Behavioral Scientist,* 52(9), 1286–1308. doi: 10.1177/0002764209332546.

Nonnos (1940/1962). *Dionysiaca* (Vol. II) (W. H. D. Rouse, Trans.). London: William Heinemann.

Pausanias (1959). *Pausanias: Description of Greece* (Vol. I) (W. H. S. Jones, Trans.). Cambridge, MA: Harvard University Press.

Pausanias (1935/1961). *Pausanias: Description of Greece* (Vol. IV) (W. H. S. Jones, Trans.). Cambridge, MA: Harvard University Press.

Perlman, D. (2002). Intersubjective dimensions of terrorism and transcendence. In C. Stout (Ed.), *The psychology of terrorism* (pp. 17–47). Westport, CT: Praeger.

Philostratus (1931/1960). *Imagines* (A. Fairbanks, Trans.). London: William Heinemann.

Plato (1914/1966). Phaedrus. *Plato* (H. N. Fowler, Trans.) (Vol. I, pp. 405–579). Cambridge, MA: Harvard University Press.

Politicrato (2008, October 15). *The Columbine killers: Part 5.* Retrieved from www.youtube.com/watch?v=bXWCjzYxxes&NR=1

Polyaenus (1994). *Stratagems of war* (P. Krentz & E. L. Wheeler, Eds. & Trans.) (Vol. I). Chicago, IL: Ares Publisher.
Pyszczynski, T., Solomon, S., & Greenberg, J. (2003). *In the wake of 9/11: The psychology of terror*. Washington, DC: American Psychological Association.
Quigley, K. (2005, September). Bug reactions: Considering US government and UK government Y2K operations in light of media coverage and public opinion polls. *Health, Risk & Society*, 7(3), 267–291. doi: 10.1080/13698570500229770.
Richey, W., & Feldmann, L. (2003, September 12). Has post-9/11 dragnet gone too far? *Christian Science Monitor*, 95(202), 1. Retrieved from http://web.ebscohost.com.pgi.idm.oclc.org/ehost/resultsadvanced
Samuels, A. (1991). Foreword. In P. Young-Eisendrath and J. Hall (Eds.), *Jung's self psychology: A constructivist perspective* (pp. vii–x). New York: Guilford Press.
Samuels, A. (1992). National psychology, national socialism, and analytical psychology: Reflections on Jung and anti-Semitism: II. *The Journal of Analytical Psychology*, 37(2), 127–148. Retrieved from http://web.ebscohost.com.pgi.idm.oclc.org/ehost/pdfviewer/pdfviewer?vid=4&sid=c44dbbe5-12c7-4f19-8934-28219c3e22ca%40sessionmgr4003&hid=125
Samuels, A. (1993). *The political psyche*. London: Routledge.
Samuels, A., Shorter, B., & Plaut, F. (2005). *A critical dictionary of Jungian analysis*. London: Routledge.
Segal, R. (1998). *Theology as psychology: An approach to the Bible*. [CD]. Evanston, IL: C. G. Jung Institute of Chicago.
Singer, T. (2004). The cultural complex and archetypal defenses of the group spirit: Baby Zeus, Elian Gonzales, Constantine's Sword, and other holy wars (with special attention to the "axis of evil"). In T. Singer and S. Kimbles (Eds.), *The cultural complex: Contemporary Jungian perspectives on psyche and society* (pp. 13–34). Hove: Brunner-Routledge.
Singer, T. and Kimbles, S. (Eds.) (2004). *The cultural complex: Contemporary Jungian perspectives on psyche and society*. Hove: Brunner-Routledge.
Singh, V. (2007). Einstein and the quantum. *The legacy of Albert Einstein: A collection of essays in celebration of the year of physics* (pp. 165–192) (S. R. Wadia, Ed.). Singapore: World Scientific Publishing.
Spencer J. W., & Muschert, G. (2009). The contested meaning of the crosses at Columbine. *American Behavioral Scientist*, 52(10), 1371–1386. doi: 10.1177/0002764209332553.
Stein, M. (2004). On the politics of individuation in the Americas. In T. Singer and S. Kimbles (Eds.), *The cultural complex: Contemporary Jungian perspectives on psyche and society* (pp. 292–273). Hove: Brunner-Routledge.
Steinhauer, J. (2013). Veterans testify on rapes and scant hope of justice. *The New York Times*, March 13. Retrieved from www.nytimes.com/2013/03/14/us/politics/veterans-testify-on-rapes-and-scant-hope-of-justice.html?_r=0.
Sundaresan, S. and Wang. Z. (2009, March). Y2K Options and the liquidity premium in treasury markets. *The Review of Financial Studies*, 22(3), 1022–1056. Retrieved from http://0-web.ebscohost.com.serlib0.essex.ac.uk/ehost/pdfviewer.
Theocritus (1999). In R. Hunter (Ed.), *Theocritus: A selection: Idylls 1, 3, 6, 7, 10, 11 and 13*. Cambridge, MA: Cambridge University Press.

Usmilitary.about.com (2013). *Careers US Military*. Retrieved from http://usmilitary.about.com/od/marines/l/aamarines.htm.

Vanderau, N. (2013). *Columbine: Understanding why*. Retrieved from www.youtube.com/watch?feature=player_detailpage&v=KikvzIlNg9g.

Van Sant, G. (2003). *Elephant*. [Motion Picture]. Fine Line Features (Producer). USA: HBO Films.

Webster's Unabridged Dictionary (1983). (2nd ed.). New York: Simon and Schuster.

World Press Review (2012). The United Nations, international law, and the war in Iraq. Retrieved from http://worldpress.org/specials/iraq.

Young-Eisendrath, P., & Dawson, T. (Eds.) (1999). *The Cambridge companion to Jung*. Cambridge, MA: Cambridge University Press.

Chapter 9

Personal myth and analytical psychology

Phil McCash

This chapter provides a fresh perspective on a highly significant but neglected area of analytical psychology: Carl Gustav Jung's Conception of the Personal Myth. In order to accomplish this, I first trace the evolution of Jung's thinking on this subject, from his early encounters with Alfred Adler's ideas on inferiority and guiding fiction through to his much later work on the personal myth, discussed in *Memories, Dreams, Reflections* (Jung, 1961/1995). Building on this, and complementing the related work of Hillman (1994) and Watsky (2002), it is suggested that a more Adlerocentric reading of Jung is required. It is further argued that Jung's work on personal myth accommodates Adler's master narrative relating to the inferiority complex and, in so doing, undermines its master status. This aligns the personal myth more clearly with contemporary thinking on the relationship between psychoanalytic studies and narrative (Frosh, 2010, pp. 69–97; Phillips, 2015). The second half of the chapter focuses on delineating the key features of the personal myth. I suggest that it represents Jung's arrival at an integrative stance in relation to his scientific and more personal works. The personal myth is an evolving lifelong and life-wide project that seeks to find a middle way between the extremes of fatalism and agency. It includes ideational and cultural material and is mythopoetic in conception. It entails coming to terms with one's distinctive life pattern and bringing it to its fullest possible expression. Overall, personal myth means to carry life and weave together the golden threads that connect us all.

Jung's reception of Adler

Jung was perhaps first exposed to Adler's ideas through the meetings of the International Psychoanalytic Association (IPA), the Jahrbuch, and Adler's early books. Adler spoke at the IPA on sadism in 1908, and psychic hermaphroditism in 1910. He wrote a paper in the Jahrbuch on the neurotic disposition in 1909 (McGuire, 1974, pp. 563–577). The private catalogue of Jung's personal library indicates it contained copies of Adler's *Study of Organ Inferiority* and *The Neurotic Constitution* but not his later works (Bibliothekskommission, 1967). Jung appears to have first read *The Neurotic Constitution* in the summer of 1912 (1913/1961, *CW* 4, p. 87). Adler was cited regularly throughout the *Collected Works* and particularly in the period 1916–1928 (Forryan & Glover, 1979, *CW* 20, p. 9).

Jung's observations on Adler are both appreciative and critical. In 1917, he attempted to explain a typical patient example from both Adlerian and Freudian perspectives, concluding,

> it is unquestionable that the urge to power plays an extraordinarily important part. It is correct that neurotic symptoms and complexes are also elaborate 'arrangements' which inexorably pursue their aims, with incredible obstinacy and cunning. Neurosis is teleologically oriented. In establishing this Adler has won for himself no small credit.
> (Jung, 1917/1926/1943/1966, *CW* 7, p. 40)

In 1921, he praised Adler for introducing the concept of compensation into the psychology of neuroses. He stated that inferiority gives rise to compensation, that is, a guiding fiction to balance the inferiority: 'The "guiding fiction" is a psychological system that endeavours to turn an inferiority into a superiority' (Jung, 1921/1971, *CW* 6, p. 418). He acknowledged this compensating function was, 'undeniable and empirically demonstrable' (p. 419) and then outlined his own views on compensation, arguing that it is an inherently self-regulating function of the psyche that seeks to balance the conscious and unconscious attitudes. He added that Adler recognised the anticipatory function of the unconscious (p. 422). In an undated note found in his posthumous papers, Jung praised Adler's,

> meticulous elaboration of the psychology and phenomenology of the urge for significance ... [he] was the first to illuminate the *social context of the problem of neurosis* ... [italics original] ... Adler's life work constitutes one of the most important keystones for the structure of a future art of psychotherapy.
> (Jung cited in Jaffé, 1979, p. 65)

Turning to more critical examples, in a letter to Freud of 1910, Jung criticised Adler for his, 'total absence of psychology' (Maguire, 1974, p. 364). Two years later, again in a letter to Freud, he plotted with him to review *The Neurotic Constitution* in a negative light and claimed, 'the man really is slightly dotty' (Maguire, 1974, p. 531). In 1955, in an interview with Michael Schabad, Jung is quoted as saying, 'Adler had only one idea. It was a good idea, but he did not get beyond schoolmaster psychology' (1977, p. 269). Perhaps the ambivalent nature of Jung's reactions is best captured by his argument, made in 1930, that Adler's individual psychology cannot be considered psychoanalytic and, in the following paragraph, that everyone interested in psychoanalysis should study Adler's writings (Jung, 1930/1961, *CW* 4, p. 328).

Adler as a point of triangulation

Jung's reading of Adler appears to have provided him with a key point of triangulation in relation to Freud and played a role in the development of several of his signature concepts. Generally, Jung developed a style of argument, whereby Adler and Freud were compared and contrasted, in order for Jung to establish his own position. This was adopted from 1913 onwards and continued throughout his life. It can be illustrated by three examples.

In 1924, Jung argued that,

> Freud and Adler can easily be reconciled if only we will take the trouble to regard the psyche not as a rigid and unalterable system, but as a fluid stream of events which change kaleidoscopically under the alternating influence of different instincts. Hence we may have to explain a man on a Freudian basis before his marriage, and on the Adlerian basis afterwards ...
>
> (Jung, 1926/1946/1954, *CW* 17, p. 82)

Here, Jung made the case for a more nuanced understanding of the psyche; and argued that the master narratives of Freud and Adler can be employed more provisionally to interpret particular episodes or periods in a life. This was developed further in 1940, when Jung argued that conscious megalomania can be compensated by unconscious inferiority just as conscious inferiority can be compensated by unconscious megalomania (Jung, 1940/1968, *CW* 9i, p. 180). Here, Jung inverted Adler's master narrative to suggest an alternative line of movement from superiority to inferiority.

In 1933, Jung stated that Adler and Freud believed the human psyche is everywhere the same, and can be explained in the same way, whereas, 'it was one of the greatest experiences of my life to discover how enormously different people's psyches are' (Jung, 1933/1934, *CW* 10, p. 137). Again, Jung contrasted Freud and Adler, in order to propose a more textured and pluralistic psychology.

In 1934, Jung compared Adler and Freud and argued they both explain neurosis, from an infantile angle and place the therapist in the position of an expert. They ignore, he suggested, the will to adapt and the potential for growth and creativity in the neurosis and enable the therapist to hide behind technique (Jung, 1934/1970, *CW* 10, pp. 160–161). Here, Jung found both Freud and Adler didactic and proposed a less technique-driven style. Related to this, in 1935, he suggested that patients may benefit from reading books by both Freud and Adler and making their own choices (Jung, 1935/1977, *CW* 18, p. 128). In 1955, he argued that, 'psychology has also the aspect of a pedagogical method in the widest sense of the word ... It is an education. It is something like antique philosophy. And not what we understand by a technique' (Jung, 1977, p. 255). This hints at a distinctively Jungian pedagogical strategy whereby grand narratives devolve to key concepts, that is, sit within the method rather than drive it.

So it was that Jung repeatedly framed his argument by contrasting the viewpoints of Freud and Adler (as he saw them) and developing a third position. He emphasised the value of both approaches but consistently refused to hang his developing sense of analytical psychology around either. Jung, it seems to me, argued for a 'pluralistic' approach to understanding the almost infinite varieties of psychological phenomena (1930/1961, *CW* 4, p. 329). He refused to explain them by using any one single theory as this would constitute a form of reductionism; writing, 'criticism of the psychological assumptions upon which a man's [sic] theories are based becomes an imperative necessity' (Jung, 1951/1966, *CW* 16, p. 114); and, 'the stubborn application of a particular theory or method must be characterized as basically wrong' (Jung, 1926/1946/1954, *CW* 17, p. 113). He consequently refused to use psychotherapeutic techniques based on a single theory as this would approximate to a kind of therapeutic fundamentalism. Jung believed that some individuals may have an Adlerian psychology just as others may have a Freudian, or both, or neither. He also inverted their master narratives; for example, he argued that the inferiority complex may be relevant to some individuals but a form of superiority complex more relevant to others. In short, analytical psychology is analytical, at least in part, because it eschews master narratives. It is a comparative approach to psychology that honours the grand myths of Freud and Adler but refuses reduction to either. Jung, in my view, is not attempting to replace the Oedipus complex or inferiority complex with a third grand narrative of psychological theory. One reason for this is his interest in enantiodromia and the play of opposites. In a limited sense, Adler's approach is enantiodromiatic because he saw inferiority turning into its opposite, namely, success. Jung, however, was more fully committed to this line of thinking and seemed to believe that all grand narratives eventually succumb to their opposites.

Adler's theory of fictions

Adler developed an explicit theory of fictions by drawing selectively from Hans Vaihinger's *Philosophy of As-If* (Adler, 1912/1921, pp. 15, 18, 38, 81). Whatever its merits, by 1912, Adler possessed a wide vocabulary of critical terms including: 'guiding line' (p. 24), 'guiding fiction' (pp. 27, 28), 'antifiction' (p. 40), and 'fictitious guiding goal' (p. 57). At that time, Jung had nothing of similar scope or depth, and was largely dependent on Adler in beginning to develop his own approach. It seems to me that Jung took on Adler's ideas to inform his own thinking. In 1916, he used the terms 'lines of psychological development' (Jung, 1916/1966, *CW* 7, p. 291), and 'life-line' (p. 293). In 1921, he again used the term 'life-line' (Jung, 1921/1971, *CW* 6, p. 170). In 1932, he referred to the 'healing fiction' (Jung, 1932/1969, *CW* 11, p. 331). In 1957, he used the expression 'fiction of oneself' to describe the persona (Jung, 1977, p. 297). The resemblance between these phrases and Adler's language of guiding lines and fictions is quite marked.

Jung's adaptation of Adler's ideas

Jung did not borrow from Adler wholesale, rather, he adapted and modified the latter's theory of fictions in his own way. In relation to life-lines and guiding fictions, Jung acknowledged Adler's use of the term 'guiding fictions' and sought to distinguish between it and life-lines.

> The construction of life-lines reveals to consciousness the ever-changing direction of the currents of libido. These life-lines are not to be confused with the 'guiding fictions' discovered by Adler, for the latter are nothing but arbitrary attempts to cut off the persona from the collective psyche and lend it an independent existence. One might say that the guiding fiction is an unsuccessful attempt to construct a life-line. Moreover – and this shows the uselessness of the fiction – such a line as it does produce persists far too long; it has the tenacity of a cramp.
> (Jung, 1916/1966, *CW* 7, p. 294)

Here, Jung explicitly criticised Adler and dismissed the guiding fiction as a failed life-line. The position in analytical psychology is that the life-line constructed by the hermeneutic method enables a synthesis with the collective psyche. It entails the elaboration of analogies and similarities in order to encourage individual and collective lines of development to appear. For Jung, the guiding fiction was too narrow a concept to accommodate the collective psyche. There is an explicitly historical dimension to Jung's critique here that contrasts with Adler's focus on the contemporary period (1912/1921, p. 24). The life-line has both synchronic and diachronic aspects, and it is the latter that provide a counterweight, or point of comparison, to contemporary events and influences.

Jung also made the criticism that the guiding fiction lasts too long. The role he envisaged for the life-line is more provisional and dynamic. Here, Jung may have been concerned that the guiding fiction can solidify into persona identification; indeed, its grounding in the resolution of a felt inferiority may make this more, rather than less likely, and therefore difficult to shake off. For Jung, the heroic overcoming of childhood problems may only be one stage in individuation and itself an obstacle to further growth. He was also interested in the dynamic nature of libido and the ways in which it can ebb and flow. For Jung, an individual may pursue several lines of development at one time, and indeed, over the course of a life. An absorbing plot can become a tiresome bore.

Adler argued that individuals wear a 'persona' or 'mask' determined by their guiding fiction just like classical actors (1912/1921, p. 39). This indicates Adler's dramaturgical sensibility and, significantly, predates Jung's first use of the term 'persona' (1916/1966, *CW* 7, p. 281). For Adler, the guiding fiction determines the persona's character traits, which then come into conflict with the anti-fiction of societal influence; whereas, for Jung, the persona is a blend of these two aspects with the accent on the latter. Adler stated that the guiding fiction is an idol, a deity, a God, holy, and divine (1912/1921, pp. 23, 41, 55). Jung acknowledged this and seems to incorporate it within his description of the persona as a petty-god (1916/1966, *CW* 7, p. 281).

Adler, influenced by Charcot, argued that the guiding fiction determines all perceptions, ideas, actions, and judgements, including the ideas of science and philosophy (1912/1921, p. 28). In this way, he anticipated Jung's elaboration of the personal equation (1921/1971, *CW* 6, p. 9). Adler also argued that the guiding fiction can appear as a second self, an inner voice, or daemon, which encourages, punishes, and accuses (1912/1921, p. 47). In 1932, Jung argued that the vocation is the voice of the inner individual and, '[a] daemon whispering ... of new and wonderful paths' (1934/1954, *CW* 17, p. 176). Adler's signature concept of individual psychology as, 'the entire psychic life' (1912/1921, p. vii) bears some similarity with Jung's evolving sense of individuation and individuality (1916/1966, *CW* 7, pp. 296–298).

Adler stated that the neurotic is nailed to the cross of his own fiction (1912/1921, p. 33). Jung subsequently argued that it is necessary to carry one's own cross in order to avoid being nailed to it (1932/1969, *CW* 11, pp. 340–341; 1977, p. 440; 2009, p. 310). As indicated above, Adler incorporated Vaihinger's threefold division into fiction, hypothesis, and dogma. Jung seems to have picked up on the idea of living out one's own hypothesis and argued this is integral to the project of individuation (Jung, 1977, p. 98). Finally, Adler argued that the guiding fiction is an individual's answer to the question of life (1912/1921, p. 23); whereas, Jung stated that the personal myth is the answer given to the question that an individual addresses to the world (1961/1995, p. 350).

Conception of the personal myth

The remainder of this chapter focuses in more detail on the personal myth and explicates the key features of it. Jung wrote only very briefly on personal myth, in an explicit way, and this took place in the 1950s when he was already in his mid-seventies. Personal myth is therefore very late work, possibly Jung's last. It may be one of his most significant contributions but it is not entirely clear what he meant by it. Huskinson (2008, p. 3) is perhaps right to argue that some of the Jungian literature has been more drawn to the analysis of classic myths than myth as personal narrative although there have been some significant contributions on this theme (e.g., Bishop, 2014; Giegerich, 2008; MacAdams, 1993; Rowland, 2005; Stevens, 1995).

In a widely quoted passage in *Memories, Dreams, Reflections*, Jung stated that he was undertaking to tell his 'personal myth' (1961/1995, p. 17). Elsewhere in that text, he referred to, 'an explanatory myth which has slowly taken shape within me in the course of the decades' (p. 371). In addition, Jung discussed a painting and a related dream set in the city of Liverpool that took place on 2 January 1927, stating that, 'out of it emerged a first inkling of my personal myth' (p. 224). Jung also retrospectively alluded to a personal myth ('my myth') in the introduction to *Symbols of Transformation* (1950/1956, *CW* 5, p. xxv). According to this account, written around 1950, the completion of the manuscript of the *Psychology of the Unconscious* in 1911 provided the spur to the development of his personal myth. In a letter to J.A. Gilbert of 1929, he referred to enabling his patients to develop their own mythology (Jung cited in Shamdasani, 2009, p. 216). These clues indicate that Jung developed a sense of personal myth over a long period, indeed, that the personal myth could evolve over a lifetime.

Scope of the personal myth and wider life

The personal myth is seen as profoundly connected with wider life. Jung insisted on the indivisible connection between his formal writings and his life.

> The 'autobiography' is my life, viewed in the light of knowledge I have gained from my scientific endeavours. Both are one ... My life has been in a sense the quintessence of what I have written, not the other way around. The way I am and the way I write are a unity. All my ideas and all my endeavours are myself. Thus, the 'autobiography' is merely the dot on the i.
>
> (Jung, 1961/1995, p. 14)

This appears to be one reason why Jung was reluctant to write an autobiography and tended not to regard *Memories, Dreams, Reflections* as one (1976, p. 550). The personal myth cannot be reduced to a short statement or pat formula. Although there are several points where Jung appears to offer a pithy summary, the personal myth should be seen as encompassing both Jung's work and wider life ('all my ideas and all my endeavours are myself'). Linked to this, the personal myth has an explicitly theoretical or ideational content. Jung wrote that making theory should be seen as an integral part of his identity, 'as vital a function of mine, as eating and drinking' (1961/1995, p. 359). In his case, the personal myth encompassed a very wide range of fields indeed including psychology, religion, literature, and philosophy. This subverts conventional distinctions between theory and practice, and further suggests that ideas should be seen as key components of narrative. It also indicates that the scope of the personal myth is vast as it potentially integrates all areas of a human being's experience.

Despite Jung's statements about telling his myth in *Memories, Dreams, Reflections*, it would be a misreading to interpret that text *as* the personal myth. *Memories, Dreams, Reflections* is, 'merely the dot on the i'. It is more of a guidebook to the personal myth and an occasionally unreliable one at that. There is also a sense in which the personal myth is always a work in progress. Shortly before his death, Jung found that he needed to revisit unresolved childhood experiences and consider their significance (1961/1995, pp. 8–9). The personal myth, then, is never complete. Its final extent is not known, and in this sense, there must remain a mysterious element to any personal myth.

The personal myth fails to wholly conform to the conventional storyline of a beginning, middle, and end; and nor does it form a purely linear plot. Jung stated, 'there is no linear evolution; there is only a circumambulation of the self' (1961/1995, p. 222); and apparently suggested that the frequent repetitions in *Memories, Dreams, Reflections* represented his peripatetic or circular modes of thinking (Jung cited in Shamdasani, 1999, p. 39). Jung's abiding interest in enantiodromia is also relevant, that is, the view that everything turns into its opposite. These clues suggest that there may be more than one way of understanding personal myth. It may be read linearly, episodically, thematically, or cyclically. It seems to me that there is an implicit invitation, on finishing *Memories, Dreams, Reflections*, to return to the start, and compare the similarities and differences between the nature visions of the old man and the child (Jung, 1961/1995, pp. 21, 252, 392). Indeed, given that Jung viewed his entire scientific works as autobiographical, one is almost invited, on finishing the last volume of the *Collected Works*, to return to volume one and start again; a somewhat more daunting challenge! In a sense, it is through the concept of the personal myth, that Jung finally integrates his personal and scientific works.

In related vein, in developing a personal myth, Jung appears to have embraced a more thoroughly mythic or mythopoetic epistemological position.

> ... I have now undertaken, in my eighty-third year, to tell my personal myth. I can only 'tell stories'. Whether or not the stories are true is not my problem. The only question is whether what I tell is my fable, my truth.
> (Jung, 1961/1995, p. 17)

Here, Jung seems to reject objectivist and positivist positions. He did not see his role as proving theories true or false, rather, he argued for the mythic nature of reality. He rejected 'critical rationalism', 'the intellect', and 'scientific man' in favour of the healing power of 'mythologising', 'the emotions', and 'mythic man' (pp. 330–331). This links with earlier statements where he argued that science was a myth (Jung, 1940/1968, *CW* 9i, pp. 179–180) and a mere 'corner' of the world (Jung, 1997, p. 611). Jung implies here that a belief in mythlessness *is itself* a myth, that is, the myth of scientific materialism. This appears to be what he meant by referring to living 'without' a myth (Jung, 1950/1956, *CW* 5, p. xxv). In a more fundamental sense, it is not possible to live outside myth. There being only two options: to recognise one lives in myth, or to live in myth unconsciously. In this sense, Segal (2011, pp. 75–76) may have overstated his case when he argued that, for Jung, science is not mythic.

Personal myth, life course development, and the carrier of life

Jung famously divided the stages of life into the morning, afternoon, and evening; with a first half of life focused on nature and a second focused on culture (1917/1926/1943/1966, *CW* 7, pp. 74–74; 1929/1967, *CW* 13, p. 14; 1930–1931/1969, *CW* 8). Although this position has some merits, it is somewhat simplistic, and has attracted criticism from later scholars. Fordham (1995) argued that traces of individuation could be detected in the lives of infants. Moraglia (1994) also proposed a less-age-linked view of adult development on the grounds that both young and old people are concerned with wider issues of the human condition as well as earning a living. He aligned Jungian adult development theory more closely to contemporary thinking in life course psychology by reducing emphasis on age-related stages in favour of more fluid understandings of the life course (Mintz, 2015; Zittoun, Valsiner, Vedeler, Salgado, Gonçalves, & Ferring, 2013). In addition, Stein (1983/2014, p. 52) criticised a strictly linear approach, arguing that the unconscious, 'resists being boxed into fixed temporal contexts and causal sequences'. The imposition of linearity is basically an act of consciousness and it may unwittingly do violence to the flow of life. Jung seemed to be aware of this and acknowledged that there were limitations to any one metaphor (1930–1931/1969, *CW* 8, p. 397). He argued that individuation was not simply a question of years and could happen at any time, 'there is the same possibility at any moment of life' (Jung, 1997, p. 761). This suggests that, whilst stage-based theories of the life course have value, they simply form part of the picture. There is a danger that over-concretised life course schemes lose touch with the nourishing life of the unconscious. The notion that consciousness can comprehend life through sequences and structures is, in the end, an act of hubris. There may even be a form of projection at play, the effect being somehow to hold life at bay or push it out of the psyche. It is not so much about the ego understanding life, as allowing life (in the sense of the wider Jungian Self) to create meaning with or from the ego. It is something more akin to Fordham's (1995, pp. 3–78) description of the deintegration and reintegration process. This focuses on the complementary deintegrating and reintegrating actions of the Self, that is, the process through which the Self reaches out and unfolds, followed by taking back in and incorporation. Jung emphasised that individuation, 'is both the beginning and the end of life, it is *the process of life itself*' (1997, p. 758; emphasis added); and, in related vein, Stein (1983/2014, p. 59) equated the psyche with this life-force. In analytical psychology, individuation is the process of life becoming conscious of itself. It reminds me of Dylan Thomas's line about, 'the force that through the green fuse drives the flower' (1988, p. 13). Jung (1929/1967, *CW* 13, p. 52) put it another way when he stated, 'it is not I who live, it lives me'. This is not life in any general or generic sense but a specific, unique form of life, 'each of us carries his [sic] own life-form within him – an irrational form which no other can outbid' (Jung, 1931/1966, *CW* 16, p. 41). Within analytical psychology, the individual is seen as 'the carrier of life' (Jung, 1955/1956/1970, *CW* 14, p. 167). In this sense, individuation and the personal myth mean to carry one's unique life and bring it to its fullest possible expression.

Personal myth, authoring, and the golden threads of culture

The idea that myths can be personal is, on the face of it, profoundly problematic. One definition of myth is that it is not individually authored. Myths come to us as the work of many hands. Jung downplayed the sense of personal authoring by emphasising the roles played by the myth itself and wider culture. It is not so much a question of writing one's myth; the 'task of tasks' is 'to get to know' one's myth and find out how it unconsciously influences one's life (Jung, 1950/1956, *CW* 5, p. xxv). It is about becoming acquainted with one's myth and, perhaps, getting on speaking terms with it. He also counselled against living one's myth and by this he means, I think, a non-agentic living out of one's fate through blind unconsciousness. It appears that the personal myth is a sort of middle way through the respective dangers of excessive agency and fatalism. Jung saw the personal myth as the living out of one's ideas and the testing of one's hypothesis in the fire of existence. It entailed developing one's own philosophy of life, an inevitably error-strewn process.

> We must make our experiment. We must make mistakes. We must live out our own vision of life. And there will be error. If you avoid error you do not live; in a sense even it may be said that every life is a mistake, for no one has found the truth.
>
> (Jung, 1977, p. 98)

On this basis, there can be no prescribed plot or route. Any prefabricated model would be an error, the surest way of avoiding individuation. Individuation is a narrative without a predetermined plot. Or, to put it in unlovely prose, the personal myth is a kind of meta-narratological project.

In similar vein, there is a further significant aspect to discuss related to the cultural and historical nature of the personal myth. Jung suggested, in 1944, that he felt disconnected, and as though he were a 'historical fragment, an excerpt for which the preceding and succeeding text was missing' (1961/1995, p. 322). He needed to find out, 'what historical nexus or my life fitted into ... what had been before me, why I had come into being, and where my life was flowing'. In relation to this, he dreamt of a figure framed by a golden chain (p. 322). Towards the end of his life, in an echo of his earlier use of the term 'life-line', he referred to seeing, 'the line which leads through my life into the world, and out of the world again' (1961/1995, p. 352). He is also reported to have experienced a final dream featuring 'golden threads' encircling the world (Franz, 1972/1998, p. 287). This can be linked with Stein's (2004, p. 221) moving evocation of the connecting 'threads in a great fabric'; and Giegerich's (2008, pp. 77–78) discussion of the personal myth as a golden chain connecting individual lives of all ages. This suggests to me that the personal myth, for Jung and potentially for everyone, entails learning about our deep historical connections with others and the wider world. It is woven from the golden threads that connect, and re-connect, the individual with culture.

Summary

In this chapter, I have explored Jung's reception of Adler and argued that a more Adlerocentric reading of Jung is required. Adler provided a key point of triangulation for Jung and influenced the development of his signature concepts. This enabled Jung to develop an analytical psychology that is subversive of grand narratives. For example, he argued that the master narratives of Freud and Adler can be employed more provisionally to interpret particular episodes or periods in a life. Jung also inverted Adler's master narrative to suggest an alternative line of movement from superiority to inferiority. In addition, Jung contrasted Freud and Adler to propose a more textured and pluralistic psychology. He developed a distinctively Jungian pedagogical strategy whereby grand narratives could become contents, that is, topics sitting within the method rather than driving it.

Jung slowly developed a theory of fictions from his encounter with Adler's system. Adler's central concepts of guiding lines, guiding fiction, anti-fiction, and fictitious guiding goal influenced the development of key ideas in analytical psychology including lines of development, life-lines, personal myth, persona, and individuation. Jung added a distinctively historical dimension to Adler's approach and an emphasis on the provisional, dynamic, and pluralistic nature of life-lines. It is in the personal myth that Jung's thinking matures. It represents his arrival at a critical, comparative theory of narrative based on a mythopoetic epistemology. The key characteristics of the personal myth are its lifelong and life-wide nature, and inclusion of cultural and ideational elements. It does not conform to a narrowly linear structure nor can it be reduced to a simple formula. It resists the contrasting pulls of extreme agency and fatalism and is, at all times, a work in progress. It entails developing a dialogue with the unconscious and getting to know one's distinctive life pattern. It is woven from the golden threads of culture and, in turn, forms part of them. The development of a personal myth means to bring one's life to its fullest possible expression and realisation.

References

Adler, A. (1912/1921). *The neurotic constitution: outlines of a comparative individualistic psychology and psychotherapy* (B. Glueck & J. E. Lind, Trans.). New York: Moffatt, Yard.
Bibliothekskommission. (1967). *Catalogue of C.G. Jung's personal library*. Zurich: Privately printed.
Bishop, P. (2014). *Carl Jung*. London: Reaktion Books.
Fordham, M. (1995). *Freud, Jung, Klein the fenceless field: essays on psychoanalysis and analytical psychology* (R. Hobdell, Ed.). Hove: Routledge.
Forryan, B., & Glover, J. M. (1979, *CW* 20). *General index to the collected works of C.G. Jung* (R. F. C. Hull, Trans.). London: Routledge.
Frosh, S. (2010). *Psychoanalysis outside the clinic: interventions in psychosocial studies*. Basingstoke: Palgrave Macmillan.
Giegerich, W. (2008). *The soul's logical life: towards a rigorous notion of psychology* (4th ed.). Frankfurt am Main, Germany: Peter Lang.
Hillman, J. (1994). *Healing fictions*. Putnam, CT: Spring.
Huskinson, L. (2008). Introduction: ordinarily mythical. In L. Huskinson (Ed.), *Dreaming the myth onwards: new directions in Jungian therapy and thought*. Hove: Routledge.
Jaffé, A. (Ed.) (1979). *C.G. Jung: word and image*. Princeton, NJ: Princeton University Press.
Jung, C. G. (1913/1961, *CW* 4). The theory of psychoanalysis (R. F. C. Hull, Trans.). In H. Read, M. Fordham, G. Adler, & W. Maguire (Eds.), *Freud and psychoanalysis* (1st ed.). Princeton, NJ: Princeton University Press.
Jung, C. G. (1916/1966, *CW* 7). The structure of the unconscious (R. F. C. Hull, Trans.). In H. Read, M. D. Fordham, & G. Adler (Eds.), *Two essays on analytical psychology*. Princeton, NJ: Princeton University Press.
Jung, C. G. (1917/1926/1943/1966, *CW* 7). On the psychology of the unconscious (R. F. C. Hull, Trans.). In H. Read, M. Fordham, & G. Adler (Eds.), *Two essays on analytical psychology* (2nd ed.). Princeton, NJ: Princeton University Press.
Jung, C. G. (1921/1971, *CW* 6). *Psychological types* (H. G. Baynes, Trans.). Princeton, NJ: Princeton University Press.
Jung, C. G. (1926/1946/1954, *CW* 17). Analytical psychology and education (R. F. C. Hull, Trans.). In H. Read, M. Fordham, & G. Adler (Eds.), *The development of personality*. Princeton, NJ: Princeton University Press.
Jung, C. G. (1929/1967, *CW* 13). Commentary on 'The Secret of the Golden Flower' (R. F. C. Hull, Trans.). In H. Read, M. Fordham, & G. Adler (Eds.), *Alchemical Studies*. Princeton, NJ: Princeton University Press.

Jung, C. G. (1930–1931/1969, *CW* 8). The stages of life (R. F. C. Hull, Trans.). In H. Read, M. Fordham, & G. Adler (Eds.), *The structure and dynamics of the psyche* (2nd ed.). Hove: Routledge.

Jung, C. G. (1930/1961, *CW* 4). Introduction to Kranefeldt's 'secret ways of the mind' (R. F. C. Hull, Trans.). In H. Read, M. Fordham, G. Adler, & W. Maguire (Eds.), *Freud and psychoanalysis*. Princeton, NJ: Princeton University Press.

Jung, C. G. (1931/1966, *CW* 16). The aims of psychotherapy (R. F. C. Hull, Trans.). In H. Read, M. D. Fordham, & G. Adler (Eds.), *The practice of psychotherapy* (2nd ed.). London: Routledge.

Jung, C. G. (1932/1969, *CW* 11). Psychotherapy or the clergy (R. F. C. Hull, Trans.). In H. Read, M. D. Fordham, & G. Adler (Eds.), *Psychology and religion: west and east* (2nd ed.). London: Routledge.

Jung, C. G. (1933/1934, *CW* 10). The meaning of psychology for modern man (R. F. C. Hull, Trans.). In H. Read, M. Fordham, & G. Adler (Eds.), *Civilization in transition* (2nd ed.). Hove: Routledge.

Jung, C. G. (1934/1954, *CW* 17). The development of personality (R. F. C. Hull, Trans.). In H. Read, M. Fordham, & G. Adler (Eds.), *The development of the personality: papers on child psychology, education and related subjects*. Princeton, NJ: Princeton University Press.

Jung, C. G. (1934/1970, *CW* 10). The state of psychotherapy today (R. F. C. Hull, Trans.). In H. Read, M. Fordham, & G. Adler (Eds.), *Civilization in transition* (2nd ed.). Hove: Routledge.

Jung, C. G. (1935/1977, *CW* 18). The Tavistock lectures (R. F. C. Hull, Trans.). In H. Read, M. Fordham, & G. Adler (Eds.), *The symbolic life*. Hove: Routledge.

Jung, C. G. (1940/1968, *CW* 9i). The psychology of the child archetype (R. F. C. Hull, Trans.). In H. Read, M. D. Fordham, & G. Adler (Eds.), *The archetypes and the collective unconscious* (2nd ed.). London: Routledge.

Jung, C. G. (1950/1956, *CW* 5). Foreword to the fourth Swiss edition (R. F. C. Hull, Trans.). In H. Read, M. Fordham, & G. Adler (Eds.), *Symbols of transformation*. London: Routledge.

Jung, C. G. (1951/1966, *CW* 16). Fundamental questions of psychotherapy (R. F. C. Hull, Trans.). In H. Read, M. D. Fordham, & G. Adler (Eds.), *The practice of psychotherapy* (2nd ed.). London: Routledge.

Jung, C. G. (1955/1956/1970, *CW* 14). *Mysterium coniunctionis* (R. F. C. Hull, Trans. 2nd ed.). Hove: Routledge.

Jung, C. G. (1961/1995). *Memories, dreams, reflections* (R. Winston & C. Winston, Trans. 5th ed.). London: Fontana.

Jung, C. G. (1976). Letter to Walter Niehus-Jung dated 5 April 1960. In G. Adler (Ed.), *C.G. Jung letters volume two: 1951–1961*. London: Routledge and Kegan Paul.

Jung, C. G. (1977). *C.G. Jung speaking: interviews and encounters*. Princeton, NJ: Princeton University Press.

Jung, C. G. (1997). *Visions: notes of the seminar given in 1930–34* (Vol. 2). Princeton, NJ: Princeton University Press.

Jung, C. G. (2009). Liber novus (M. Kyburz, Trans.). In S. Shamdasani (Ed.), *The red book: liber novus*. New York: Norton.

MacAdams, D. P. (1993). *Stories we live by: personal myths and the making of the self*. New York: Guilford.

McGuire, W. (Ed.) (1974). *The Freud/Jung letters: the correspondence between Sigmund Freud and C.G. Jung*. London: Hogarth Press and Routledge & Kegan Paul.

Mintz, S. (2015). *The prime of life: a history of modern adulthood*. Cambridge, MA: Belknap Press of Harvard University Press.

Moraglia, G. (1994). C.G. Jung and the psychology of adult development. *Journal of Analytical Psychology*, 39(1), 55–75.

Phillips, A. (2015). Against self-criticism. *London Review of Books*, 37(5), 13–16.

Rowland, S. (2005). *Jung as a writer*. Hove: Routledge.

Segal, R. A. (2011). Jung on myth. In K. Bulkeley & C. Weldon (Eds.), *Teaching Jung*. Oxford: Oxford University Press.

Shamdasani, S. (1999). Memories, dreams, omissions. In P. Bishop (Ed.), *Jung in contexts: a reader*. Abingdon: Routledge.

Shamdasani, S. (2009). Liber Novus: the 'Red Book' of C.G. Jung: Introduction (M. Kyburz, Trans.). In S. Shamdasani (Ed.), *The Red Book: Liber Novus*. New York: Norton.

Stein, M. (1983/2014). *In midlife: a Jungian perspective*. Asheville, NC: Chiron.

Stein, M. (2004). Spiritual and religious aspects of modern analysis. In J. Cambray & L. Carter (Eds.), *Analytical psychology: contemporary perspectives in Jungian analysis*. Hove: Routledge.

Stevens, A. (1995). *Private myths: dreams and dreaming*. Cambridge, MA: Harvard University Press.

Thomas, D. (1988). *Collected poems 1934–1953* (W. Davies & P. Maud, Eds.). London: J.M. Dent.

von Franz, M.-L. (1972/1998). *C.G. Jung: his myth in our time*. Toronto, Canada: Inner City Books.

Watsky, P. (2002). Alfred Adler's influence on the work of C.G. Jung. *Journal of Jungian theory and practice*, 2(Spring), 43–56.

Zittoun, T., Valsiner, J., Vedeler, D., Salgado, J., Gonçalves, M. F. D., & Ferring, D. (2013). *Human development in the life course: melodies of living*. Cambridge: Cambridge University Press.

Chapter 10

On the spirit and the self
Chagall, Jung and religion

J.A. Swan

> *There is the thought that, if one lives with patience, hones an appreciation for engaging the increment of moments, and imparts a self-reflective attitude across lifespan, then the patterns of one's unique developmental process – and, professionally, even, the developmental process of others – may be experienced in visual tones; tones that vibrate not only with colour and ornament, but with visceral perception. In their cyclical tempos, the circles in each individual lifespan, that begin and end, and begin again, hold the capacity to ring true to an archetypal tone re-composed, now, in new and different ways. The Jungian instrument is a life-lens that illuminates archetypal expression as it resonates with the tones of the visual patterns created. In Time, such a perspective perpetuates an understanding of the archetypal nature of our collective existence.*
>
> J. A. Swan, inspired from a passage in *The Plural Psyche* (Samuels, 1989, p.25)

Images are the dominion of the psyche. We live in an imaginal world, and our lives are filled and coloured by the imagery that surrounds us as we move through our lifetimes. The ways in which we experience image and the imaginal world remain a complex and debatable understanding of a cyclical life-processing-life-reflecting experience. Finding a path towards such Understanding begins at the intersection of the physical sciences and psychologies, the study of aesthetics, and Faith. This is Jungian territory, wherein the borders between the individual psyche and the collective world are indistinguishable: wherein images become as a symbolic state, holding the capacity for illumination, and emerge as the life markers and the visual imprints of the psychic current called change through which all transformation takes place (Swan, 2019, p.11).

This as-yet-incomplete Knowing of the imaginal experience remains a curious human process, as we interact with material images (and, in our dreams) through an encountering of sorts: the observing of a visual "observance" in the material world. The familiar and demonstrative human emotions we gauge our life responses through, and by, are present in such imaginal encounters; Rarely, though, do visceral emotions – such as one being brought to tears or to verbal exclamation – surface in definitive or completed ways as we observe our imaginal history during visits to a museum or picture gallery, a library, or even whilst observing the natural vistas of our earth and skies. Yet, the imaginal world affects us deeply, and collectively: We are united through all Time as human beings by our symbolic Life images. We hold onto – and carry away – these images that live (now) within us, whether in physical form,[1] or by thought, alone. We revisit or refer to an image in us, ongoing, perhaps by using its given name in the material world, or through the essence of description: the idea of this image, what is behind this image, the story which it holds, what it communicates, collectively or to one alone (Swan, 2019).

Most often, what remains of our imaginal encounters is an imaginal feeling, a particular presence evoked, provoked, or emoted through an individual encounter with imagery. Creating form through feeling is the spirit of the artistic process. Visual art remains among the most powerful – and demonstrative – imaginal provocateurs of life feeling: the neutrality of creative materials, and the unity present in a cohesive application of the Principles of Design, open a psychic window for the Observant to gaze through, into the symbolic life of mankind (Swan, 2019, pp.11–12).

The collective vista is a neutral space – as the sum of materials from which it was birthed – yet, in linear time, this organic view contains images that may unite, as well as divide, human perceptions of life observations. The creative spirit has a rhythm of bringing forth such spirit, enriching (or, destroying) polarities for artists and writers to explore and to re-create, to re-imagine, over, and again. Engaging this life-spirit with creative materials is perhaps the initiation of the imaginal journey – raw image (and, colour pigment) connect with the capacity for openness, creating a visual portal with the potential to stimulate and invigorate our psychic lives. Whether naturally, or through force (e.g., "forcing" an image upon us), the connection between our individual selves and the collective expression of mankind's world is illuminated through exploring image. In this connecting space (or, psychic vista), the patterns of Life – mankind's symbols – live through the processes of repeating, distorting, changing, transforming, and re-merging images over the course of our own lifetimes, and through the ongoing movement of human history (Swan, 2019, p.12).

There is a human tendency to categorise objects in the material world; visual art is not an exception: there are faith-based images, Antiquities, Period pieces, Modern works, popular images, realistic images, abstract images, Important images, Lesser works, and so forth. In secular life, an auction catalogue or exhibition guide explains the provenance of the image, its creator and their creative process. Yet, even the most secular of exhibition rooms is treated as a sacred space, once the pictures are hung. The human appreciation of the imaginal world is rooted deeply in that which is sacred and, even, that which is Unknown. We are reverent, in our observing an observant reflection of Life. There is the understanding, that the imaginal world continues to reveal and reflect far more about our lives in Time, and an understanding of human life, than we are each able to know (ibid.).

Some of the earliest images of human lifetimes that remain survive within the earthly temenos of caves that have lain undisturbed for millennia. The imaginal here is re-imagined, regenerated by our Times, through an understanding of shared symbols: the hunted animals, the worshipped gods, the recording of an ancient lifetime in images. We continue – perhaps now, more than ever before – to reflect and to record our own becoming process in the imaginal world. (There is even the thought that our youngest generation is becoming too image-saturated.) We seek out unique places and find curious spaces to record (and then, to present) our personal experiences of a lifetime in the imaginal world (ibid.).

The connection between images and experiences is potent. There is the understanding of an ongoing, experiential contact – image encounters – with the imaginal world. There is, too, the thought that, across the lifespan, one comes to understand an experience of life through a particular image – or a series of images. Whether such imagery arises with the study of Neolithic forbearers – the story of an historic figure, the life of a Prophet, the miracles of a Saint, or the Wonder of the Universe – a psychic connection to an image of a symbol in one's own personal transformation path is formed, through what one experiences when one is life-observing. Life's symbols remain alive and potent human connectors in the conscious world – and, between unconscious life – through the creative spirit recording human experiences with images, for the Observant to observe: they are carved into stone and stained in glass, sewn together with fabrics and knitted in threads. They are scratched into parchment, rendered on paper, painted onto canvas and tooled into wood. They are sculpted with clay, poured in metal, are photographed, developed, and now, are displayed on electronic screens. The creative Movements of the latter nineteenth and twentieth centuries (and, beyond) have continued to reinforce the thought that image – whilst itself, timeless – is receptive to, and reacts with, collective patterns of change. Moreover, that the organic expression of the imaginal world holds – and continues to contain – reflections of the transformation process for both collective, and individual lifetimes (Swan, 2019, pp.12–13).

Jung and Chagall were twentieth-century individuals, whose lives did not coincide, yet they share much, in their respective experiences, of an individualised lifetime spent observing in the imaginal world. As creative individuals, they each held an understanding about the necessity of communicating their life observations to others, and were both gifted in the ways they individually went about "making" their ideas known. The Jungian conceptualisation of religion, and, the exploration of the imaginal world through archetypal theory, together form a particular understanding of creative and religious life through images: Jung characterises the universality of religion, and the interiority of the artist's creative spirit in a way that is both psychologically and visually pertinent when considering the imagery of Marc Chagall. Chagall's work is seen through the presence of religious experience in creative expression (Swan, 2019, p.15).

There is the thought that the telling of any story is not without certain challenges: Chagall, a prolific writer and speaker, particularly during his later life, clearly communicated his views on the application of Depth Psychology in theorising his works, "I have slept well without Freud" (Harshav, 2003, p.173). There are, also, no written accounts nor documents from the Artist to support the suggestion that Chagall had been directly acquainted with Jung or with Jungian theory ... Yet, within Chagall and Jung's visual art and writing, in their talks and speeches, and in interviews, coincidences emerge, over, and again: the shared presence of a universal religion in their lives, the shared imagery of the transforming Self, and the shared creative spirit that engaged their imaginal observations and recordings of life experiences (ibid.)

It is with the thought that connections extend beyond coincidences in the imaginal world that this story of Chagall as a religious artist begins. "To my way of thinking, these paintings do not illustrate the dream of one single people, but that of mankind ... it is not up to me to comment on them, works of art should be able to speak for themselves" (Chagall, 1973,[2] in Harshav, 2003, p.173). Chagall's process of painting, and the works he created through ([his specific)] technique and style, supported the idea that: ([the Artist's)] visual language reflects a projection (or, vista) of the collective and personal unconsciousness, that emerges in the compositional understanding of the Artist's technical application of form, and is translated visually to the exterior world. Chagall continued throughout his career to utilise and return to particular groups of images: architectural structures (windows, houses, and cities), animals, zoomorphic creatures and bi-morphic figures, brides and wedding couples, hermaphrodites, and crucifixions. These images appear in the background matrix and as part of the compositional focus (Swan, 2019, p.16).

Artists have the capacity through their use of creative languages to illustrate their reflections into and out from the experience of life. The appearance and use of these creative images is the process of symbols and the symbolic. Samuels et al. (1986) remark that, "the symbolic process is an experience in images and of images" (p.45). This is most essential to an understanding of how and why a material product of art is able to stimulate and interact with its human audience. This also explains why specific works of art appeal across cultures and remain fresh and relative in contemporary times, independent of when and where they originated (Swan, 2019, p.17).

Within this process of manifestation or emergences, and through the unconscious processing of image connection, the nature of creative and religious life – the *wholeness* of lifespan – is present. Jung's theory of archetypes develops the numinous features experienced in human imaginal connection, and makes the reasoning as to why this archetypal level of expression is an important part of understanding the way to see a human being *becoming* throughout their lifetime (ibid.).

Samuels et al. (1986) explain the prevalence of the transformation concept in Jungian theory: that it is a concept which is central to Jung's collected works; that transformation symbolism is used to describe both clinical and metaphysical transitions, as in the example of Jung's writing on alchemy and religious rites; and, that the transformative process can manifest as either a positive signal of psychic growth, or a negative experience of psychic breakdown (Swan, 2019, pp.19–20). The analytic process examines the content and presentation of such archetypal images or experiences in an effort to reintegrate the understanding of their symbolism within the conscious layer of the psyche. The personal unconscious psyche works through its contact and unification with imagery of the collective unconscious, and through this, the individuation process is reflected as a transformative and whole experience (Swan, 2019, p.21).

For the artist Marc Chagall (1887–1985), a lifetime of image-making and creative writing produced both visual and narrative paths through which it is possible to follow the transformative nature of the individuation process: for both the Artist as creator, and the collective passage of change in a twentieth century of lifetime (Swan, 2019, p.20).

In Chagall's oeuvre, the most prominent example of a sacred archetypal image and the transformative metaphor is the Crucifixion, which Chagall revisited in various forms and materials from 1909 until his death, in 1985. The appearance and strength of the crucifixion theme became an important finding in the research process: Chagall's natal faith was found in the traditions and culture of Hasidic Judaism; and, the artist experienced anti-Semitism whilst living in Russia and France. He was among the Jewish "Artists in Exile" who fled from the Holocaust to America in 1941, with the support of Varian Fry and the sponsorship of the American Emergency Rescue Committee. In the historical and biographical context of Chagall's natal faith and life experiences, the repetitive use of this most familiar of sacred Christian images provides a curious visual paradigm from which to begin to explore Jung's conceptualisation of the artist and aesthetics:

> Art is a kind of innate drive that seizes a human being and makes him its instrument. The artist is not a person endowed with free will who seeks his own ends, but one who allows art to realise its purposes through him. As a human being he may have moods and a will and personal aims, but as an artist he is "man" in a higher sense – he is "collective man" – one who carries and shapes the unconscious, psychic life of mankind.
> (*CW* 15: par. 157)
> (Swan, 2019, p.21)

In *The Plural Psyche*, Andrew Samuel's (1989) post-Jungian thought approaches the transformative dynamic in its relocating Jung's archetypes to the contact experience of the imaginal within the personal unconscious's connection to life. An internal filtering process, or personal life lens, is present and concordant within the processing of an individual's engagement of and with various external realities. Samuels describes his concept of the archetypal experience as a result of an "affect" or "archetypal filter" belonging to and operated through an individual and their personal experiences: This filter engages with continuous, external reality, and "converts experiences onto the archetypal level" (1989, pp.25–26).

Samuels (ibid.) states that:

> ... the archetypal may also be seen as a gradation of affect, something in the heart and eye of the beholder, and not what he or she beholds or experiences ... An analogy would be a filter that is always in place, colouring or otherwise influencing what is seen or experienced. There is a sense in which the filter is the experience, or in which the filter is dead without the experience. The filter is what we term archetypal. The implication of this is that depth lies in the filter. The filter is a kind of disturbance of attention, distortion even. It is a way of introducing imagery to the world and imposing imagery on the world so that the world becomes an experienced world.

The concept of filters "filtering" within and through the unconscious realms of the psyche remains a challenging, if not [still[3]] controversial, concept. Yet, more than twenty years since this idea (Samuels, 1989) came to be discussed, and debated, terms such as "filter" and "filtering" are now invited into the story of post-Jungian thought, and utilised universally as technology vernacular to discuss the ways in which human beings capture, and process the (mainly, photo) images we choose: our filtering the life imagery of ourselves, within the infinite threads of technological tapestries ... Presently, the possibility of technologically filtering the Whole world in which we live, is imbued, and accepted, in the experiential processes of visually capturing and disseminating the imagery of our lifetimes. In the technological encounter, rapid exposure to image is the remit of the Internet plane. The twenty-first century is a world wherein the authenticity of image is difficult to define, and is, more often than not, indeterminately filtered through individual (and, collective) means as a way to control what is understood to be Known. There is the thought that Samuels' (1989) approach to archetypal theory may find resonance within the world of technology, wherein the concept of hyper-saturation of imagery exists. The hyper-saturation of imagery in the psychic world brings with it new paradigms for psychic structures and their functioning. It is possible that the growing (and future) generations may demonstrate a new paradigm through evolution of the filtering of life images. Image hyper-saturation has the potential to create a new psychic state: in this paradigm one may not – or no longer – be able to discern or distinguish between true "connection" to image without the evolution of the psyche to facilitate a filtering of the connection between the unconscious and conscious imaginal world. We continue in this digital realm, to connect images of ourselves to images of others to understand who we are as human beings (Swan, 2019, pp.18–19).

In visual art, Samuel's (1989) descriptive language holds a connotation that is compatible with the translation of the personal stages of creating art, from its origins in the unconscious, through the conscious aspects of the image-making process. The "lens" is simultaneously Chagall's viewfinder and viewpoint in the psychic process of "being found" by imagery, capturing the findings, and reproducing a work of art. In Chagall's "Later Life" period (1952–1985), this psychic process predominates his personal experience of contact with archetypes and archetypal life. This observation connects with Stein's (2005, p.10) thinking that, in the last third of lifespan development an individual may undergo a second transformative period wherein the process of an individual becoming is characterised through the elevated presence of interior religion and religious expression (Swan, 2019, p.19).

To further examine Stein's (2005) theory, the historical and personal details of Chagall's biography were compared with the dates of the initial visual emergences and subsequent repetitions of particular images as they formed into a group or theme. A correlation found between the patterns of emergence and repetition, and the convergence of internal and external changes in the artist's biography was consistent across lifespan development. Central to this corollary relationship was the concept of transformation: during critical periods in Chagall's biography, the imagery in the work reflected a greater percentage of transformation metaphorically and literally, through the visual content of shape and form. These "transforming" works contained both secular and sacred content, and included images and themes of:

(1) natal faith and The Bible
(2) zoomorphic animals, bi-morphic creatures, and anthropomorphic beings
(3) hermaphroditic figures, bridal couples, and conjoined lovers
(4) the image of Christ, and crucifixions.

(Swan, 2019, p.19)

For Chagall, a lifetime of image-making and creative writing produced both visual and narrative paths through which it is possible to follow the transformative nature of the individuation process, for both the Artist as creator, and the collective passage of change in a twentieth century of lifetime ... The post-Jungian concept of "archetypal" (Samuels, 1989) has its essence in the personal processing of connecting through emergences, which are understood through the life filter of the personal unconscious. The emergence is treated as archetypal through the expression of content, though is not considered – as it is particularly in Jung's early career (Samuels et al, 1986) – independent of the individual's personal unconscious.

Whilst Jung's own theory of archetypes changed during his lifework, his position remained and is reflected in the classical thought that, true "archetypes" are linked always to the collective unconscious of mankind and thus spontaneous in their emergence (*CW* 7: par. 185; *CW* 11: pars. 82, 893). The numinous quality of archetypal emergence finds connection to the presence of religion, whether through ancient or contemporary traditions. Thus, the identification of "sacred" or "secularised"[4] archetypal imagery, for example, is helpful when considering images which are consistent with Chagall's concepts of religious attitude, ritual and practice (e.g., Christ, Crucifixion, Holy Family, Marriage Rites), or are related to "secularised" images within the artist's personal biography (e.g., Home, Family) (Swan, 2019, pp.20–21).

The analytic process examines the content and presentation of such archetypal images or experiences in an effort to reintegrate the understanding of their symbolism within the conscious layer of the psyche. The personal unconscious psyche works through its contact and unification with imagery of the collective unconscious, and through this, the individuation process is reflected as a transformative and whole experience. Stein (2005, p.56) considers the transformative image as:

> An image that has the capacity to redirect the flow of psychic energy and to change its specific form of manifestation. The way in which this image relates to the instinctual needs of the individual is critical, for this will determine whether the constellation supports balance and wholeness or represses aspects of human nature.

Identifying the transformative images and defining their functioning as visual or experiential markers – across both biographical and historical timelines – is most critical for an understanding of Chagall's body of religious art (Swan, 2019, p.21).

Jungian aesthetics emphasises the separation of Chagall's images from his role as an accomplished image-maker. The image-making process is the catalytic element in the emergence of archetypal imagery, with the artist functioning as a conduit for the collected unconscious and its contents. Philipson (1994) considers that, "Jung conceives the primary concern of an analytical psychological interpretation of art to be with the nature of the psychic significance of works of art" (p.80), and that the interpretation, "is achieved not by beginning with the process of the artists' act of creation [psychoanalytic aesthetic[5]], but by an inquiry into the different 'roles', 'ends', and 'effects' of works of art" (Philipson, 1994; Swan, 2019, p.22).

Jung's observations differed when describing the role of connection within an individual's interaction with archetypal images. There is a distinction made between the capacity for archetypal images to appear in physical form through the process of image-making, and the exploration of dream and active imagery through an analysis. The Jungian differentiation between process and product as two separate psychically driven phenomena in the birth of a work of art is accepted here, with the thought that an artist's creative instinct – the combining of technical craft and their external and internal realities with the personal unconscious – builds an imprint upon the archetypal imagery during the physical process of image-making. The artist as a conduit is creating a physical portal for the visual expression of a psychic concept. The phenomenon of exchange is dependent upon the artist's active and passive engagement and re-engagement with the contents of his personal unconscious psyche, and the collective unconscious. Jung uses the term, "transcendent function" to describe this exchange of contents between these two psychic realms (*CW* 7: par. 159). The archetypal images which actively come into focus on a canvas have been experienced through the personal unconscious of the artist, and acknowledgement and discussion of the psychic presence or imprint of the artist is significant to an understanding of the ways in which a particular work of art came into being.

Earlier, I explained that in Chagall's oeuvre, a correlation exists between the patterns of emergence and repetition of four distinct themes. The convergence of internal and external changes in the Artist's biography and historical lifespan of the twentieth century was proximate to the increase in the emergence cycle. In the context of the individuation process, the expression of such [visual emergences[6]] surrounding critical points in development is suggestive of transformative imagery. That Chagall's transformative images often literally reflect and repeat the "transforming" process (i.e., bi-morphic creatures, hermaphroditic figures, the Crucifixion) reinforces and strengthens the connotations of their expression (Swan, 2019, p.23).

Of these archetypal images, the Crucifixion is identified foremost with the dogmatic traditions of the Christian faith, and thus translates to an active "sacred" archetypal image. For Jung, Christ is a universally symbolic image and corresponds to his conceptualisation of the archetype, *the Self* (*CW* 11: pars. 226–242; *CW* 9ii: pars. 68–126). That this image of self could be recognised across a timeline of Chagall's lifespan – and, that its emergence correlates with convergences of interior and exterior transformative events – is most significant in providing an understanding of Chagall's creative lifespan, the processing of image, and the Artist's experience of religion in a century of quickening decline in faith (Tacey, 2004; *CW* 9ii; *CW* 11).

This [study[7]] is the first exploration of Chagall's crucifixion-themed body of work presented through a Jungian perspective. The topic has been addressed within the art history community previously, and it is not without scope or strength, as contemporary art historians have directed their arguments concerning Chagall's use of Christ through a variety of conditions.[8] There is an element of inclusivity particular to the collective and symbolic nature of archetypal expression ... The argument here, and throughout this [study[9]], is that as an artist, Chagall's process of individuation development is able to be explored visually through the emergence of transformative imagery, including the [appearance of, and[10]] use of Christ and the Crucifixion. That the first emergence of the crucifixion theme occurred in 1909 [see, PLATE 1], in a sketchbook self-portrait illustration – and in Chagall's poetry – whilst still an arts student in Russia, and, that a consistent re-imagining of this form continued for a further eight decades, is evidence of an archetypal expression and evocative of the transformative process. Such a symbolic expression is universal: it holds the capacity to transcend associations with the specificity of creed. Therefore, the appearance of the crucifixion in Chagall includes, as well as transcends, the microcosm of the artist's – and Christ's – natal faith. Chagall has stated, "Christ is a poet ... one of the greatest – through his incredible, irrational manner of taking pain onto himself" (Kamensky, 1989, p.131; Meyer, 1964, p.16). In his writing and speeches, Chagall has emphasised the importance he places upon Christ's ideas about life and mankind as, in his words: "the man possessing the most profound comprehension of life, a central figure for the 'mystery of life'" (Meyer, 1964, p.16; Swan, 2019, p.126).

Between 1909 and 1985, Chagall completed more than fifty works of art that each depict the image of Christ and the Crucifixion. A "lifetime of art" for some creative individuals, was, for Chagall, a devotion to exploring one image. The crucifixion theme appears in different styles, colours, and media, and corresponds in its visual changes to particular and critical points in the Artist's biography and career. The symbolic emergence is consistent with what Jung has described as an archetype of the Self: the appearance at different times and in different ways is as a "portrait"[11] of a symbol,[12] and as such, it corresponds to the concept of a self-referential image or imago. The image of Christ was perhaps the most important symbol for Chagall. It expressed in one single form the symbolic connection to life, which the Artist experienced through religion (Swan, 2019, pp.130–140).

Notes

1 A visit to any museum or picture gallery gift shop reveals the printed postcard-sized reproductions from a given collection, that may be purchased, taken away, and kept by the observer.
2 Excerpt from Chagall's 1973 speech at the official opening of his Museum of the Biblical Message, later, Musee National Marc Chagall, in Nice, France.
3 The brackets are present – inserted by the author – as they serve to clarify the already (Chiron) copyrighted text, for readers who have no familiarity with either the Chiron book or the subject/topic.
4 The "secularising" of an image is a product of cultural change in religious perspective.
5 Spitz (1985) remarks that, "Almost from its origins, psychoanalytic theory has been applied outside the clinical sphere to works of art and used as a mode of

understanding in art in at least three areas of major concern to aestheticians: namely, (1) the nature of the creative work and the experience of the artist, (2) the interpretation of the work of art, and (3) the nature of the aesthetic encounter with the work of art" (p.ix).
6 The brackets are present – inserted by the author – as they serve to clarify the already (Chiron) copyrighted text, for readers who have no familiarity with either the Chiron book or the subject/topic.
7 The brackets are present – inserted by the author – as they serve to clarify the already (Chiron) copyrighted text, for readers who have no familiarity with either the Chiron book or the subject/topic.
8 These include an emphasis upon: Chagall's self-identification with this symbol through Christ's historic association as prophet of Judaic heritage; Chagall's particular use of this "Christianised" symbol as a means to reflect upon and commentate about his own life, as a "Jewish man"; and, the specific expression of Jewish "persecution" – within Chagall's lifetime – surrounding the anti-Semitic campaigns of the eighteenth- and nineteenth-century European pogroms and the atrocities of the twentieth-century European Holocaust.
9 The brackets are present – inserted by the author – as they serve to clarify the already (Chiron) copyrighted text, for readers who have no familiarity with either the Chiron book or the subject/topic.
10 The brackets are present – inserted by the author – as they serve to clarify the already (Chiron) copyrighted text, for readers who have no familiarity with either the Chiron book or the subject/topic.
11 Both PLATE 2, and PLATE 3 are self-portraits, in title.
12 PLATE 4 is particular to the symbolic interpretation through the alchemical (here, Viriditas) Christ: One of the curious life facts the author provides in his autobiography was that he was a stillborn baby. Chagall describes his birth: "The town was in flames ... The bed and mattress, with me at Mama's feet was carried off to safety ... But first of all, I was born dead. I did not want to be alive. Imagine a pale bladder that doesn't want to live in the world ... They pricked it with pins, threw it into a bucket of water, and finally it gave out a squeal. But what's important is that I was born dead. I certainly don't want the psychologists to draw any unfavourable interpretation for me Please!" (Harshav, 2004, p.86).

References

Harshav, B. (Ed.) (2003). *Marc Chagall on Art and Culture*. Stanford, CA: Stanford University Press.
Harshav, B. (2004). *Marc Chagall and His Times* (B. Harshav and B. Harshav, Trans.). Stanford, CA: Stanford University Press.
Jung, C. (1959). Christ, A Symbol of the Self. In *Aion: Researches into the Phenomenology of the Self* (*Collected Works*, Vol. 9ii, pp.68–126) (R. Hull, Trans.). Princeton, NJ: Princeton University Press.
Jung, C. (1966). *Collected Works* (Vol. 15: *The Spirit in Man, Art, and Literature*) (R. Hull, Trans.). Princeton, NJ: Princeton University Press.
Jung, C. (1966). *Collected Works* (2nd ed., Vol. 7: *Two Essays on Analytical Psychology*) (R. Hull, Trans.). Princeton, NJ: Princeton University Press.

Jung, C. (1969). *Collected Works* (2nd ed., Vol. 11: *Psychology and Religion: West and East*). (R. Hull, Trans.). Princeton, NJ: Princeton University Press.

Kamensky, A. (1989). *Chagall: The Russian Years 1907–1922*. London: Thames & Hudson, Ltd.

Meyer, F. (1964). *Marc Chagall*. London: Thames & Hudson.

Philipson, M. (1994). *Outline of a Jungian Aesthetics*. Boston, MA: Sigo Press.

Samuels, A. (1989). *The Plural Psyche*. London: Routledge.

Samuels, A., Shorter, B., and Plaut, F. (1986). *A Critical Dictionary of Jungian Analysis*. London: Routledge & Kegan Paul, Ltd.

Spitz, E.H. (1985). *Art and Psyche*. New Haven, CT: Yale University Press.

Stein, M. (2005). *Transformation: The Emergence of the Self*. College Station, TX: Texas A & M University Press.

Swan, J.A. (2019). *On the Spirit and the Self: The Religious Art of Marc Chagall*. Asheville, NC: Chiron Publications.

Tacey, D. (2004). *The Spirituality Revolution: The Emergence of Contemporary Spirituality*. Hove, England: Routledge.

On the spirit and the self 155

1 Der Sturm (Cover), 10 February, 1920
(from a 1909 school sketchbook drawing) Vol. 10, No. 11, Editor: Herwarth Walden c Marquand Art Library Archive Princeton University, Princeton NJ

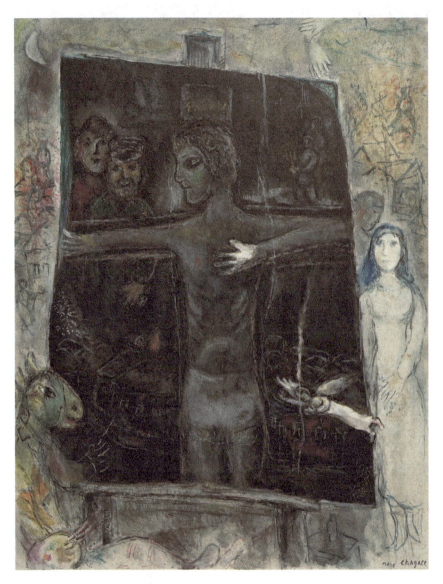

2 In Front of the Picture, 1968–1971
Oil on Canvas, 116 x 89 cm Foundation Marguerite et Aime Maeght, St. Paul, France

3 Self Portrait with a Clock, 1947
Oil on canvas, 86 x 70.5 cm Private Collection

158 From the PhD theses

4 L'Obsession, 1943
Oil on canvas, 76 x 107.5cm
Musee de Beaux-Arts, Paris

Chapter 11

Marriage as a psychological relationship in China

Huan Wang

In 2016, the Chinese government replaced the one-child policy with a new two-children policy, and stated that in the near future, policies that set limits on reproduction would be abolished entirely. A year later, the Chinese government began to place an emphasis on mental health, abolished the old examination to become a psychotherapist, which was overseen by the Ministry of Labour and Social Security, and instead placed the Ministry of Health in charge of the training and qualification programme for psychotherapists. In terms of these two changes, the first has massive repercussions for society at large, giving young parents more choice in relation to their family planning, while the second offers more guarantees to people seeking psychotherapy due to the higher requirements of the training and qualification programme.

These two changes could be viewed as indicating progress in China. Nonetheless, the new policy has not been welcomed by young Chinese women as anticipated, and the birth ratio of girls and boys amongst second-born children is even more skewed in favour of males than amongst first-born children. According to the Sixth National Population Census of the People's Republic of China (2010) in Anhui province, amongst first-born children, the ratio of female to male babies is 100:108.78 in urban areas, while the same ratio amongst second-born children is 100:155.37 in urban areas, rising to 100:171.38 in rural areas. In 2016, the official website Xinhua.net reported that, since the implementation of the two-children policy, secret foetus gender testing has been prevalent, despite its illegality. Amongst ordinary Chinese families, the preferable family structure comprises one boy and one girl; however, the birth ratio demonstrates that, amongst second-born children, sex-selective abortion mainly targets girls. It is rare for male foetuses to be aborted based solely on gender, due to the traditional son-preference which has had deep historical roots. Hence, it may be imagined that in future generations, it will become even more difficult for men of marriageable age to find spouses, and marriage issues will increase as a result.

Regarding the new standard for training and qualification in psychotherapy, this has also been met with ambivalence. On the one hand, the increased government attention on this field means increased financial investment and more convenient procedures for handling relevant issues, which in turn brings more security to professionals. On the other hand, in the area of depth psychology, there is concern as to whether the typical terms and ideas, such as 'the unconscious', 'free association', 'individuation', etc., can fit within the remit of government ideology, not to mention the fact that healthy relationships, which are based on separation between children and parents, might challenge the traditional value of 'filial piety' which has once more been emphasised by the government. The question thus arises: under government supervision, will therapeutic methods oriented in depth psychology, which are rooted in Western culture, develop in accordance with their original pattern, or will government intervention force them to develop in a way that is more 'suitable'?

Currently in China, there is a feverish clamour for psychotherapy, and psychoanalysis in particular. In the coming years, will Freud's theory, like that of his fellow German, Marx, be applied in a 'Chinese characteristic' way? And if this does occur, will such psychotherapy, which is either explicitly or implicitly interfered with by the government, really help those who seek it out, as it does in the West? What results will accrue for clinical work in China? The answers remain, as yet, unclear.

The Chinese notion of 'integration'

For many years, China has been good at localising ideas from other cultures. During these years, the concept of integration has been welcomed in the realm of psychotherapy. In 2017, I attended the fifth Chinese psychoanalytic congress in Wuhan, a city in the middle of China, for which more than 800 people were registered. The keynote speeches included studies from the Freudian, Kleinian, Jungian, Lacanian, and Winnicottian schools, amongst others. The techniques discussed at the congress covered infant observation, sandplay therapy, dream interpretation, family therapy and hypnosis; in short, almost every topic that was considered relevant to depth psychology. Most of the psychotherapists attending the congress followed a psychodynamic or psychoanalytic orientation, with most purporting to be integrated psychoanalytic therapists, which means that they learn and apply all techniques and theories known to them, regardless of the differences or even conflicts between them. In terms of 'integration', they might also profess to be interested in Buddhism, Taoism or Confucianism, while Chinese medicine was mentioned several times. The attendees were applying these relevant ideas to their psychoanalytic work. The most popular themes at the congress were how to understand these Western-rooted psychological ideas from a Chinese cultural perspective. The idea of 'localisation of psychotherapy' means that all ideas in Western psychotherapy have a counterpart in Chinese culture; therefore, the ideas and technologies of Chinese culture can be applied directly to clinical work without the need for adaptation. In discussing 'localisation' and integration, emphasis was placed on the similarities amongst different theories and how they can work together, while differences amongst them were ignored, conflicts denied, and disagreements set aside.

A similar attitude to integration can be found throughout Chinese daily life, such as the government propaganda of 'establishing a harmonious society' and its suggested panacea for marital difficulties – adapting to and tolerating each other. Here, the definition of 'integration' is similar to that in the Longman Dictionary of Contemporary English:

1. the combining of two or more things so that they work together effectively;
2. when people become part of a group or society and are accepted by them;
3. the process of getting people of different races to live and work together instead of separately.

From this definition, it seems that 'combination' and 'desegregation' are essential for 'integration'. In China, all of these words (integration, combination, and desegregation) represent an inclusive attitude, with its underlying ideology of collectivism, which emphasises similarities, cooperation and the sameness within the group while ignoring individual differences and conflicts between individual members. People seek to have a common voice, and if new issues and conflicts emerge, they try their best to assimilate the new issues into the existing structure and to immediately annihilate potentially explicit conflicts.

To illustrate this further, let us examine the attitudes towards female images in China. When they are in high school, girls are required to wear school uniforms that are usually oversized to cover the shape of their young bodies. Schoolgirls generally have one of several basic haircuts, wear no makeup, and are asked to believe that a natural appearance is the ideal form of beauty.

Later, however, when they grow up, and in particular when they reach marriageable age, women are told that there is another standard of beauty, which is demonstrated in the pictures of Fan Bingbing, a Chinese star: big eyes, wide double-fold eye-lids, small faces, a straight nose and pointed chin – these comprise the standard attributes deemed desirable for young women. However, these features are influenced by the Western aesthetic and are not natural for Chinese people, not to mention that they demonstrate the opposite standard to that promulgated at school. However, both standards of beauty express the same idea: there are certain ideal criteria that everybody should attempt to fit within.

More importantly, young people are expected to marry before age 30, but preferably before age 28 so that they can have a baby before 30; this is believed to be good for the baby. Once married, they should have a baby immediately and thereafter devote themselves to child-rearing. If there is severe disagreement between the couple, they should remain together even if they do not talk for weeks on end. Filing for divorce is usually considered a bad choice, particularly for women. If a woman does divorce, she should find a new husband as soon as possible, although she is automatically devalued in the marriage market and therefore her new husband will often be a man who is 'below' her first husband. Beebe, an experienced analyst who has worked with many Chinese patients, told me of his shock when he realised the obsession with marriage amongst Chinese people and the cultural tendency to force young women into the mother role in a 'suitable' marriage (2017, personal communication). This could be called an archetypal expectation of Chinese marriage – finding someone who is 'suitable' and with whom one remains together permanently and engages in the task of reproduction as soon as possible. This is not solely a woman's task, however; Chinese men are also expected to fit within a given pattern. Schoolboys wear the same oversized school uniforms as their female counterparts. As they mature, they are expected to be 'Beckhams' (a reference to the English footballer and fashion icon, David Beckham) – tall, high earning, with a high social status, and preferably spending time with their wives and children. The female and male images have certainly been affected by Westernisation but marriage between Chinese women and men is nevertheless very traditional, with specific Chinese characteristics. In other words, as has occurred in the therapeutic world, in Chinese daily life, Westernisation might comprise a surface-level cosmetic persona. Chinese people adopt what they have learned from the West in a conscious and superficial way, but the deep-rooted Chinese cultural principles on ethical ideas and behavioural patterns have always dominated in Chinese society, both consciously and unconsciously.

However, as times goes by, with more and deeper interaction with the rest of world, such cosmetic Westernisation has gradually changed. In recent years, the divorce rate has soared amongst the younger generations and an increasing number of young couples are seeking help from psychotherapy. This does not mean that young Chinese people have more marriage issues than their parents. It indicates, rather, that they realise that 'integration' will bring many painful and intolerable issues to their lives. This notion of 'integration' can be observed in the Chinese persona – 'a mask of the collective psyche, a mask that feigns individuality, making others and oneself believe that one is individual, whereas one is simply acting a role through which the collective psyche speaks' (Jung, *CW* 7, para. 245). Individual will is sacrificed to the cultural expectation of marriage and how a marriage should work. The older generations cannot see any other option or way of being 'married', that is, being independent yet still together, role reversals, etc. However, the younger generations do not want to yield to such sacrifice and attempt to find their individual positions within marriage and family. Here, the idea of 'integrity' has emerged in working with them.

The psychological notion of integrity

Integrity is an idea that is less common in China nowadays. From a philosophical perspective, Calhoun (2015) says that, as a personal virtue, integrity means, '[that it is] for the sake of my autonomy, my character, my agency that I stand by my best judgment'; acting with integrity is 'intimately tied to protecting the boundaries of the self', while 'loss of integrity signals loss of some important dimension of selfhood' (pp.145–146). As Calhoun describes, integrity focuses firstly on the self, stands for individual differences and one's best judgements, and values personal autonomy and boundaries. It is the basis of self-awareness, which allows a person to know who he/she is and what he/she wants to do and to be responsible for that, thus distinguishing self from others.

On the other hand, Calhoun continues, 'integrity is ... not just a matter of the individual's proper relation to herself but is a matter of her proper relation to common projects and to the fellows with whom she engages in those common projects' (ibid., pp.148–149). In terms of relationship, integrity emphasises the proper relationship to the self and to others and this is exactly what the many young people who meet with relationship difficulties lack: without proper relationships to themselves or to their partners, they are full of disappointment with their spouses, complain about their lack of autonomy and free choice, and refuse to take responsibility and even blame their parents for their failure, which is sometimes, but not always, warranted.

Calhoun describes integrity as referring to a proper relation to the self and others from an ethical perspective. But what does 'a proper relation' mean? Regarding this question, the psychological notion of integrity can provide more detail. As Beebe (1992) notes, '[i]ntegrity involves our dealings with others, and ambition to win their respect is part of its archetypal constellation; integrity is a self-consistency that is effective interpersonally' (p.10). It demonstrates that there are two dimensions of relation in integrity: one is self-consistency, which is the elementary dimension; the other is relating with others and earning their respect. Self-consistency is highly relevant to the ability to choose freely and take responsibility for that choice, not to be easily affected by others and not to be too flexible, always seeking to fit in within a group. In a word, being loyal to the self and protecting its boundaries are the basis of receiving respect from others. This does not mean, however, that integrity implies a self-defensive attitude towards others. In examining Jane Austen's definition of integrity from a feminine perspective, which suggested that integrity comprised 'amiability', 'constancy' and 'self-knowledge', Beebe concluded that 'integrity is part of the genuine interest in others ... and of continuity of identity' (ibid., p.70). Integrity implies the development of friendly and authentic relationships to others based on self-knowledge and self-consistency.

However, when we turn to the relationship between the individual and the group, integrity demonstrates a certain antagonism to collectivism. Even Calhoun (2015) highlights that integrity has social traits, but the community members to whom she refers comprise a group of 'deliberators who share the goal of determining what is worth doing' (p.151). Such a group is more likely to be selected by the individuals who join the group of their own free will and fit within its subjective criteria, rather than comprising a group determined by objective or external factors, such as blood, gender, geography, or social status. In a word, it is a group composed of independent individuals. Beebe (1992) expresses the clash between integrity and the collective in a more explicit way: 'we have to take the notion of integrity out of the realm of collective counsel, which supports a false self of superego expectation' (p.100). Hence, integrity should remain separate from collective influence; otherwise, individuals will be trapped in a rigid and inauthentic moral model and one's ability to face oneself honestly might be harmed by the wish to fulfil collective expectations.

How individual integrity can be eroded by collective power is revealed in Rangell's study of the Watergate scandal. Rangell (1980) thought that Nixon and his cabinet's attempt to lie to the public and cover up the truth of their decision-making demonstrated that the strength of the masses can force individuals to compromise their integrity. Such strength occurs not only in major events but also in daily life. Rangell suggested that it is essential for individuals to have the courage to maintain their integrity if they are to oppose collective pressure (pp.11–12). Here, the collective opposes integrity. The individual must make a great effort to maintain his/her integrity under collective pressure and this is no mean feat. Calhoun (2015) depicted in vivid detail how 'our own vulnerability to others' leads us to compromise our integrity and noted that 'people without integrity … trade their own views too readily for the views of others who are more authoritative, more in step with public opinion, less demanding of themselves' (pp.142–144). Such scenarios are common in a society which always places the group above individuals, sometimes leading to disasters. In another article, Rangell noted that the consequence of compromising one's integrity is the 'forestages on the path to psychopathy or impulsive disorder' and may 'result in neuroses' (1974, p.7). Under such circumstances, an individual's judgement may be clouded by the decision of the group and his/her behaviour may become psychopathological in a bid to correspond with collective action. This is well illustrated in the insane pictures of mass violence against 'suspected reactionaries' during China's Cultural Revolution and of the huge number of coerced abortions under China's one-child policy. On the other hand, there are many stories of people with integrity who, in extreme circumstances, fought against the atrocity of the masses to tell the truth and protect victims.

In sum, integrity implies an exclusive attitude that stands for autonomy and separation, values consistency over flexibility, encourages people to deal honestly with difficulties, and places individual wills over collective requirements. Only when they have integrity can people be independent individuals, and only then can they establish decent relationships with other independent individuals.

Integrity in marriage

For many years, due to the typical Chinese marital expectation, integration – adjusting oneself to a long-term relationship which secures the happiness of the natal families – has been overemphasised, while integrity – being loyal to individual wills and choices – has been lacking. Hence, marriage lies beyond the unity between the two partners and carries with it many collective decisions of the two extended families and the burden of social expectations, including the following: people should marry at approximately the same age; reproduction and child-rearing are the main tasks of marriage; and the young couple's parents should be highly involved in both their daily affairs and major decisions, particularly for only children. There is a well-known joke that the wedding bed of a couple comprising two partners from one-child families must be large enough for six people. In my clinical work, on one occasion, an only-daughter came to me to seek help for her depression caused by her marriage. When she arrived, six other people squeezed into my office with her: her husband, her parents, her parents-in-law, and her one-year-old son who was held in her mother's arms. After speaking to her, I realised that her marriage difficulties were due very simply to the fact that there were too many people in her marriage, which should have been composed solely of herself and her husband.

Hence, how to relate with the other and other members in the extended family is essential for our clinical work on marriage issues. Regarding the different modes of relationship in marriage, Colman (2014) distinguishes between 'non-relating' and 'anti-relating'. The former refers to the need for 'space and solitude', which is 'an inherent – and essential – aspect of all relationships'; the latter comprises 'the intrusiveness of the other – when others intrude their difference and their own needs and demands into the private space of the self' (p.23). In a typical Chinese marriage and family, the unity and harmony of family members, which need to be demonstrated explicitly, are so important that private space and other possibilities of the relationships are excluded. Hence, the relatedness that occurs in a traditional Chinese family is, in fact, the anti-relating described by Colman, in which individual members are forced 'to be what is wanted to be under the control' of the collective will, while non-relating, or relating to others within certain limits, maintaining one's own autonomy and remaining beyond intrusion and invasion (ibid.), which is highly relevant to integral attitudes, is new to Chinese marriage.

In line with this development of a possible space of non-relating in marriage, two further archetypal patterns could prove useful complementary approaches. Schmidt (1980) suggested that the old parental model, which projects parental images onto the spouse as the basis of marriage, is not suitable on its own for modern relationships. A viable alternative could be the 'sister–brother' pattern, in which the two spouses are equals. In this model, 'the brother and sister archetype would serve as a meeting place for the man and woman', covering 'fighting, testing, challenging and sexuality' between each other (p.18). In China, due to the one-child policy, many young people lack the direct experience of having siblings, but they do have cousins, other children in the neighbourhood, and their peers at school, who have competed with them for praise from adults and their teachers' attention. Of course, the tension in such competition cannot compare with the tension in competition for parents' love, but it is nevertheless an opportunity for boys and girls to build relationships together and recognise each other as equal and real.

Another option in marriage relationships is to adopt the friendship pattern. As Johnson (1983) highlights, 'friendship ... within marriage, between husband and wife' which does not judge 'each other's difficult points and weaknesses and offers help, affirmation and support to each other, is necessary for human love and for a long-term relationship. The friendship pattern without romantic drama and intensity also takes away egocentric and unrealistic fantasy in marriage' (p.197). Friendship may be a more familiar experience for a child from a one-child family and could help couples to rid themselves of the ego-centred role cultivated by their parents. This would allow them to learn how to share, thus facilitating their ability to get along with their spouses.

Compared with the parental model, both the 'brother and sister pattern' and the 'friendship pattern' are established through equal relationships between peers. One does not have to yield to the authority of the other, thus creating space between the two partners and excluding parents from the children's marriage. This has the potential to bring integrity into the marriage. However, each of these patterns has its own flaws, which is why I stated that, while they may be useful as complementary approaches, they cannot serve for marriage alone. In the brother–sister pattern, as Schmidt conceded, the two spouses 'are permanently connected with each other; one does not divorce one's siblings' (1980, p.18). Such a pattern does not allow for the breaking up or failure of the marriage. In the friendship pattern, meanwhile, Johnson (1983) overemphasised the positive aspects of friendship, such as being nice to each other, acceptance of non-perfection, and offers of affirmation and support, while neglecting the necessary tension between couples and ignoring the difficult, negative aspects of marriage, such as disagreements, conflicts and fights.

However, in any real relationship, negative feelings are undeniable and failure is sometimes unavoidable. As Beebe (1992) says,

> failures in relationship also serve integrity ... Real work on integrity ... includes accepting the shadow and taking the impure parts of the

collective human and animal character consciously into oneself ... [This] leads to a more conscious relationship to envy, shame, and anxiety.

(p.124)

In this view, none of the aspects of shadow in our inner world or our relationships with others are ignored or denied. Instead, they are seen and accepted, and even failure in relationship is a viable option. This comprises a very authentic attitude that is open to disagreement. Getting married and remaining in a marriage are no longer of primary importance. Moreover, adapting to and tolerating grievances and complaints cannot fix marital problems and initiating communication without real dialogue cannot serve to connect husbands and wives. With such recognition, our clinical work on marriage would be helpful and practical for couples trapped in marital difficulties. Otherwise, a relationship without integrity can only be constructed on the false-selves of the two spouses and no real intimacy or security can develop between them. Therefore, for couples who meet difficulties in their relationships, a new approach would be to try to integrate their voices less, while demonstrating more integrity. This means, first, listening to one's inner voice, standing by one's best judgement, even if such judgement includes the possibility of breaking up, and taking responsibility for one's own choices. This is the basis for the further negotiation and cooperation, which are necessary even in divorce cases.

Marriages as a relationship beyond gender difference

For negotiation and cooperation, recognising difference is the first step for any relationship. Saban (2016) compared Jungian psychology with psychoanalysis and noted, '[t]he single necessary condition for any healthy relationship is a clear awareness of the fundamental difference between the two partners; fusion, and especially unconscious fusion, is always an obstacle to relatedness' (p.345). Such a proposition can also be applied in marriage. The two partners in a marriage should realise and accept the differences between them. This is the basis of their recognition of the independence and subjectivity of each other and the establishment of their authentic relationship. However, the question arises: are such differences due to their biological body, or in other words, are they relevant to the differences between men and women? Further examination of this is required.

Williams (1989) noted that 'marriage itself is based on the archetypal theme of the union of complementary opposites' (p.257). Based on her understanding, the difference between the feminine and masculine – the opposites – and the complementary relationship between them are the two basic elements of marriage. Schmidt (1980) expressed a similar idea in a more explicit way, saying that 'marriage is the problem between a man and woman' and sets 'a stage where the problem between man and woman may be worked out' (p.17). However, while most marriages in the modern world are comprised of a man and a woman, a real man and real woman do not embody femininity and masculinity respectively, and the notions of masculine and feminine vary in different cultural/social settings. Thus, it is very difficult to define conclusively that the different identities of a man and woman, or the opposite stance of the feminine and masculine, are necessary for modern marriage.

It has been traditional to distinguish between the development of girls and boys in psychoanalysis and between the functions of the feminine and masculine. Benjamin (1995) noted that although the binary gender oppositions 'play a major role in organising our experience, that frame reveals many conflicts and provides a background for many other differences' (p.12). This is to say femininity and masculinity are two different elements that help us understand the complexity of the world in a familiar and simplified way. The terms 'Yin' and 'Yang' also describe this role without the necessity of any gender implication. (In the system of 'Yin' and 'Yang', although 'Yin' is more often related with the feminine and 'Yang' with the masculine, both men and women have 'Yang' and 'Yin' sides within their biological bodies. Hence, these two terms are beyond opposite and binary gender certainty and difference). Benjamin considered that 'the terms of binary opposition men-women is likely to be as constricting as [it is] liberating' for women and suggested 'we may recognise that "Women" is not a unitary identity, and we may continually test the frame of gender' (ibid., p.11). I would add that such a constriction also applies to men and that we also cannot say that 'Men' is a unitary identity. The stereotype and certain category of the terms 'man' and 'woman' deprive all individuals of their potentials. Samuels asserts that 'gender certainty forms the oppressive heart of much neurosis' (1989, p.85). Based on past experience, it has brought to both men and women more constriction than liberation and made both sexes suffer from the narrow expectation of what a man or a woman should be like. Further, gender certainty can be viewed as a defence against gender confusion and the latter 'comes closer to capturing what contemporary people feel about their gender identity' (Samuels, 2001, p.41).

When we enter the realm of relationship, the tendency to distinguish gender roles within a marriage is prominent. Saayman, Faber and Saayman (1988) interviewed 62 parents, and described how marriage is 'ascribed to the intensely patriarchal orientation of Western Culture' (p.269). Thus, they concluded that the 'couple personified the clash between the impersonal feminine and masculine' and that in the failure of this marriage, the husband's 'instrumental and power aspects of Logos' constrained him from expressing any feminine affect to his wife and offspring, frustrated his wife and caused her to seek revenge by removing her affection from him and instead giving it to their child or another lover (ibid., pp.264–267). Based on these arguments, man and woman, husband and wife, feminine affect and masculine logos are in a split and opposite position, and the marital problem has always been due to the lack of the feminine principle – the principle of relatedness, which is quite essentialist.

However, in China, the principle of relatedness is essential in the Chinese family, while the Western feminine virtues of constancy, amiability, humility, etc., are as valuable for Chinese men as they are for Chinese women. In other words, such virtues do not have gender implications in Chinese culture. Further, as Dien says, 'Chinese society shares the same social structure of women mothering and men dominating in terms of social power', but 'Chinese women are psychologically more independent' than Chinese men (1992, p.105). Sun, a historian who studied Chinese immigrants in the US, came to the same conclusion that Chinese women demonstrated more confidence and ego-strength in adapting to the new environment, while their husbands demonstrated a prevalent sense of disorientation and kept asking to return home (2004, pp.341–345). Such characteristics do not fit within the catalogues of the Western feminine, which refers to relatedness, or of the masculine, which refers to separation.

A common modern conflict found amongst young Chinese couples in my interviews and clinical work is that the husband asks his wife to relate more with his parents and to care for other members within the two extended families, while the wife wants to lead a life that is more separate from the parents and to maintain boundaries between their small nuclear family and the larger extended family. Hence, because the notions of feminine and masculine vary amongst cultures and societies, the Western 'feminine principle' based on the binary opposition of man and woman is not a universal solution for marital difficulties.

Moreover, even in the West, Samuels has challenged the overemphasis on the 'feminine principle', stating that, 'celebrating the feminine has raised it to the status of an ego-ideal, leading to a simple and pointless reversal of power positions' (1989, p.100). Hence, the emphasis on the difference between the feminine and masculine and the opposite positions of man and woman are based on the patriarchal ideology – situating man and woman in a rigid gender frame and asking them to behave according to certain patterns, thus devaluing behaviour that lies outside of such expectations.

Schmidt (1980) proposes that to apply 'quantitative differences (e.g. more or less "hard", more or less "soft")' to discuss the differences between feminine and masculine is more appropriate than applying 'contrast qualities (e.g. "hardness" for masculine v. "softness" for feminine)'. She also concedes that 'instinctive [sexual] differences have receded from today's young adult life' even though such differences can be observed in small children (pp.23–25). The differences between men and women have become increasingly vague today and, as noted by Samuels, have reached a position of 'fluidity or flexibility, or even androgyny' (2001, p.41). Hence, in modern times, it is difficult to state that modern marriage, as a relationship comprising two adults, demonstrates and resolves the conflicts between men and women. The difference between the two spouses in a marriage is not due to the difference between men and women as specific gender groups; rather, it is due to the differences between individuals. Moreover, the conflicts that occur between a couple are not due to the fact that one carries the feminine principle while the other carries the masculine; rather, they are due to the fact that each is a distinct and separate human being. Thus, it is natural for them to have conflicts and disagreements. Hence, the core issue for contemporary Chinese marriage is how to be a grown-up and find a balanced position between individual independence and interdependence with surrounding family members.

Further, as Guggenbuhl-Craig (1977/1981) notes, '[m]arriage involves not only a man and a woman who happily love each other and raise offspring together, but rather two people who are trying to individuate, to find their "soul's salvation"' (p.124). This points to another direction: as a psychological relationship between two human beings, marriage not only requires individual independence and integrity but also serves and fosters individuation and integrity.

The way in which love and relationship can give people the courage and determination to fight against totalitarianism is not a new theme in literature or film. In George Orwell's *1984*, after the lead character, Winston, fell in love with Julia, he began to recall what had really occurred in the past, realised the manipulation of the Party and found his own recognition. In their love relationship, both were facilitated to have a sense of awareness, approached the truth and made attempts to fight against Big Brother. Their love stimulated their awakening integrity and fostered their attempts to become individuals and not to be 'infected by the leprosy of collective thinking and ... an inmate of that insalubrious stud-farm called the totalitarian State' (Jung, *CW* 14, para.194). However, when their integrity was damaged by torture, their love disappeared, and they became totally subordinated to Big Brother and lost their sense of self.

The Chinese film, *Hibiscus Town*, which is based on historical reality, shares a similar theme but with a more positive ending. The two lead characters, Hu Yuyin and Qin Shutian, were unfairly accused of being counter-revolutionaries and enemies of the people during the Cultural Revolution. In a difficult and persecutory situation, moved by the kindness of Shutian, Yuyin fell in love with him and they made an attempt to get married despite the government's rejection of their marriage application. In this uncertain and difficult situation, they insisted on marrying by their own means and had a simple ceremony even though the people around them claimed that they did not deserve it. This determination to reveal their relationship rather than having a secret affair that would avoid trouble demonstrates their integrity, and also serves as a form of protest against the collective insanity. With such integrity and determination, both held onto hope and had the resilience to get through the most difficult period when they were forced to separate and were finally reunited.

While *1984* is a dystopian novel that portrays a pessimistic view of human nature, *Hibiscus Town* attempts to reflect on and heal the psychological trauma of recent Chinese history. Both share the mutual influence of attempts at integrity and love relationships. Marriage, which should be the most officially recognised love relationship and, beyond that, a private matter, inevitably involves many complicated interactions between the two spouses, between the members of their natal families, between each spouse and his/her family-in-law, and even between the individual wills and collective expectations and requirements. Hence, marriage affords us the best opportunity for maturity but also has great potential to demonstrate the deficiencies and limitations of our characters. As Beebe (1999) notes, in analytical relationships, integrity embraces the limitations of the patient's character and contains its deficiencies 'in the midst of ambitions for [the patient's] psychological growth' (p.624). Marriage, as a psychological relationship, which also follows the model of 'container and the contained', albeit in a more flexible way (Jung, *CW* 17), could do the same.

A very Chinese dilemma?

In China, a very typical modern dilemma is how to achieve a balance between integration and integrity. Although the respective meanings of 'integration' and 'integrity' differ, and delving into these differences lies beyond the scope of this chapter, their linguistic resources are similar and they share a common epistemological root. This commonality serves the discussion of the ethical notion of each, which is provided in the following section.

As noted, there has been a long tradition of focusing on integration – the ideology of inclusive collectivism – and this has brought benefits to Chinese people. In the clinical world, therapists in contemporary China have many opportunities to learn techniques from different schools. Unlike their Western colleagues, few set limits on their study from the outset; new therapists find that they can learn techniques from different orientations at the same time, and even if they later identify themselves with one or more schools, they still have opportunities to dialogue with other schools and rarely develop hostile attitudes towards a certain school. These open attitudes by candidates during their training programmes bring a lively energy, and the tendency to integrate every school fosters their curiosity. They may lack the spirit of criticism, but they also lack prejudice and bias, and do not reject from the outset the understanding or accepting of different perspectives within psychotherapy. This open attitude nurtures their future potential.

To return to the issue of marriage and family, it must also be noted that the close bonds within natal families are not unilaterally negative. The strong support that parents provide to young couples may constrain the internalised space within the family but gives young people more space in their lives outside of the family. In China, it is quite usual for parents to help the young couple with payments for their apartment and car, or at least to help them with the down payment. It is also the norm for parents to take care of grandchildren, particularly of only children. With such support, young couples have less financial stress and less burden on rearing children, and this gives them more security as new parents. They also have more opportunities for career development, and more time for their social lives. Most young couples do not have to give up their careers because of the birth of a new baby; if they wish, they can rely on their parents to take care of the baby during the daytime, not to mention cooking, doing laundry, cleaning, tidying the apartment, and other housework. Typical Chinese parents will do whatever they can to help their children and are not merely 'guests' in their children's homes. This brings particular benefits for their children, in making life physically easier for them. In China, a single woman is under a great deal of pressure, but a pregnant woman and the mother of a son will be carefully looked after and may accrue privilege in her husband's home where she can ask for whatever she wants. Chinese women are rarely moved to fight for their individual rights, as women in the West do, perhaps due to the fact that when she gives birth to a son, a woman gets the opportunity to take charge of her husband's family, has a stable sense of security on the property and gains respect. Hence, in a certain way, integration brings security and means that the Chinese family constellation is organised in a mutually supportive pattern.

On the other hand, there is a danger of such integrity being misused. As Beebe warned, there is persona integrity, whereby 'the mask for the ambitions to respectability which severs the status quo looks more attractive' and 'such integrity has grown rigid and inauthentic in the course of advancing psychological and moral development' (1992, pp.101–102). Here, integrity, and more precisely 'integrity in depth', does not comprise a rigid demand for morality, nor an adaptive attitude that serves for relationship. Both of these can be seen together in a collective persona of so-called 'integrity' that applies a single moral criterion to everyone and criticises those who are not adaptive to such a model. For example, while independence is essential for integrity, persona integrity overemphasises the financial independence and importance of careers for women, to the extent that women who prefer to be housewives or full-time mothers are looked down upon; or, the simple criterion that a man's mental health necessarily involves him maintaining a distance from his parents and that his affection for his mother renders him an abnormal 'mummy's boy'. Asking people to be independent from their families in this way comprises pseudo-independence from a concrete small group, while remaining dependent on an abstract bigger group, or submitting to a consciously or unconsciously held collective belief. During the Cultural Revolution, the Red Guards jumped at the opportunity to challenge, or even beat up, authority figures, such as their parents, teachers, or even some government leaders; in so doing, however, they were being manipulated by higher authorities. These rebellious behaviours of adolescents allowed them to be valued within their gangs. Here, another dilemma arises: how can we know that for a woman the struggle to gain more financial independence in her marriage is her own choice rather than being forced to do so by the belief that 'all housewives are losers'? For a man, meanwhile, is his love for his mother and attempts to take care of her an aspect of the goodness of his human nature or is he simply possessed by his mother-complex, or a cultural obligation?

The concept of 'moral imagination' can help us to answer these questions. Moral imagination covers the attitudes of forgiveness without blame and embraces conflict and pluralism. It comprises a creative moral space, in which dialogues occur without the 'certainty [of] who speak for what' (Samuels, 1989, pp.201–207). It also allows for illogical combination. As Samuels describes, '[w]hat we admire and value in ourselves and others need not follow any logical format: warmth and openness together with careful attention to detail, driving ambition with pervasive self-doubt' (ibid., p.204). Simplification places both integration and integrity in a dangerous position, but with moral imagination, which places our moral choices in an imaginative space, an open and ambivalent space, wherein dialogues between different voices are facilitated. In such spaces, integration does not simply combine everything and integrity is not a single criterion; hence, people can find their individual positions within a collective context. The following vivid picture of the ideal Chinese relationship between young couples and their parents illustrates this space: the best distance between the home of a young couple and the home of their parents is that if freshly boiled soup were delivered from one home to the other by walking, the soup would still be warm upon arrival: not too hot, not too cold, just warm. This beautiful metaphor demonstrates that warmth lies on a spectrum between hotness and coldness. It is a complex and ambivalent temperature that is difficult to define, in which tension, challenges, arguments, debates, conflicts, and even clashes first occur to increase the heat, and then gradually calm down so that dialogue can continue in a sustainable way.

Moral imagination has to, and will, be achieved gradually in China in the coming years. In previous years, the traditional belief in integration has been greatly challenged. The first generation of one-child families, as 'the first world youth in the third world' (Fong, 2004, p.154), demonstrates more obvious self-awareness than previous generations and subsequent generations have even more self-awareness because they live in better circumstances. With the development of the economy and the employment of the Internet, information is delivered in various channels and people can see different aspects of the world and listen to a variety of voices. The younger generations have opportunities to communicate with people from other countries and regions around the world and have a broader vision with which to facilitate the creative space described above.

When my mother was young, she watched a film about twin sisters who lived separately in North Korea and South Korea. The sister in North

Korea, as an ordinary person who was the owner of the state (referring to the communist idea), led a happy life; meanwhile, her sister in South Korea was a slave to the rich and lived a miserable life. Together with her peers, my mother totally believed this story because she had no other channels of information and had to believe everything she was told. Today, however, no young person would believe such a story and Seoul is one of the most popular cities for young Chinese people to go shopping. They have more direct experience of what is happening both inside and outside of China. Hence, the simple combination of exterminating disagreement, repressing conflicts and creating harmony on the surface is becoming increasingly difficult to sustain.

The same phenomenon is apparent in the clinical world. Most of the first generation of therapists completed their training in China. They learned from Western teachers who visited China and whose interests lay in China. By remaining in a Chinese setting and having lecturers whose passion was for Chinese culture, their unavoidable tendency was to focus on the similarities and to assimilate what they had learned with the world they saw around them. Although some trained in Western countries, upon returning they would practise in accordance with their preferences in an adaptive way, particularly if they received funding from the government. However, young therapists today have many more opportunities to study and train abroad with private funds and with local lecturers and trainers who may not have a particular passion for China. This increases their awareness around the differences between each school and rids them of the inclination towards 'localisation', because they are in a location outside of China, both physically and psychologically.

Under such circumstances, when young generations speak of 'integration', they have more potential to discover a pattern with which to integrate what they have learned with 'integrity', creating a space to balance separation and combination with an attitude of first admitting the difference. This will lead to the individuation process – 'open conflict and open collaboration at once' (Jung, *CW* 9, para. 522–523).

The most popular history book in contemporary China, *Stories about the Ming Dynasty*, which was first published on the Internet in 2006 and completed in 2009, was written by an author who was born in 1979. It has now sold more than 5 million copies and is the best-selling history book since Chinese open reform. As such, it has had a phenomenal influence on Chinese readers. Instead of relating the termination of the Ming Dynasty, the stories of the Emperor and national heroes, the young author concludes the book with the story of a traveller, Xu Xiake. In this story, Xu does not consider it important to be filial to his parents, to get married, to have offspring, to be rich and famous, or to be recognised by the government – all of those things that are considered valuable in Chinese culture. Instead, Xu spent most of his time travelling around China taking notes because that was where his passion lay and thus he preferred to devote his life to this. This was his personal choice. The author says that after he had finished writing stories about major political events, about emperors, ministers and heroes, he finished his book by telling people: the most important thing for a human being is to spend your life in your favourite way. In Chinese culture, this is a rebellious statement and calls upon the young Chinese psyche. Individuation often entails a battle with one's culture. For young Chinese people who attempt to find their individual position within a context dominated for thousands of years by collectivism, and trapped by the dilemma between integration and integrity, balance is sometimes difficult to achieve. That being the case, choosing integrity over integration is another solution.

> ... individuation (becoming who you authentically are) ... is very different from mental health or social adaption and may, for some individuals, involve a non- or even anti-relational passage through life.
> (Samuels, 2017)

Is this only a Chinese dilemma?

While writing this chapter and researching the issue of coerced abortion amongst Chinese women, I noticed that women in other countries, such as the US, Ireland and Brazil, were also fighting for the right of abortion. Basic individual rights, even the right to own and take charge of one's own body, has not been fully achieved around the world. Collective forces are difficult to bend.

In the past years, the world outside of China has also undergone many changes: the Trump presidency, Brexit and the emergence of the new Tsar in Russia. Suddenly, nationalism seems to have become prevalent in every corner of the world. Upon studying the madness that has occurred throughout history, Zoja (2014/2017) came to the following conclusion: 'the psychological space occupied by collective paranoia is the same one in which nationalism resides' (p.345). Nowadays, the fever pitch of nationalism has spread dramatically: the overemphasis on the term 'we' and the suspicion and hostility towards the 'not we' form the basis of a collective narcissism that threatens to poison individual independence and harm integrity. There is great danger that extreme forms of collectivism are being fostered – a totalitarianism in which there will be no space for integrity.

That being the case, a major challenge for China and for the whole world, in the coming years,

> will be that of maintaining, amid the indifference of the masses and anaesthesia of consumerism, a capacity for indignation. This should have two directions: an impulse towards rectifying wrongs committed by others, but at the same time shame for our own transgressions. Ultimately,

the mobilization of credible moral feelings arises in the solitude of the individual conscience; and it mistrusts crusades aimed at the masses, propagated by media multipliers.

(Zoja, 2014/2017, p.327)

References

Beebe, J. (1992). *Integrity in Depth*. College Station: Texas A & M University Press.
Beebe, J. (1999). 'Integrity in the Analytic Relationship', *Psychoanalytical Review*, 86: 607–625.
Benjamin, J. (1995). *Like Subjects, Love Objects: Essays on Recognition and Sexual Difference*. New Haven, CT and London: Yale University Press.
Calhoun, C. (2015). *Moral Aims: Essays on the Importance of Getting It Right and Practicing Morality with Others*. New York: Oxford University Press.
Colman, W. (2014). 'The Intolerable Other: The Difficulty of Becoming a Couple', *Couple and Family Psychoanalysis*, 4(1): 22–41.
Dien, D. (1992). 'Gender and Individuation: China and the West', *Psychoanalytic Review*, 79(1): 105–119.
Fong, L.V. (2004). *Only Hope: Coming of Age under China's One-Child Policy*. Stanford, CA: Stanford University.
Guggenbuhl-Craig, A. (1977/1981). *Marriage: Dead or Alive*. Thompson, CT and Dallas, TX: Spring Publications.
Johnson, R. (1983). *We: Understanding the Psychology of Romantic Love*. New York: HarperOne.
Jung, C.G., references are to the *Collected Works* (*CW*) and by volume and paragraph number, edited by H. Read, M. Fordham, G. Adler and W. McGuire, translated in the main by R. Hull. London: Routledge & Kegan Paul; Princeton, NJ: Princeton University Press.
Rangell, L. (1974). 'A Psychoanalytic Perspective Leading Currently to the Syndrome of the Compromise of Integrity', *International Journal of Psychoanalysis*, 55: 3–12.
Rangell, L. (1980). *The Mind of Watergate: An Exploration of the Compromise of Integrity*. New York: W.W. Norton and Company.
Saayman, G.S., Faber, P.A. and Saayman, R.V. (1988). 'Archetypal Factors', *Journal of Analytical Psychology*, 33(3): 253–276.
Saban, M. (2016). 'Jung, Winnicott and the Divided Psyche', *Journal of Analytical Psychology*, 61(3): 329–349.
Samuels, A. (1989). *The Plural Psyche: Personality, Morality, and the Father*. London and New York: Routledge.
Samuels, A. (2001). *Politics on the Couch: Citizenship and the Internal Life*. London: Karnac.
Samuels, A. (2017). 'The Analyst is as much "in the Analysis" as the Patient (1929)', *Jung as a Pioneer of Relational Psychoanalysis*. San Francisco, CA: The Relational Institute.
Schmidt, L. (1980). 'The Brother–Sister Relationship in Marriage', *Journal of Analytical Psychology*, 25(1): 17–35.

Sun, L. (2004). *The Theodolite of a History*. Guilin: Guangxi Normal University Press.
Williams, M. (1989). 'The Archetypes in Marriage', in A. Samuels (ed.), *Psychopathology: Contemporary Jungian Perspectives* (pp.245–259). London: Karnac.
Zoja, L. (2014/2017). *Paranoia: The Madness that Makes History*. London and New York: Routledge.

Part II

Andrew in 1000 words

Part II

Andrew in 1000 words

Chapter 12

Mary Addenbrooke

I was one of Andrew's first PhD students. I had been pleased to learn that, after a considerable period of to-ing and fro-ing in the arguments for and against linking a bequest to the Society of Analytical Psychology to the foundation of a professorial chair, this had actually come to fruition.

Apart from being an analyst, I had worked in medical research with colleagues in the NHS, but our published papers had been mostly quantitative, in spite of the fact that the material we had gathered over the years into the long-term outcome of treatment of heroin injectors was also rich in the personal narratives of the patients. Andrew's appointment at the university jogged me into wondering if I could pursue a qualitative approach, bearing in mind that I was an analytical psychologist, and that Jung had had a relevant, though oblique, part to play in the initiation of Alcoholics Anonymous in the 1930s. I phoned Andrew. Things moved very swiftly – meeting, discussing, forming the proposal and registering at the university. I found the speed and enthusiasm with which he took up my idea encouraging. It set me off to a really good start.

I then spent a day at the Centre accompanying Andrew on his seminars, and became aware of how much I would have to plunge again into the pond of psychoanalytic and Jungian theory. All that detail, all those dates and references! A useful awakening.

As I was a part-time student, I spent over six years working with Andrew as a supervisor, and it is fascinating to recall how this unfolded. My main recollection is that Andrew consistently respected my feelings for my material throughout that time, and treated me as a colleague. Each time we met, I left with the sense that we were looking at the challenges together, and this enabled the welter of material that I had to fall gradually into various patterns. Rather than being a set of intricate stories, themes began to emerge and these led the research. Instead of finding the relevant theory a drag, it became one of the by-roads of the work, which began to grab me in a way I hadn't anticipated. I believe this was a result of Andrew's generosity in trusting that I could actually think, when I probably often gave him the impression that I couldn't!

Of course as the months went by, I became a willing victim of what Robert Romanyshyn has more recently described as transference on to the research. I felt as if I owned it, but actually, *it* owned *me*. It became incredibly important to me, alongside seeing patients every day and still working with addicted people in the hospital. Andrew and I never discussed this, but it underpinned the development of the thesis and was, I believe, implicit in the course of supervision. Being trusted does great things for building confidence.

By the end of my time as a student, I found I had managed to cobble together a picture for myself of both common and divergent factors in the various stages of addiction and recovery, and also to convey that picture in writing in terms of Jung's idea of *spiritus contra spiritum*.

Andrew was always flexible about timing, which I appreciated, but near the end, I suddenly got cold feet and, feeling overwhelmed, phoned him, saying I couldn't possibly meet the deadline for submitting the thesis. He advised me to postpone for a few months. In retrospect I wish he had just told me to get on with it and stop being a wimp, but I did learn from that that it was up to me if I wanted to behave like a wimp.

I have lovely photos of the sunny day I was awarded the doctorate at the university, amidst a field of daffodils, although the people giving out the hired gowns were convinced that it was my daughter who was the prospective graduate (which she already was). The Addenbrookes all had a great time that day, and I felt amazing.

What has happened since? I think Andrew's perspective on how people best thrive in the supervisory duo was the gift that enabled me to publish the thesis, having played around with it a bit, to make it accessible, particularly, I hope, to people who are afraid they are becoming out of control of their drinking or drug use, and the other people in their families. Now I realise that forming the thesis was a jumping-off point in my development. I never got bored during my years as a student, and never felt patronised by a supervisor who knew reams more than I did, and had written many papers and books I had read. I am writing another book now, which emerges from a different aspect of my work on that thesis and people who come to hear me speak publicly about my findings respond with enthusiasm, even when they don't agree with me.

So, thank you, Andrew.

Chapter 13

James Alan Anslow

Andrew Samuels and I are about the same age, but from starkly different social and professional worlds. When I sat down opposite him in his London flat for my first doctorial supervision, I was a nervous sixty-something street-trader's son who had spent most of his working life as a tabloid newspaper journalist, whereas the assertive and cultured university professor guiding my research was an esteemed psychotherapist, leading academic light in depth psychology, who had brushed youthful shoulders with a knighted judge to whom I later referred in my study. We were an unlikely match, which, I am sure, challenged even his proven expertise in the field of human relationships. And yet, with the help of the Trickster, it worked.

I was eager, even desperate, for Andrew to supervise my PhD, which sought to divine the archetypal forces that drive the tabloid phenomenon with which I was so familiar. Inspired by his published work, and a brief collaboration with a mutual colleague, Helena Bassil-Morozow, the Trickster had already sneaked into my thoughts, in the initially imperceptible way that this potential so often does. It was Andrew's paradigmatic recasting of thought derived from, or relatable to, analytical psychology as 'post-Jungian', and his demonstrations that its insights – partnered with those drawn from other theoretical fields (a methodological framework I later came to know as transdisciplinarity) – could be applied successfully to societal phenomena, notably politics, that led me to dare hope I could invoke this scholastic spirit for my psychological 'deep dive' into my besieged journalistic tradition. Chapter 4 of Andrew's *The Political Psyche, The Lion and the Fox: Morality, Trickster and Political Transformation*, was to serve as my shamanic rattle.

For the Trickster, I was to discover, lurked not only in journalism and politics, but also in the relationship soon to evolve between my celebrated supervisor and my still uncertain self. The thesis I was to write characterised that archetypal principle, among other things, as 'the third', the psychosocial space relatable, I argued, to Habermas's public sphere, and to Jung's transcendent function. Journalism, my trade and Bourdieuian habitus, occupies that space, and the 'third person' phenomenon is a familiar visitor to the consulting rooms of psychotherapists and counsellors. The third, engendered by my interactions with Andrew, spoke directly to the Trickster my research was investigating – although I did not identify that correlation until after my doctorate was achieved.

If the third that is Trickster is spawned by oppositional forces striving their way to PhD individuation, then Andrew and I were the perfectly imperfect pair. Andrew is the 'radical theatre' professional who morphed into a psychotherapist, and then an academic – although, as our supervisions continued, I began to regard him rather as an anti-academic, a paradox which was often the midwife to insights that proved most useful to my doctoral inquiry. For example, when early in my quest I was struggling to encapsulate the disruptive imperative that I 'felt' propelled all journalism, but particularly the phenomenon's bawdy, image-rich, tabloid manifestation, he talked to me of 'Trickster energy' in a way made more convincing by his own mercurial presence than by the books and academic papers to which he helpfully directed me. Later, when a small library in the American Mid-West kindly located for me an obscure anthropological paper about a native American Trickster figure, he immediately recognised the importance of that research journey, rather than simply its product, and encouraged me to make more of it than I would otherwise have done. I concluded later that this was him drawing on his theatrical background as well as his psychological insightfulness: he knew the dramatic value of a strong story.

According to his Wikipedia page, Andrew ran a 'commune-style radical theatre company' in the 1960s and 1970s 'directing plays in and around Oxford'. He never discussed that part of his life with me, but a dramatic air always seemed to accompany my supervisory meetings with him (although I have since concluded that any interpersonal histrionics were provided by my own projections and insecurities), and it often informed the content of our discussions, notably those concerning the Trickster principle. I later contemplated how Turner's work on theatre and the liminoid reflected aspects of the archetypally disruptive potential that shared our relational space so comfortably. I was once sitting in a theatre in Madeira, waiting for the curtain to rise on a performance, when, as I reached down to turn off my mobile phone, I noticed a notification from Andrew. All doctoral students will recognise the jolt of anxiety that drove me to leave my seat and read a succinct message from him that could be fairly summed up as, 'Where is the writing you owe me? I want it by midnight.' Needless to say I provided it, although my wife watched the show alone. If that sounds like a critical anecdote, then it is mirrored by another theatrical occasion whereby, once I had been formally awarded my PhD, Andrew invited me to a London theatre to see Ink, a play about the launch of *The Sun* newspaper, where I had worked for many years, and which played a major part in my PhD thesis. Thus, for me, theatre trips neatly characterised two complementary zones of the Samuels spectrum.

Andrew guided my work, like the best theatre directors, with a stick here and a carrot there, continually clearing a pathway to doctoral individuation. He displayed an encouraging faith in my unlikely thesis, and ultimately steered me to a heroic victory. The passage from it I include here exhibits my use of the archetypal tool I would not have dared to wield without his support. As I wrote, 'The primary hypothesis of the work, that the subject manifests the archetypal Trickster principle, borrows an investigatory model frequently used by post-Jungian, and more broadly cultural, scholars for explorations in associated areas, notably film studies'. Andrew's work, both on and off the page, gave me the nerve, however tentative, to apply depth-psychological insight to my own rough trade. I shall remain immensely grateful for that inspiration for the rest of my life, and once a year I find time to silently raise a commemorative glass to the three Tricksters of my doctoral journey: me, him and it.

References

Bassil-Morozow H. and Anslow J. A. (2014) Faking Individuation in the Age of Unreality: Mass Media, Identity Confusion and Selfobjects. *Analytical Psychology in Conversation with a Changing World*. London and New York: Routledge.

Graham J. (2017) *Ink*, London and New York: Bloomsbury.

Samuels A. (1993) *The Political Psyche*, London and New York: Routledge.

Turner V. (1982) *From Ritual to Theatre*, New York: PAJ Publications.

Chapter 14

Elizabeth Brodersen

I am delighted to contribute to this collection in honour of Professor Andrew Samuels' *Festschrift*. As one of his former PhD students from 2008–2014, my thesis topic on twins describes well the relationship with Andrew as my 'self-regulating other.' My thesis topic, called *Laws of Inheritance: On the Psychology of the Relationship between the First and Other(s) – A Post-Jungian Perspective*, was published by Routledge in 2016 under the slightly different title: *Laws of Inheritance: A Post-Jungian Study of Twins and the Relationship between the First and Other(s)*. For the research on twins, I used an archetypal perspective, which opened up new channels to explore the phenomena of twin-ship on both micro and macro levels. Andrew and I share a 'twinning' relationship: Andrew's birthdate is near mine and we are the same age; I come from Wales and Andrew spent time in Wales as a social worker. We attended The London School of Economics at the same time and studied similar courses. Like Andrew, I have a social work background and we are both Jungian analysts, albeit from different training schools. But prior to 2008, we had never met.

When I finished my training at the C.G. Jung Institut Zürich to become a Jungian analyst I wanted to expand on my diploma thesis, then supervised by Professor Verena Kast. I sent the thesis to the department of Psychoanalytic Studies at Essex University in the hope that I would find a supervisor. The diploma thesis fell onto Andrew's desk and from then on, a creative twinning relationship developed between us, which gave me, as a second born twin, a new opportunity to develop further ideas on the archetypal aspects of twin-ship within a symbolic twinning, transference–counter transference dynamic.

During the research on twins at Essex, I perceived other twinning phenomena at play. In chapter 4 of the thesis and the book, I used Edgar Allan Poe's short story *William Wilson* (1839) which, to my mind, is one of the best descriptions of twin-ship written by a non-twin to illustrate the dynamics of the 'self-regulating other' in actual twins. To my astonishment, I noticed that Edgar Allan Poe had the same birthdate as Andrew and the same birthday as William Wilson! Added to these synchronicities, in chapter 7 of the thesis and book, I used F.W.J. Schelling's theosophical work on the essence of human freedom (1809) and saw that Schelling's birthday is the same date as mine! Thus, throughout my research I felt the support of twins as 'first' born and the 'other' which accompanied me to find out more about their hidden archetypal dynamics.

For this publication, I have chosen chapter 3 of the published book from my PhD thesis as it gives a historical overview of the anthropological evidence of an affective archetypal twinning process that moves through cultural forms, redressing and redistributing the balance between the twins as 'first' and 'second' born.

References

Poe, E.A. (1839). William Wilson. In *The Fall of the House of Usher and Other Writings*. London and New York: Penguin Classics, 2003.

Schelling, F.W.J. (1809). *Philosophical Investigations into the Essence of Human Freedom*. Albany, NY: State University of New York Press, 2006.

Chapter 15

Stefano Carpani

Andrew and I met for the first time in Berlin in April 2015, where he was giving a series of lectures on 'How to Choose Your Therapist', 'Polyamory', and other themes. Several days before his workshop I had received an email from one of his former MA students, saying: 'There is a very important Jungian in Berlin. You cannot miss him …' Almost as if it were an order, I followed, signing up without hesitation, and attended. *Ça va sans dire* I had never even heard of him before! Although on that Saturday I was only supposed to take part in one section of his workshop, I ended up staying the full day (which annoyed my wife and friends as I missed our planned afternoon activities and arrived late for dinner). But it was worth it! Without a doubt, it was a *coup de foudre* (at least from my side), and I spent the entire dinner talking about Andrew to my wife and friends. I clearly recall the puzzled expressions on their faces…

Now, several years later, I can certainly say that meeting Andrew was meaningful, and I am grateful to my friend for inviting me to attend his workshop. Jungians call this synchronicity. The moment I spoke to him *vis-à-vis*, I had the feeling I had found the mentor I had been seeking since my twenties (or even before!). The encounter was a moment that changed my life. Something clicked, and I started fantasizing about beginning training analysis with him (although this was not possible for various reasons). At the end of 2015, I began to imagine finally 'setting right the time out of joint' (Heller, 2002), which had been interrupted following my completion of an MA and MPhil in Sociology, at Manchester and Cambridge, respectively. Setting right the time out of joint for me meant re-initiating my PhD work – having dropped out of a scholarship at Lancaster University and Frei Universität in Berlin – by employing a psychosocial look at the formation of narratives of self-identity; in other words, a merging of sociology and psychoanalysis.

With great respect and a bit of bravado, I wrote an email to Andrew. He answered me within 24 hours with words of interest, encouragement and opening my initial idea to so many levels. Slightly overwhelmed, it took me six months to pull all of his suggestions together into a formal proposal. This is how my PhD and relationship with Andrew began. '*Es ist nur eine frage der Zeit*'[1] is written on the building where Wim Wenders lives in Berlin-Mitte. Setting right the time out of joint had not been a possibility at Manchester and Cambridge; because it was there that time went out of joint. To meet Andrew, my *Doktorvater*, was certainly only a matter of time. Meeting him helped me set right the time out of joint.

In October 2016, I officially enrolled as a PhD student at Essex University and my new (although second) academic life began. Memories, feelings and emotions from previous studies and difficulties were always present and haunted me, almost to the point of dropping out. Yet Andrew was always there to support me and to persuade me to go on (although, in March 2017, when I was going through a very difficult financial and personal stage of my life and was not able to put together a good enough first chapter, he also suggested that I give up!). The first year, chapter one, was incredibly difficult, but paid off, as everything else that followed became easier and possible. And Andrew was right. He helped me to learn how to write academically, to trust my instincts and to not give up (a good idea). He was the first person in my academic career to *read through* what I was writing and to support it, polish it, and push me to go deeper. His guidance and support also helped me to lose my stage fright, and to learn to stand in front of an audience of strangers and share my ideas without being afraid. He helped me to learn to do so without letting my inferiority complex take me, with all its consequences; or without, as John Beebe would say, losing my integrity.

Working with Andrew has been fundamental from an intellectual point of view. This is because, while at the C.G. Jung Institut in Zürich I had the opportunity to study Jung, with Andrew I was gently pushed towards the post-Jungians and non-Jungians. It became very clear to me that all Jungians are also Freudians, although with distinctions. It also became clear to me that we, neo-Jungians, need to work hard to place Jung back at the core of psychoanalytic investigation, which is the investigation of the soul – of the logic of the soul. Andrew, therefore, opened my eyes to areas I hadn't explored before, including psychosocial studies, feminist psychoanalysis, and relational psychoanalysis.

I am grateful to Andrew for having supported me, even when I felt lost and was unable to write. He remained there and accompanied me until I found my own way. I am grateful to him because he supported me in being able to say what I think (instead of borrowing opinions from others) and to say it aloud. And he was also there when my training analyst, Günter Langwiller, passed away in March 2019. Andrew, who knew Günter well, offered to talk to me, and this is what a mentor does. He did so with generativity, which is – in the words of Mauro Magatti and Chiara Giaccardi (Routledge, 2018) – a generative (psycho)social action accomplished in three movements (bringing into the world, taking care and releasing). This is, for me, Andrew's legacy. To be able to bring something into the world, and to nurture and care for it until the time comes for its release (because that something – whatever it is – has to live an autonomous life).

Note

1 *It is only a matter of time.*

Reference

Heller, A. (2002). *The Time is Out of Joint: Shakespeare as Philosopher of History*. New York: Rowman & Littlefield.

Chapter 16

Laner Cassar

In 2008, I started the process of applying for a PhD in psychoanalytic studies at the Centre for Psychoanalytic Studies at the University of Essex. Often, starting a research degree marks a transition in the lives of students and mine was no less different. I was 35 years old and very much interested in studying further analytical psychology. Although the educational system in Malta (my country) is very close to that of the UK I still had to get used to new ways of learning as a distance-learning student. Furthermore, I was not yet a Jungian analyst and had a lot of ground to cover before I could understand well and criticise Jung's work. However, the biggest hurdle was finding an original PhD topic and a supervisor for the thesis.

According to Sverdlik, Hall, McAlpine and Hubbard (2018) the supervisor is one of the external factors that influence PhD students' successful completion of their thesis. I had asked for a specific supervisor, one who I had come to know during some seminars delivered in Malta. However, I was instead proposed to work with Professor Samuels as the other professor was not able to supervise any more theses. I did not know Samuels personally, only through his books. I was also aware of his rather provocative stance in criticising the establishment of the Jungian world. Being an introvert I was not so sure our characters could fit, working together on such a task for at least seven years. When I asked other PhD students for their opinions I received different comments. Some worked really well with Samuels while others found him either very busy or too informal for their liking. Research has found that there is a high number of PhD students who fail to complete their studies in the UK, with the most frequently cited problems being the nature of the supervision given (Delamont and Eggleston, 1983; Marsh, 1972). As Dinham and Scott observe: "the student–supervisor relationship has the potential to be wonderfully enriching and productive, but it can also be extremely difficult and personally devastating" (Dinham and Scott, 1999, p.2). I looked forward to meeting Professor Samuels in person to make my own judgement about working with him or not.

When I met my assigned supervisor at University he seemed very busy and had very little time available. He immediately went straight to the point and after hearing my ideas for my research he suggested that I do a theoretical piece of work and insisted that I find something original for my research. His last words were clear, firm and to the point. Professor Samuels immediately showed me that he possessed excellent research skills, yet his Hestian "spiritual" flame left me wanting more of his guidance and direction. He underlined the fact that, at the PhD level, initiative and independent work were necessary although he was ready to accompany me on my journey. Those were not the words I wanted to hear at the time, but looking back, his words were more like the paradoxical language of a Zen master. He gave me responsibility for my research and immediately threw me in deep waters I was hesitant to face.

In spite of the negative comments I had heard from some quarters, I took a gamble and decided to stay with him as my supervisor. Time proved my decision to be right. The journey of my dissertation was indeed a journey with Professor Samuels. The supervisor initiates the student through a journey of transformation, from a novice researcher to a professional researcher. Mouton (2001) relates the nature of the post-graduate thesis supervisor to the four dimensions of research supervision, that is, the advisory role; the quantity control role; the nurturing supportive relationship role; and the guidance or what we term as the coach role. An accomplished supervisor is able to adapt and switch between various dimensions as the situation demands. Overall, I have to say that Professor Samuels did tick all the boxes. He encouraged me to deepen the quality of my writing while directing me to a wealth of books to expand my knowledge on the subject. He seemed interested in creative therapies. I have a background in humanistic psychotherapies and was pleased to discover that Professor Samuels had developed a blend of Jungian and post-Jungian, relational psychoanalytic and humanistic approaches. He encouraged me not to hesitate in deconstructing the notion of free and spontaneous aspects of active imagination as described by classical Jungians and to put active imagination in dialogue with other guided imagination therapeutic methods. He was open and interested in forging new approaches to Jungian psychology and very interested in the creative arts, given his past work in theatre groups. His theoretical syncretic stance motivated me further in my research.

Furthermore, Professor Samuels responded positively to the integrative comparative methodology of my research, which highlighted pluralism. He believed this was a better approach in comparative research since it enables therapists to use a variety of theories without the need to reconcile differences. I found his ideas of holding "unity and diversity in balance" (Samuels, 1989, p.33) innovative and contemporary. In his research supervision, Professor Samuels was a trickster, helping me shift through different perspectives rather than stick to one approach. This staying with ambiguity opened me to the domain of the trickster archetype, which in turn brought new developments to my work. This led me to develop a unique integrated-hybridised theoretical framework of clinical practice, that is, a RED-based approach to active imagination.

Professor Samuels was also very much interested in the historical part of my research, which continued with the tradition of historical revisionism which he himself promoted, with the apology to Jung's anti-Semitic comments in the 1930s (Samuels, 1994). Likewise, though on a different note, I felt freer to argue that Jungians may have to accept Jung's failure to acknowledge the other European pioneers of imaginative therapies who were present in his time. The same would hold for the hard comments made from some of Jung's close disciples against practitioners who worked with guided imagery in order to protect their new emerging discipline of analytical psychology.

Over time, Professor Samuels and I felt more comfortable with each other. Sometimes I met him in Essex and sometimes in London. I appreciated his flexibility and hospitality, given that I was a distance-learning student. I got used to the informality of his mentoring. Whenever I forgot and used the title of 'Professor' when addressing him, he would remind me to call him 'Andrew'. Back home I would email Andrew with my questions or latest drafts of my chapters or my latest historical archival discoveries, which he found exciting. I appreciated very much his immediate replies to my emails even during the time when he had a horrible accident whilst on holiday abroad. He was available and ready to encourage me when I felt stuck and discouraged. Andrew knew how to foster trust, maintain motivation, play the devil's advocate and celebrate success.

Looking back I can say that I was lucky to have had the opportunity to work with Andrew given that I was one of his last students before his retirement from Essex. My supervision experience with Andrew, as a distance-learning student, was a fruitful one and was crucial to the successful unfolding and completion of my PhD.

References

Delamont, S. & Eggleston, J. (1983). A Necessary Isolation? *Qualitative Studies in Education,* 9(4), 481–500.

Dinham, S., & Scott, C. (1999). *The Doctorate: Talking about the Degree.* Sydney, Australia: University of Western Sydney.

Marsh, A. (1972). *Postgraduate Students' Assessment of their Social Science Training (SSRC Survey Unit Occasional Paper No. 2).* London: Social Science Research.

Mouton, J. (2001). *How to Succeed in your Masters and Doctoral Studies: A South African Guide and Resource Book.* Pretoria: Van Schaik.

Samuels, A. (1989). Analysis and Pluralism: The Politics of the Psyche. *The Journal of Analytical Psychology, 34*, 33–51.

Samuels, A. (1994). Jung and Anti-Semitism. *Jewish Quarterly, 40*(5), 59–63.

Sverdlik, A., Hall, N. C., McAlpine, L., & Hubbard, K. (2018). The PhD Experience: A Review of the Factors Influencing Doctoral Students' Completion, Achievement, and Well-Being. *International Journal of Doctoral Studies, 13*, 361–388.

Chapter 17

Martyna Chrzescijanska

Andrew is one of those people one hears about before ever meeting them. There are stories and anecdotes, some true, some false, but all of which contribute to the atmosphere of the first meeting. This was also true of my first meeting with Andrew. When I started my training in Jungian psychology in Poland, we read Andrew's papers and some chapters from his books as part of our seminars. His status was somewhat legendary, although I guess there is always something legendary about Jungian analysts from one part of Europe, from the perspective of those from the other part of Europe! All in all, Jungians are a rare species.

When I decided to move to the UK to do a PhD in Jungian psychology after completing my Master's degree, most likely by fate or perhaps simply luck, Andrew became my supervisor.

If I say it was luck, it is only a half-truth (or less) however, as it was also down to Andrew's kindness and engagement. I remember having a conversation with Kevin Lu from the University of Essex about a possible PhD supervisor. He said that there may be a place with Andrew but he was on his annual leave so we would need to wait. I could not wait, however, because my scholarship deadline was fast approaching. So Kevin said, let's try emailing Andrew, but there were no guarantees.

So we did. Andrew not only welcomed my application, but from the very beginning he became involved in improving my application to the point that it actually won a scholarship. Even two.

All this happened during Andrew's annual leave, when he was prioritising not only his current PhD students but also his future PhD students, like me. This is something that everyone probably knows about Andrew – his job is not only his passion, it is his life.

It was some time later that I met him in person for the first time. If indeed a (subjective) image of who somebody is can be illustrated so briefly, I will refer to two short episodes to describe the impression Andrew made on me – as a person and as a supervisor.

Shortly after completing my PhD application, I went to the 7th biennial Andrew Samuels Lecture that hosted Roger Brook and Mark Saban that year. This was a few years ago and I was new to both London and the Jungian world in London, but I recognised Andrew and approached him to introduce myself. He was busy talking with other people (those who know Andrew know he is always busy during conferences, a true people person). I did not really expect him to be too bothered, and I was surprised by his kind and warm reaction when I introduced myself as a PhD student that he would be supervising in the upcoming academic year.

I guess this first kind reaction and the fact that he was able to find time to chat with me at a very busy moment, made a lasting impression that was reinforced by my later experience. I can say that although Andrew is always busy – with conferences, writing, old friends, new friends, colleagues, students, patients, and the numerous projects with which he is always involved, he was always able to find time for me when I needed it the most.

This is where my second mini-vignette comes in to show how I see Andrew. It was few years later and I was halfway through my PhD journey when I applied for training at one of the Jungian training societies. Andrew is one of those supervisors who support their students in the most "holistic" way – he was always interested in my non-PhD-related plans, particularly my training in psychotherapy. As I had stopped my training in Jungian psychology in Poland, I wanted to give it a try in London. I applied and my application was rejected, which was a rather bitter experience. When life gives you lemons, make some lemonade, and the best lemonade is served in the sunshine of South Africa. Shortly after I received the rejection letter, I went to the Jungian conference in Cape Town (again, greatly supported by Andrew, who read my abstract and encouraged me to keep improving it until it finally reached its best form). I dropped him a line in an email, telling him about the rejection I had received before going to Cape Town. Again, I remember so well, when we met in Cape Town, that he found extra time, in the midst of all his meetings and presentations, to sit down with me and discuss it. He was probably the most supportive person at that time.

A PhD is a long journey, with ups and downs, and having somebody to provide the continuity of support and belief in the value of your work is pivotal. This is what Andrew did for me – there were numerous moments when I lost track and was unsure whether my PhD research was meaningful and if it was, what this meaning might be. Andrew very often understood my PhD more than I did, always seeing the bigger picture. If I forgot or lost understanding of my own research, he did understand it and he believed in me.

I think we were both surprised on many occasions by how our interests, ideas and perspectives coincided with each other. I did not realise at the beginning that my critique of containment in psychotherapy fits a broader perspective, one that is critical toward the many well-established categories in psychotherapy that Andrew promotes. Andrew is a rebellious and independent thinker, changing the landscape of Jungian and psychotherapeutic thought with a great determination and persistence. He is also dedicated to supporting young people, critical minds, revolts and transformations. This is unique in the world of analysts and academics, each of whom sooner or later turns into a senex. Andrew, on the other hand, is a puer, and, simultaneously, he is more than that. That being the case, we await the next step and I can already bet that it will be inspiring.

Chapter 18

Clare Crellin

Andrew was my PhD supervisor for a very long time, almost ten years, on and off, between 2001 and 2011. This takes patience, endurance even. We are the same age. I saw my PhD project as a kind of 'swansong' begun towards the end of my career and the product of 30 years of reading. It grew out of my involvement with both the history of psychology and critical approaches to psychoanalysis. The PhD thesis was more like an expression of what I had done and where I had been. Andrew saw this as an important function of a doctorate program and encouraged candidates for whom the work had a closing function at the end of a working life. I was at a very busy point of my career as a consultant clinical psychologist and psychotherapist and had increasing family responsibilities. Andrew understood this. Since I lived in Sussex, UK, one thing that was helpful in a practical way was that Andrew was able to give supervision sessions in London rather than Essex.

What I most appreciated was Andrew's belief in the project. He supported it and defended it. He fought my corner, especially in relation to my linking Jung's work on alchemy with Jung as a personality theorist. Andrew saw my project as a re-visioning of Jung as a personality theorist and as a contribution to debunking myths about Jung and his theories. He always grasped what I was getting at, and he was playful with ideas and enthusiastic, amplifying my original thoughts.

Circumstances at the end of my period as his supervisee meant that he was less available to me in the later stages. The work was largely completed by then, although I lacked the confidence to realise this. It was not an ideal end. But until then Andrew had stuck with me and tried to be helpful. I was not the easiest student to help. I was stroppy in the annual 'Boards'. I did not gel with their approach. I objected to having board members who were from other psychoanalytical orientations. They and I seemed to be at cross-purposes. Andrew was a good mediator. His practical advice was very valuable as I struggled to reconcile the demands made by my board with what I wanted to do, and when I wanted to give up.

I was already familiar with Andrew's work so there was a comfortable cross-referencing in our discussions. He introduced me to Jungian scholarship that

I was not familiar with. In this way, he amplified my ideas. Perhaps his influence was most evident in my chapter on Alchemy and Individuation, especially in his way of thinking about alchemy as a metaphor for the process of psychotherapy and for all developmental approaches where a transformative process is involved. That is why I have chosen to put together extracts from that chapter for inclusion in this volume.

Most importantly of all, Andrew understood that I was working through my dual position as scientist practitioner and Jungian scholar, and that I was trying to find ways of reconciling the two.

Andrew's promotion of the value of publishing PhD theses was significant in Routledge's decision to produce a series of scientific monographs on psychoanalytical subjects. This ensured that many Essex PhD graduates, like me, who were new authors, not already known in the psychoanalytical field, were given an opportunity for publication by a well-known and world-renowned publishing company.

I hope that my PhD and its subsequent book 'Jung's Theory of Personality: A Modern Re-appraisal' (Routledge/Taylor & Francis 2014) demonstrates one way in which clinical and analytical psychology can be integrated. More than this, Andrew believed that I had a unique perspective and a message that was important for the Jungian world and for Jungian scholarship as it was then.

Chapter 19

Sukey Fontelieu

I met Andrew *after* I was accepted into the Psychoanalytic Studies program as his student. I'd already begun my research and apparently was the first transfer student into the program. I came from the University of Lancaster (even though I'm American). After over a year of work there, researching the Greek god Pan, my plan to defect began when one of the members on my committee wanted to know why I wanted to use mythology in a psychological study. Rather than ask him if he had ever heard of the Oedipus myth, I decided I needed to find a supervisor who knew more than I did. At this, I certainly succeeded.

The Fairmont Hotel, in San Francisco, was where we first met in the flesh. We had coffee. He was jetlagged. He leaned back in his chair, got as close to lying down as a person can in a chair (a position I found was a familiar one during our talks and which helped me to relax), eyes nearly shut, and listened to me ramble on about what I was trying to articulate about the unconscious influence of Pan everywhere. For the paper, the focus was to be on America and how Pan can be seen in climate change, sexuality and power, bullying, school shootings, wars, and so forth. He sat up.

So, "Pan stalks America" he said. Three words summed it up. Brilliant. They became my title and my plumb line keeping me on track for the next years. They also allowed my brimming confidence, that I was actually on to something, to burst out, and I chattered on about how important this all felt.

"Don't be a vicar," he chided and started telling me about a British TV show I'd never heard of. I had to ask him what a vicar was. He then gave me a quick outline of how to organize my thoughts, told me to give it 8–10 hours a week, and we were done.

That was it for a while. The long story about my parents' illnesses will now be skipped but as soon as I started I had to take a leave of absence. "People like you," Andrew informed me, "never finish." I took this as a challenge. Especially for me, a woman with four planets in Aries in her natal chart, finishing is a sore point. Once the family duties were complete, I started working and finished early. So there. I had to leave out climate change, which I regret to this day, and may just tackle before I'm done.

As it turned out, Andrew's sudden, intuitive bursts were all uncannily useful. His direct and, at times harsh-feeling, criticisms were actually some of the most helpful bits of advice I've ever been given. They still are. Currently, I'm teaching research at Pacifica and I repeat many of my Andrew stories to the students, who listen with big ears to the words that helped me as I stumbled up a steep learning curve and managed to write something that, with all my heart I hope is one drop in the wave that will turn the American ship of state away from the greedy, power hungry, sexualized condition that it now is in. I know, I know, don't be a vicar.

Chapter 20

Phil McCash

It is a tremendous honour to be invited to contribute to this *Festschrift* for Professor Samuels. I would also like to express my appreciation for the opportunity to share some of my own work. It is typical of Andrew's generosity that he wished to use this collection to highlight the work of others. It is impossible to do full justice to his seminal scholarship and activism but I would like to make some brief observations on both topics as they relate to my PhD experience. I would also like to share some remarks relating to my personal experience of supervision.

I was originally attracted to Andrew's democratising project in relation to Jung, that is, the goal of sharing analytical psychology as widely as possible by applying its insights in academic fields outside of traditional psychotherapy. This was attractive to me as my project related to improving the dialogue between Jungian studies and career studies, with a particular focus on enhancing the work of career coaches.

I read several of Andrew's books and found they all enriched my thinking in various ways. In particular, I enjoyed reading *Jung and the Post-Jungians* (Samuels, 1985) as it demonstrated a way of engaging with analytical psychology as an admirer but also a contemporary critic. The *Critical Dictionary of Jungian Analysis* (Samuels, Shorter, & Plaut, 1986) provided a regular source of insight. *The Plural Psyche* (Samuels, 1989) probably shaped my thinking the most, and its influence can be detected in my chapter contribution (Chapter 9).

I find events and conferences a useful way to balance the relative isolation of research. Andrew is tirelessly involved in organising a wide range of such activities. Shortly after I started on the PhD, I woke up one morning to hear him on the BBC Radio 4 Today programme with Sonu Shamdasani, announcing the publication of *The Red Book* (Jung, 2009). It felt like an exciting and important time to be studying analytical psychology. I attended several events he helped to organise, including a conference on Jung and film studies, and another exploring the work of Carl Rogers and Jung. I found them stimulating and enjoyable. The former helped me more fully understand how Jungian ideas could be translated into another discipline. The latter was very relevant, given the long-standing influence of Rogers in the training of career development professionals, and helped me to explore new points of connection and difference.

During the first year of my PhD, I audited a module on Jungian concepts, led by Andrew, on the MA in Jungian and Post-Jungian Studies at the University of Essex. He used his unrivalled network of contacts to bring in a range of distinguished guest speakers. I learnt about the poetry of Hafiz from a beautiful talk by Gottfried Heuer, and the ideas of Giegerich through Ann Shearer's inspirational session.

Andrew is sufficiently confident in his own scholarship not to feel compelled to insist that you cite him. In fact, he would rather you did not unless it is important to the work. Nor is he doctrinal in terms of developmental, archetypal, or classical orthodoxy. He encouraged engagement with all strands of thought where relevant and helpful. I also found him very open to broadening the scope to include other ideas from psychoanalytic studies. This was particularly helpful to me, as I needed to more fully appreciate Alfred Adler's individual psychology. His background in therapy gives another string to his bow as an academic. Sometimes he brings insights from the therapy context that have not yet surfaced in the academic literature. This helped clarify my thinking at several points.

Andrew is always direct in his remarks. If he finds something rather uninspiring he tells you. Sometimes, he may even yawn! When he finds it exciting, he communicates that too, usually in an animated and inspirational way. His response to the extract below was like that. I argued for a more Adlerocentric reading of Jung, advancing the notion that some of Jung's concepts, such as the personal myth, the persona, and the personal equation, are foreshadowed in Adler. I am sure he did not agree with every dot and comma of it but he could see the argument and liked the direction of it.

It is common for supervisory relationships to go through a honeymoon period followed by a few bumps in the road and ours was no exception. I needed to adjust to our psychological type differences. He is as strong in extraversion as I am in introversion. It also took me a while to appreciate how creative and direct he is in the moment. He is comfortable sharing his immediate responses arising from engaging with your work but, as I came to realise, fairly relaxed about whether you take these ideas on or not.

Andrew resists the pull of stereotypes such as the omniscient professor or mysterious Jungian analyst. I feel he is very present as a whole person in his varied roles as academic, analyst, citizen, and man. He is a good example of the adage, 'be yourself, everyone else is taken'. This helped me to be present in my work. I am sure that is true for some of his other supervisees too.

The extract that forms Chapter 9 of this volume was selected from my PhD and focuses on personal myth. This aspect is just part of my thesis but significant to it for two reasons: firstly, the importance of the (re)turn to narrative in the social sciences in general (Bruner, 1986; Polkinghorne, 1988; Sarbin, 1986); secondly, and relatedly, the influence of Adlerian narrative ideas in career studies (Cochran, 1997; Savickas, 2013). I wanted to understand Adler's individual psychology in more depth and trace its influence on the evolution of Jung's thought. I then subsequently used this to critically evaluate existing ideas in career studies.

I have also selected this extract because I enjoyed writing it and felt it may be of wider interest in the Jungian community. I would very much welcome dialogue on any of the ideas discussed. I am sure there are many other aspects to the personal myth and areas of debate. It would be very helpful to know if there are others with interests in this area.

References

Bruner, J. (1986). *Actual minds, possible worlds*. Cambridge, MA: Harvard University Press.

Cochran, L. (1997). *Career counseling: a narrative approach*. Thousand Oaks, CA: Sage.

Polkinghorne, D. E. (1988). *Narrative knowing and the human sciences*. Albany, NY: State University of New York Press.

Samuels, A. (1985). *Jung and the Post-Jungians*. London: Routledge.

Samuels, A. (1989). *The plural psyche: personality, morality and the father*. London: Routledge.

Samuels, A., Shorter, B., & Plaut, F. (1986). *A critical dictionary of Jungian analysis*. Hove: Routledge.

Sarbin, T. (Ed.) (1986). *Narrative psychology: the storied nature of human conduct*. Westport, CT: Praeger.

Savickas, M. L. (2013). Career construction theory and practice. In R. W. Lent & D. Brown (Eds.), *Career development and counseling: putting theory and research to work* (2nd ed.). Hoboken, NJ: John Wiley.

Chapter 21

J.A. Swan

In a life spent dreaming, one may find a preference remains for dreams in which persons one has known are present as themselves. There may be time, months or years between dreams, before the same individual reappears (or, visits) in a similar corporeal way, in a different stage or life circumstance. One might observe, when such corporeal familiarity emerges, initially – and particularly, when it returns to the dream state – that the momentum of psychic phenomenon may accelerate: noticeably, externally, for participants in the dream.

We wake from different dreams, in different ways. I recall being still on the pillows for a time longer than typical.

I was in a setting not dissimilar to the random variety of classrooms, used early on by the Centre, at Essex. The dreich[1] day complimented the fluorescence of the aging Plateglass space.[2] The room was unoccupied, except for one standing figure in neutral clothing, central with their back to the wall of windows. The figure in the room wore glasses. I knew this person[3].

In the afternoon of that same day, I opened my email account, and read an invitation from Stefano, to participate in this project about the figure in my dream.

The English word that I associate most with my experience in supervision with Andrew Samuels is, Generosity. Generosity appears in many forms, and throughout the experience I was aware that Andrew is a generous scholar. He is a busy person, with a complicated set of responsibilities: The fact that every email or letter I have ever composed to him and sent, over the course of fifteen years now, was replied to within minutes, or hours, or days – before, during, and beyond the official timeline of the supervisory process – speaks to his commitment to studentship, and scholarship, ongoing in the context of an experienced, active life. (He is a person that one is able to reconnect with, as if no time had passed.)

Although time has changed into the way we are now, there is an image of Andrew that has remained an indelible construct: A gentleman whose firm professional reputation appeared in first instance to my Year, to fit as only bespoke tailoring will, into the angles of a fine wool suit, an unusual dove grey, grounded unexpectedly by the artisan tooling of a cowboy's tanned leather boots. The theatre of aesthetics is difficult to capture effectively; here it was pure, and alive.

Andrew genuinely shares with his students the belief in the vitality of the supervision process. I remember the grey London morning meetings in his office, offset by colourful art books tiled across the rugs. We spent much time animated in discussion about The Arts and aesthetic life: It is a pleasure to work in this way with someone who understands the creative process well, from his perspective of the Artist. Whilst Andrew's own studies of archetypal theory, and the alchemical colouring of the transformation process are woven thickly through my thesis, much of his essence, too, remains in my work about temenos sites, especially the Moscow GOSET Theatre set designs (Chagall completed in 1920). Andrew has an excellent eye; the importance of colour resonates for him, to the extent he went searching, and found, his only copy of a response paper he gave, to James Hillman's, 'The Yellowing of the Work' (1991). Years later, he sent to me abroad, unsolicited, a copy of Tate Liverpool's Chagall exhibition catalogue (2013), as I was unable to travel then.

Andrew's commitment to the supervisory process with his students always prevailed. In this situation, the responsibility of working together included a time when the need arose for my contribution to pause, through a period of unforeseen life circumstances, when it was not possible to continue along as before. Life does sometimes become too disconnected, or disrupted, to produce what is needed, well. Andrew saw me through the academic process during this time, insisting upon my completion of the degree: He is a Good Man. He understands the value of continuation in scholarship; he is willing, to the end, to support the quality work of his students and the sharing of their ideas.

In my own estimation of the supervisory encounter, the thesis would not be here, in this way, if at all, if not for Andrew's support in the creative process across more than a few selected years.

Andrew has retired from his work in university now. There is an understandable professional void, though the memory of this time will remain with me in the continuation of scholarship, the love for aesthetic derivations of venerated theories. For me, Andrew is a part of the collective works, always.

What a long, strange, and beautiful journey into visual life it has been. Thank You.

Notes

1 'dreich', adj. A Scottish word used to communicate the daylight weather as 'dreary or bleak'. "There is a stillness to a dreich day that is matched by no other. It is not extreme weather in any sense ... Dreich days are not days of excess. They are quiet

days, melancholy but not depressing. They are a blank canvas on which to project future hope." (McCredie, 2016, pp. 1–2).
2. Michael Beloff's (1968) review of seven English university sites erected during the early to mid-1960s in rural settings (including, a chapter on the University of Essex) is the initial British study of such buildings to utilise the term, 'plateglass', beyond the architectural vernacular of Modernism: Beloff's metaphor outlines and characterises the changes in the social politics of education and the alternative educational structures built not to resemble the more familiar institutional buildings in Victorian bricks, or ancient stones.
3. This is not the first time such coincidences have been generated in connection with the particular activity of writing this thesis, or, as the supervisee in the supervisory process. The form is a cycle of connections, available within the content of dreams, active imagination, and the coincidence of conscious ideas about the work and happenings around the research process itself. The thought, of unconscious connection and coincidences brought forth through the supervisory experience, fi nding translation in its own versions, in all academic disciplines. In a Podcast *Rant* concerning students and the supervision process, Andrew presented and discussed this thought in his own detail.

Bibliography

Beloff, M. (1968). *The Plateglass Universities*. London: Secker & Warburg.
Chagall: Modern Master. (2013). Simonetta Fraquelli, Ed., London: Tate Publishing.
Hillman, J. (1991). "The Yellowing of the Work". *Spring*, 77–96.
McCredie, A. (2016). *Scotland the Dreich*. Edinburgh: Luath Press.

Chapter 22

Huan Wang

The first time I met Andrew was in a restaurant in Macao, a city famous for its casinos. At this meeting, we discussed the possibility of my becoming a PhD student at the University of Essex. As a woman from China, single and in my early 30s, the idea of going abroad to spend the following four to five years, writing a dissertation in a second language, and, more importantly, using unfamiliar academic methods to organise my thoughts, was rather daunting. It was a life-changing decision and a real gamble for my future. I don't remember what we discussed at that meeting, but our dialogue catalysed my decision. Now, having finished my dissertation and at a point when I am working to turn it into a book, I look back at what has happened over the past several years and I must say, I feel so lucky that I chose the right path: the whole process of working with Andrew on my PhD has been quite transformative for me.

The beginning of my study was not at all easy: at first, I felt quite confused and struggled. Previously, when I had written a thesis or essay in China, I was used to collecting all the materials I needed to support my views while discarding or ignoring those which seemed to contradict my assertions. In other words, I didn't know how to develop a real argument. As I wrote in my dissertation, this may be a habit rooted in our culture – the Chinese tend to focus on sameness and similarities and are fond of a harmonious voice, while disagreement and challenges are not welcome and disparate voices bring unbearable anxiety. Hence, when I realised I had to develop 'critical thinking' in my work, I felt quite nervous and had no clue how to begin to criticise others' work. This prospect seemed too hostile in the context of my culture and hence was difficult for me until Andrew clarified that critical thinking more accurately means trying to develop independent thinking. Although this change of expression seems simple, at that moment, it brought me great relief and changed my attitudes when reading others' work, including that of Jung and of Andrew himself. In a short time, I no longer struggled with how to write an academic paper in English: his advice not only changed how I organised my thesis, but also how I read and think to this day.

To be honest, Andrew has been the most inspiring supervisor I have ever met. During the years of my PhD study, each time I finished my supervision with Andrew, the discussion between us allowed me to hear my own voice more clearly. At the same time, the more of Andrew's own work I read, the more I came to understand how to be critical – seeing various possibilities, hearing plural voices, developing my own thoughts, and challenging ideas that may be prevalent but stereotypical, and without hostility. Andrew is a brilliant writer and his strong, authentic, intellectual curiosity opened a new world to me. Although I previously considered the Chinese to be a very open-minded and flexible people who attempted to integrate all that they had learnt, compared with Andrew, I realised that my previous education, both in psychoanalysis and analytical psychology, was too fixated on classic works and showed too much loyalty to great Western masters; this made it very difficult to establish authentic, fresh and original ideas that belong to the real world and to the present moment in which we live. In my own dissertation, I attempted to change this and for this reason, I affirm that this process of PhD study with Andrew was a life-changing and transformative process for me.

The other struggle I had was with writing in English. English academic writing was a major challenge for me and the difficulty I faced was to far exceed my own preconception before I arrived in the UK. As a foreigner, although I tried to find a proofreader, it was very difficult for me to judge my proofreader's work. Andrew rejected my first proofreader, then recommended another to me. However, when he realised the second one, despite having very good skill, was not careful enough, he told me to stop working with him immediately and tried very hard to find a third for me. Based on my observation, no other supervisor makes so much effort with their students' language skill. I must say that even at the beginning, I found the process very stressful, but by the end, when I had finished my dissertation and passed my Viva with the result of no correction, I was extremely grateful for Andrew's insistence on finding me the best proofreader. It made me feel more secure, certain and confident about expressing my ideas and it is in small details such as this that Andrew shows his authentic, warm and real care as a supervisor to his students.

Westerners, and Jungian psychologists in particular, are very familiar with the Chinese term Tao. It is the path to individuation, while 'Te is the integrity we bring to our participation in Tao ... [Te] is the moral weight of a person' (Beebe, 1992, p.30). Te, integrity, means consistency within oneself while being sincere and engaging with others. Andrew and his work showed me the embodiment of Te and working with him helps me to find my own way for Tao.

Reference

Beebe, J. (1992). *Integrity in Depth*. College Station, TX: Texas A & M University Press.

Part III

Psychoanalysis in the 21st Century

Chapter 23

Stefano Carpani and Andrew Samuels in conversation

Personal biography

SC: This interview is divided in three broad sections. To start with, I would like to focus on your personal biography, then on your intellectual biography and your own contribution to the field. And, last, on psychoanalysis in the twenty-first century.

Who is Andrew Samuels? I am particularly interested to hear from you about your childhood, values (family and individual), fantasies when a teenager, Philosophy, Politics and Economics (PPE) at Oxford (and why you dropped out), activism and 1968 in London, theatre and your move into psychoanalysis.

AS: Jung famously wrote that 'every psychology is a personal confession' and that remark guides me here. You've specifically invited me to be personal and so I'd like to show why – to the best of my conscious knowledge – some of the themes in my work came to be there from a personal angle.

Starting in 1967, between school and university (in American terms, between high school and college), I lived in Swaziland for over a year, exactly 50 years ago. At that time, the small country, completely surrounded by South Africa, was a British Protectorate. I got a job with the British Colonial Office as a District Officer, complete with ceremonial sword and solar topee (like you can see Jung wearing in the photos of his African trip).

In short order, I was secretly recruited by the African National Congress (ANC), in part because I had been involved with the Anti-Apartheid Movement in Britain. I performed certain tasks for the ANC that, as you'd expect, totally contradicted my task as a District Officer. I comprehensively broke the Official Secrets Act. Eventually, I was found out and fired. They threw me out of Swaziland and when I entered South Africa I was arrested and flung into Pretoria Central Prison (of Steve Biko infamy). Of course, the British had betrayed me.

I stayed in jail for a few weeks and it was not a pleasant experience. Still, attending a British public (that is, private) boarding school prepares one for such ordeals as being kicked, hit and shouted at.

In 1967, at about the age of eighteen, I was a highly political young man, but trying to realize my political dreams through the arts – specifically, theatre. We were a radical theatre company, influenced by Jerzy Grotowski and Peter Brook. The group was composed of university drop-outs and draft dodgers from the Vietnam War. Those were remarkable days at the end of the 1960s, when you could get money from the English Arts Council for radical theatre companies. Then, after becoming a youth worker and a counsellor working with young people and an encounter with humanistic psychology – a serious option career-wise for a while – I went into analysis, and dropped out of the political world for a decade. So, when Thatcherism came in in the 1980s, there was I, a former Trotskyist and student radical, busy writing Jungian books!

Gradually, the political side of my personality, and my interest in society, came back in and merged with my clinical concerns, leading to the formation in 1994 of Psychotherapists and Counsellors for Social Responsibility. Then, when I began to have children, as often seems to happen with men, a third strand came in, which we could call 'spiritual'. Psychotherapy, politics, and spirituality – three sides of a coin!

SC: Tell me about the influence of your family and background on your work:
AS: I agree that my account up to now is somewhat external and avoids my beginnings in the family. I have always struggled to find a vigorous to-and-fro in my image of my parents' marriage. I am not saying it was never there, only that I had an image of a conventional togetherness without much passion or risk-taking. They were kind to each other but never went near (in my fantasy anyway) the grotesque and divine experimentations I found a need to write about in my paper on 'The image of the parents in bed'.
(Samuels, 1989)

I will talk about my mother in a moment. My father was a gentleman, and I mean this in two senses. First, that he was well educated, had been through the war (ending up in both Italian and German prisoner of war camps), and enjoyed a cultivated and comfortable lifestyle ranging from golf to classical music. But he was also, for me, what I came to call in my writings (e.g. 2001) a 'dry' father, not using his body to give out much erotic or aggressive playback – but a decent and polite man. In fact, I felt he depended on me to provide a kind of excitement and, via my rebellious, bad and rejecting behaviour, that is what I did. His father was a self-made immigrant tycoon type, though the family business went bankrupt in the end.

My concern – even obsession – with relations between women and men stems, I believe, from this respectable but emotionally constrained background.

Hence, I found it hard to buy into Jungian essentialist approaches to gender because they felt so limiting. That was why I wrote 'Beyond the feminine principle' (2001). And I have been strongly influenced by feminism in what I wrote over the years about the relations between women and men. Amongst my influences were Susie Orbach, Jessica Benjamin, and my late former partner Rozsika Parker.

I am a competitive person, who delights in negotiation and bargaining. But over time I have become able to agree with Gerhard Adler that there is a 'principle of complementarity' at work in life: some people are better than others at some things. But when it comes to other things, other people are more adept. These three principles, stemming from my personal psychology, also lie at the heart of pluralism: competition, negotiation, bargaining, complementarity. Pluralism gave me an opportunity to be aggressive and tolerant *at the same time*. Those three principles are relevant to many levels of experience, you see.

Although my classification (1985) of the schools of post-Jungian analytical psychology was developed before I developed pluralism as a theory in 1989, it was the former project (post-Jungians) that got me going. In 1985, the Jungian analytical field was even less cohesive than it is today – I mean in terms of any beginner being able to find their way around in it. There were huge differences in approach and things only held because each segment of the field claimed to derive something from the connection to Jung.

I experienced it all differently from most of my friends and fellow students. I really liked the fragmented nature of the field, with its dispute, polemic and lack of clarity. What looked like totally inimical perspectives were in fact linked by their desire *to go beyond Jung* whilst *retaining a critical connection to him*. This meant that each of the revisionary or revolutionary tendencies (Developmental, Archetypal) could be seen as having a similar relation to the more settled centre (Classical). But the model did not rule out evolutions within Jungian classicism.

SC: You said you would talk about your mother in a moment…

AS: For a novice analyst to write an overview of the field into which he had just arrived was, of course, an inflation. But I certainly made a name for myself. This does lead me to comment a bit on my mother's influence on me. It was she who spotted, with her down to earth intuition and generally savvy approach to life, that writing could be a way for me to make my mark. She went on and on about this, and, unusually and amazingly, I listened even though I knew that my success was for her glory.

This brings me to the not inconsiderable matter of my relationship, on all levels, to Tricksters in general and to Hermes in particular. What attracts me to the Trickster actually is his very lack of a political or psychological project. In fact, he lacks integrity or ambition. If he does good, it is entirely by accident. There can be no 'cleaning up' of the Trickster act. His primitivity makes him what he is. And 'he' is not only a 'he'. I do not really know why I was the first to spot the potential of the idea of the 'female Trickster' (1993).

I deplore that there is these days so much idealistic, sentimental and romantic writing on the Trickster as a creative and constructive force (especially the female version).

Be that as it may, Hermes speaks to me, as to many analysts I suspect, because he links the base, corrupt, grotesque aspects of the Trickster ('dirty tricks' in politics) with some kind of skill at making creative connections. But the story of Hermes/Andrew remains resistant to a wholly positive reading because the shadow of being an emissary of the Gods is that the messenger becomes (or seeks to become?) more important than the message. A power trip, then? So, behind my pluralistic tendency to pop up in many fields of psychotherapy beyond the post-Jungian one (humanistic psychology, body psychotherapy, relational psychoanalysis), and in both mainstream and activist politics, there is, like there was for Hermes, assuredly a quest for power.

SC: Power is a political theme and you are known for your work on political strands in Jung's work.

AS: I don't think it was only the need for power that motivated my controversial work on Jung and anti-Semitism from the mid-1980s until the publication of *The Political Psyche* (1993). This material, and other, later discoveries, was originally published in the *Journal of Analytical Psychology* though not without having to overcome attempts to censor me by Michael Fordham and Judith Hubback.

If there was a personal background to this project, it was simply to do with the plain fact of being Jewish in a community whose founder had written objectionable things about my people. Fred Plaut and I discussed this all the time. In addition, there was also some kind of background wish to be more accepted as a contributor to academic, psychoanalytic and political discourses, which was undermined by being seen as an adherent of that notorious anti-Semite Jung.

The reactions to my early essays into the allegations of Jung's anti-Semitism really pissed me off, though on a good day I could also empathize with them. It did feel like being in my family in which I was always the 'black sheep', the *Rosha* – the wicked son who seeks to opt out of the Passover Seder ceremony. In the early stages of our community's engagement with our problem, there was a closing of the Jungian ranks, a repetitious argument that Jung was merely a man of his time, and even some pathologizing of me as a Jew with a complex.

Well, Jung was not exactly a man of his time (as you can see from the detailed research I and others did), and it is those kinds of knee-jerk defences that even today sometimes represent our problem (the Jungians' problem) and not Jung's problem. Nevertheless, gradually, the Jungian community realized that apology and reparation was needed and the informal alliance of concerned people that emerged has done a pretty good job in this regard. Some are here today. Of course, for those who need us as a tribal enemy, such as the psychoanalysts, the unfortunate legacy provides a marvellous base.

Nevertheless, much explicatory and reparative work still needs to be done on Jung's racial attitudes and his theories and utterances about 'Africans', and I hope to return to this later in the interview.

SC: Power is also a psychoanalytical theme. When did you realize (and decide) you wanted to become a Jungian analyst?

AS: To be honest, I didn't decide. I applied to all of the psychotherapy institutes in London (at the time, 1971, there were only three!) The psychoanalysts said I was too young. The Jungians didn't reply but I found myself walking aimlessly one day in the street where the Society of Analytical Psychology had its offices and I went in. When I emerged I had the name of a training analyst.

But it wasn't quite as aimless, Stef. I had read *Jung's Psychology and its Social Meaning* by Ira Progoff (2013 [1955]) and it inspired me in many different ways, enabling me even then, right at the beginning, to conceive of coupling my activism and my interests in psychology.

One thing to add is that I had two options for training. One was the SAP. The other was to go on to complete my apprenticeship as an Encounter Group facilitator. I found my theatrical background suited Encounter work. But the behaviour of the senior trainers was appalling and unethical and it put me off.

Nevertheless, I've retained an interest in humanistic and integrative psychotherapy alongside my Jungian and relational psychoanalytic interests. Every lecture I give has an experiential component, even in the university context. I would never have done this without exposure to humanistic psychotherapy. And one of the best conferences I ever curated was linking humanistic and Jungian psychologies.

SC: Activism and being an activist is important to you as well. It is in your veins. I remember your speech in April 2017 at the Association for Psychosocial Studies conference at Bournemouth University ... when you showed a picture of the demonstration in London when you got arrested for the first time. Which are the key themes for you and how these mingle/link with being a psychoanalyst and a political advisor?

AS: My political preoccupations change. I cut my teeth in the Anti-Apartheid Movement. For a time, I was a Trotskyist. At the moment, I am interested in the rights of the Palestinian people and also in defending the onslaught in Britain against disabled people. Above all, these days I am exploring what it means to be a white 'ally' of people of colour in their struggles.

I have a great loathing of too much abstraction when it comes to politics. But it is interesting how personal politics such as sexuality and gender, and macro politics such as the economy or climate catastrophe, are ever more easily linked in people's minds.

Other themes that continue to preoccupy me include leadership (my work on the 'good-enough leader') and the role (if any) of an individual in radical politics. Here, Jung's ideas, intellectually wrong, about the relations between an individual and the society are, emotionally speaking, very useful and intuitive.

Intellectual biography

SC: You are considered one of the most important, influential post-Jungian psychoanalysts. You describe yourself as a relational-Jungian with a strong interest in psychosocial studies. Can you share with us the central steps in your intellectual biography/journey?

AS: When you asked me this, I immediately began to think in terms of BOOKS! That is so typical of an intellectual, a Jewish intellectual even. I am not a true academic in that my education was never completed and I dropped out. But the word 'intellectual' resonates for me.

One book was Joseph Heller's novel *Catch-22*. I instantly got the anti-authoritarian message when I read it in about 1965 when I was 16. (The book was published in 1961). The hero Yossarian stays with me all the time.

A similar book was Albert Camus's *The Rebel* with its punch line 'I rebel therefore we exist'. This book constituted a cornerstone of my rejection of my parents' values. It is sad, but the rifts that began then never healed and both of my parents died with relations being very estranged.

SC: Which are the authors that, and the research areas which, you consider essential for your own development and work? In particular, what was Jung's role in these areas? Why Jung and not Freud or Adler, etc.? Which other areas do you consider fundamental in your own intellectual biography (also beyond psychoanalysis)?

AS: Jung was a bit of an accident but, as I mentioned, a consultant recommended Ira Progoff's *Jung's Psychology and Its Social Meaning*. This was my entrée into Jungian things, not *Memories Dreams Reflections* or *Modern Man in Search of a Soul*. So the much later 'political turn' really was there from the start. No turning at all!

SC: Earlier I mentioned that you are a relational-Jungian with a strong interest in psychosocial studies. Through my PhD work – also thanks to your guidance – I came to the formulation of a Jungian-relational-psychosocial model.[1] What are relational psychoanalysis and psychosocial studies?

And why are they important in your latest intellectual development as well as a clinician?

AS: My favourite phrase regarding the relations between the clinic and the social world is 'a two-way street'. People like me are pretty inflated really. We want to illuminate the political scene with our psychological insights. Well, OK, if we can do it. But what about the other direction of travel, how political thinking and processes influence clinical work? More modesty is needed from us activist analysts!

SC: You suggested that within both the microcosm of an individual and the macrocosm of the global village, 'we are flooded by psychological themes' and that 'politics embodies the psyche of a people' (Samuels, 2001: 5). Thus, you remind us that 'the founders [of psychoanalysis] felt themselves to be social critics as much as personal therapists' (Samuels, 2001: 6) and in this respect, you recall Freud, Jung, Maslow, Rogers, Perls, the Frankfurt School, Reich and Fromm. You also noted that in the 1990s, psychoanalysts such as Orbach, Kulkarni and Frosch began to consider society once more, but noted that although 'the project of linking therapy and the world is clearly not a new one [...] very little progress seems to have been made'. Thus, you stressed that today 'more therapists than ever want psychotherapy to realize the social and political potential that its founders perceived in it', but are aware of the 'large gap between wish and actuality' (Samuels, 2001: 7). I argue that psychosocial studies might fill this gap. Do you agree?

AS: Yes, the development of psychosocial studies in universities is the most helpful thing. The problem is that, especially in Britain, the psycho bit is carried pretty much exclusively by British psychoanalysis – Klein and object relations. There is little relational or attachment-based thinking in psychosocial studies. No body-based psychotherapy or transpersonal psychotherapy. And certainly, no Jungian and post-Jungian psychology. This is a great opportunity.

SC: In 2014,[2] you opened the discussion on the role of the 'individual in contemporary progressive and radical political discourse', engaging with Giddens, Beck and Beck-Gernsheim, who are also key to my work. In this paper,[3] you – concurring with Jung – underline that 'individuals are socially constructed, even when they believe themselves to be autonomous and inner directed entities' (Samuels, 2014: 100). Therefore, referring to Giddens, Beck and Beck-Gernsheim on the so-called 'self-invented identity,[4] cut off from traditional context' (Samuels, 2014: 100), you claimed that although challenging and useful, these authors offer only an 'experience distant' perspective (Samuels, 2014: 100), and add – quoting Layton (2013) – that 'sociologists today [...] have reached the conclusion that individuals need to be better theorised, though this is usually in order to make a deeper and more fecund contribution to their own discipline of sociology' (Samuels, 2014: 100). Why is mainstream sociology unable (afraid?) of the unconscious?

AS: Most politics, not only progressive/radical politics, is done by groups. Most political thinking is groupish, collective, whatever word one uses to side-line the individual. Yet everyone is wondering what they can contribute. What I did in that 2014 paper was redefine what we might mean by an individual, making her/him less unified and pristine than liberalism usually does. Jung got an intuition that an individual was vital to political generativity and I built on that. I often build on something that Jung chucked out and then left.

SC: In contrast to Hillman, you actively demonstrated 'how useful and effective perspectives derived from psychotherapy might be in the formation of policy, in new ways of thinking about the political process and in the resolution of conflict' (Samuels, 2001: 27) and you claimed that 'our inner worlds and our private lives reel from the impact of policy decisions and the existing political culture'. In considering why policy committees do not include psychotherapists, you noted that 'you would expect to find therapists having views to offer on social issues that involve personal relations' (Samuels, 2001: 2). This is, I propose, your most innovative aspect: to see psychoanalysts (as well as individuals) as activists, with a fundamental role to play within society.

Am I right sensing that you attempted to 'repair' Hillman's error in leaving the consulting room in order to theorize, without considering societal development and the claim of individuals? Instead, for you, the psychosocial turn is imperative for its ability to approach the *individual* from a psychological and social standpoint. Examining the individual through this lens, you sought to recover the aim of the founders of psychoanalysis: to examine the individual within the social environment and the complexities arising from this relation. Therefore, you worked to regain the revolutionary *quid* of psychoanalysis and to remind us – as alchemy suggests, and in contrast to Hillman – that *our Art* comprises both theory and practice.

AS: If I answer with a plain 'yes', it could seem offensive. But the long question just posed is such a well-expressed summary of what I, also, think – that I will just say 'yes'.

SC: You are both a scholar and a clinician. What are the pros and cons of this in your own work, as a thinker, and a therapist? For me, both are two sides of the same coin and cannot be separated.

AS: Funnily enough, I am writing a keynote presentation for the next conference of the International Association for Jungian Studies[5] on the relations between the clinic and the academy. Here's what I shall do: Simply paste my Abstract here and you can take it from there. I think this is justified by the fact that this *Festschrift* is seemingly rooted in the academy. But is it really, or only like that?

The politics of Jungian studies: clinicians can't think, academics can't feel – towards the emergence of good-enough all-rounders

Professor Andrew Samuels (Society of Analytical Psychology, London)

This is not about the application of Jungian therapy thinking to political, social and cultural problematics. It is about the politics of the relationship between Jungian analytic clinicians and academics working in Jungian Studies. Andrew believes that, despite folk who are active in both of these activities, there have been tensions approximating to splits (in the psychoanalytic sense of the word, including mutual projections) between these two broad groupings. This has been marked since the foundation of the International Association for Jungian Studies in 2002.

Dictionaries and thesauruses are not kind to the all-rounder. They are said to be 'generalists', 'jacks of all trades and masters of none', and so forth. The Notes on 'the human sciences' provided to those submitting proposals use the word 'eclectic'. As a pluralist, if not exactly an eclectic, Andrew believes that we need, in the spirit of the human sciences, seriously to interrogate this network of prejudices, mining the gold buried in the shit therein.

The same dictionaries and thesauruses are much kinder to the whole notion of the 'good-enough'. This notion stems from the work of the British psychoanalyst D.W. Winnicott and characterizes the shift in an infant's perception of their parent(s) from a split state alternating between idealization and denigration towards something more realistic and humane.

The paper is delivered in the full knowledge that the binary – clinic and academy – is simplistic. But entering the world of the binary may also be heuristic. For, as Andrew sees it, there is a serious turf war bubbling under, and the prize is legitimacy – meaning things to do with power, authority and influence.

Hence, the audience is asked to enter a space in which the following (absurd, overblown, exaggerated) generalizations may be explored. Let's not forget Theodor Adorno's *apercu* that 'In psychoanalysis, nothing is true but the exaggerations'.

From the analysts, they say that (i) academics can't really feel or suffer complex emotions because they suffer from precocious intellectual development (a point taken from Winnicott who writes about it); (ii) many concepts developed in analytical psychology are clinical in nature or can only be appreciated if one has a clinical outlook and, above all, clinical training and experience; and (iii) whether the academics like it or not, analysts have special knowledge even Gnosis.

As far as Jungian analysts are concerned, we are helped in the above characterization of the academics by the various things Jung said about intellectuals and it is still seems hard for intellectuals to feel they have been treated justly by admissions committees on clinical training.

From the academics, we hear that (i) analysts can't really think systematically or rationally; (ii) analysts assert things rather than argue them through; (iii) that they misuse authority in both the treatment and training environments; and (iv) that their main research tool – the case study – is badly flawed.

The idea of the good-enough all-rounder is floated with considerable awareness of what would be missing if this became a goal. For what this idea implies is that not only do we need people who struggle with the field of Jungian Studies as well as that of Jungian analysis, but that *they might not be excellent at either enterprise.*

In 1968, the first generation Jungian analyst Gerhard Adler published a paper entitled 'Depth Psychology and the Principle of Complementarity'. Adler picked up on the physicist Niels Bohr's point that something can't be a wave and a particle at the same time. Adler tweaked this idea to engage with what was the main hot issue in Jungian analysis at the time, and maybe it still is. This is the tension between (a) those who work with the numinous, classical models of individuation, dreams and active imagination – and (b) those that analyse infancy and transference–counter-transference and valorize the therapeutic alliance.

In plain language, Andrew is saying in his paper that *some people are better at one and some are better at the other.* This is how he sees the field of Jungian Studies at the moment. Those in it who are entirely devoted to academic research may be better at that than those who spend all or most of their days in a clinical office. And vice versa.

Following this declaration, Andrew will show that he is nothing more than a good-enough all-rounder by presenting a historical and personal account of how such splits have been handled within the overall field of depth psychology. Of interest in itself, this study is also to be considered an analogy. The intent is that those of us engaged in Jungian Studies can find models in these historical phenomena to facilitate the emergence of the good-enough all-rounder.

Your own personal contribution to analytical psychology and psychoanalysis

SC: Now, in the concluding section of this interview, I want to look at your own contribution. Particularly at the father and at plurality. In your own words, what is your unique contribution to analytical psychology and to psychoanalysis at large?

AS:
- The schools of analytical psychology;

- The political turn in Jungian analysis;
- Challenging Jung's positions on gender and 'race, with special reference to Jews' and 'Africans';
- My 'new anatomy of spirituality';
- Building bridges between the Jungians and groups of others.

SC: In your book *Jung and the Post-Jungians* (1985), you claimed that there are three main post-Jungian traditions – the 'classical', 'developmental' and 'archetypal'. In my PhD thesis and in the introduction of this book I proposed it may now be time for a fourth: the plural. This approach, encompassing eclecticism and integration, is rooted in your work and aims to restore and enhance Jung's work and analytical psychology at the core of depth psychology, by studying the psyche as plural and, therefore, as political. What is your take on this?

AS: It is a good idea. Nowadays, what I say is that within the professional mind of a contemporary Jungian analyst are elements of all the schools. A process or separation and division was needed back in 1985 (and, of course, long before). But now we can start to develop a plural version of the analyst, just as you depict in your question. Your language is very creative.

SC: That being said, I propose that this is, however, not the only new approach. I call this new approach: neo-Jungians. This is a heterogeneous, international, and multicultural group of scholars who, on the one hand, base their work on the teachings of Jung (and the post-Jungians), while on the other hand have opened their investigations beyond analytical psychology. Therefore, the *neo-Jungians* are able to balance the teachings of Jung and the post-Jungians with those teachings coming from other schools and traditions (both within and beyond psychoanalysis) in a mutual and plural, enriching exchange. In fact, contemporary neo-Jungians can be linked (although not limited) to relational (and post-relational) psychoanalysis, feminist psychoanalysis, the intersubjective approach, psycho-social studies, and cultural studies, to name a few. Thus, there are many ways to be Jungian (or to be a Jungian), and this is very good news. It signifies that analytical psychology is alive, and reflects the continuing interest in, as well as perhaps even rejuvenation of, Jung's theory at the beginning of the twenty-first century.

AS: Whilst I could quibble at the prefix 'neo', the important thing is that you, a member of a different and younger generation, are also engaging with a central problematic of huge importance to me and to my generation: How to relate to Jung on the basis of knowledge and passion – and how to distance oneself when that is required.

SC: In 1989 you coined the term PLURAL PSYCHE. How do you see this concept 30 years after? We live in very rigid times now, where neo-populism is gaining power. Is plurality *passé* or could current rigidity and populism be considered a regression before development?

AS: Pluralism, as I developed it, is a way to hold the tensions between unity (like the state) and many-ness (like the various identity politics groups within the state). But the state is also an interest group within the state, if you see what I mean. It is not above or always bigger than its component parts. Jung got at this when he said that the Self was both the centre of the psyche and also its circumference. The Self, like the state, is BIG. But it is also a little thing within something bigger, which, paradoxically, we also call the state. Pluralism is not 'the many'. It is the relations between 'the one' and 'the many'.

SC: To put the understanding/study of the psyche in relation to politics was ambitious. Therefore, to claim that the psyche doesn't constitute a marginal aspect in politics and policy making was innovative. You claimed that the psyche is a fundamental tool in politics. When/How did you come to that?

AS: Well, I wasn't the first, as you know. Others went before, and so I demur from the question. But it has been and always will be a somewhat marginalized element in depth psychology.

SC: You underlined (1989: 1) that the plural psyche is a concept necessary to both analytical and depth psychology to 'hold unity and diversity in balance', because pluralism is an 'instrument to make sure that diversity need not be a basis for schismatic conflict'. This is, in my opinion, what makes you a relational psychoanalyst *ante litteram*.

AS: You are right that I understand pluralism as a way, not to avoid conflict, but to prevent conflict from being only destructive.

SC: You have underlined that the psyche is an unavoidable tool for looking at politics. Was your message understood? I propose that it was not (although not because of your own failure) – because, to understand what you were trying to say, you have to have a deep understanding of the unconscious. And this is why, Blair preferred to follow Giddens' advice and not to adventure to understand politics psychologically. I propose that his election as Prime Minister, inaugurated a long series of political shooting stars (e.g. Zapatero; Sarkozy; Trudeau; Renzi; Macron and perhaps even Obama), who are politicians that appeared on the international stage and that inspired change and transformation, although they colluded with the existing system instead of changing it radically. Does this mean that the system cannot be changed? It is puzzling that Clinton and Blair came into power to contrast (even compensate) Reagan and Bush Sr. and Thatcher, but failed to make chance happen and to build a new system that would resist in time. And now ... looking at politics today with Trump, Brexit, Salvini, Le Pen, Orban, Bolsonaro and the possible return of Kirshner's dynasty at the Casa Rosada in Argentina, etc...

AS: I worked with Blair and his team between 1995 and 2001, and they understood the role of psychological thinking in the following areas: leadership, male issues such as structural unemployment, and public apologies (e.g. for the Irish potato famine and the Slave Trade).

I also worked on both Obama election campaigns in 2008 and 2012. Again, the question of leadership, with special reference to leadership by a Black man. Also, he wanted to be 'the father of the nation' and I proposed that new variants of the father, such as a more nurturing, related and democratic father might be more use than the disciplinarian, patriarchal father we were all used to. I also valorized failure and this led to Obama saying 'I'm not perfect'.

This is the first time I have allowed the detail of this work to appear in print

SC: Thank you for sharing this detail about your work with Blair and Obama here. I truly appreciate it. But you haven't answered my question about what I call *political shooting stars* and the current emergence of populists or neo-fascist leaders.
AS: To be honest, I think that the question of 'neo-fascist leaders' was really well addressed in your Abstract for the Analysis and Activism 4 conference in Berkeley, California in October 2020, where the upcoming US Presidential Election was a key focus. Why don't you paste that Abstract into this interview?
SC: I didn't expect you to suggest that, but why not ...:

The fascist among us / the fascist in us

When the analyst's attitude is problematic: untamed complexes and counter-transference in training analysis

This paper has been inspired by works on fascism by Austrian writer and dramatist Thomas Bernhard, Italian poet Giovanni Raboni and (Czech-born) former US Secretary of State Madeleine Albright.

In her book titled Fascism: A Warning (2018), Madeleine Albright underlines that 'There is no consensus definition, which may explain why the term is so indiscriminately tossed about. In my book, fascism is not an ideology of left, right or center, but rather an approach to seizing and consolidating power by an individual or party that claims to be acting in the name of a nation or group.'

In the piece titled Heldenplatz (1988), Thomas Bernhard wrote: 'There are more Nazis in Vienna now / than in thirty-eight.'

Now, more than 30 years after its premiere, we know that Bernhard was right, although his vision cannot be limited to Vienna. In fact, if we swap the word Nazi with fascist, we have a picture of 2019's scenario (Trump/USA, Putin/Russia, Orban/Hungary, Bolsonaro/Brazil, LePen/France, Salvini/Italy, Farage and Johnson/UK, AfD/Germany, and of course Austria). The list is still longer, if other continents are taken into consideration.

Raboni, in his poem entitled *Politica estera* (Foreign Politics), wrote that: 'The speaker has to say / the things he says and maybe not / or maybe others. But it is a fact that those who keep silent / let everything happen to them and what is worse / let what has been done to them / be done to someone else.'

Both authors propose that holding a silence (remaining silent) is not an option. Both insist that it is an ethical duty to speak up, so that what might have happened to one, will not happen to anyone else. Both Bernhard and Raboni wrote a *j'accuse* against the collective shadow of their own country.

I propose that today in 2019, fascism it is not a party. It is a *forma mentis*. It is trans-national, trans-cultural, trans-religious, trans-gender and transpersonal, etc. And if we are unconscious and unable to tame our complexes, we all – at some point – become fascist. Therefore, I will demonstrate that a fascist is a person of any sex and gender, of any colour, religion, ethnicity, age, nationality and place of birth, etc.

With this paper, I wish to propose a *j'accuse* against the fascists among us (in us); and hence the fascist in the analytical room: when the fascist is the analyst (not the fascist de jure, or the other or the patient).

I intend to ask, looking at my colleagues: Are you a fascist? Have you ever been a fascist? I will ask myself the same question and I will propose that the answer is – unfortunately – YES. Where the answer is yes, lies the basis for self-criticism, transformation and – following Watkins, (Lorenz and Watkins, 2003) – liberation. Because it is too easy to see a fascist in the other: in the true fascist. But it is very difficult to see the fascist in us and among us.

My own personal *j'accuse* is against the fascist analyst, who becomes a fascist *de facto* (therefore unconsciously in the encounter with the other/patient), though perhaps only for a moment, but sufficient enough to cause/repeat (or reinforce?) trauma.

Because both Bernhard and Raboni insisted on speaking up, I shall share a fictional case (in line with James Hillman's and Susie Orbach's work) that will serve as an example. I will do so keeping in mind von Franz, who said that the shadow is 'what we are although we don't like to be.'

My fictional vignette builds on John Beebe's courageous statements on the concept of the anima, individuation and homosexuality at the 'Jung and Activism' conference in Prague 2017, about a hypothetical encounter between a training candidate and training analyst. This vignette is about a meeting and confrontation in the analytical room and looks specifically at the problematic behaviour of the analyst.

It is problematic because his comments (in an email to the candidate months after their first and only meeting) are offered with veiled hostility, and because he seems to be unaware of (or not interested in) the impact on, and context of, his statements to the candidate (especially because the analyst has no way of evaluating his statements' impact). Particularly problematic is the way the analyst shared highly charged analytic observations in an email to the candidate; to do so being un-analytic in nature.

Secondly, the analyst mixes psychodynamic impressions with moral evaluation – implying that there is something immoral in the trainee's approach. While this may not be unethical, per se, again, this is not analytic in nature.

I will propose that the problematic and hostile behaviour of the analyst (who is well-known and respected internationally, and is considered to be a 'leftist') helps me uncover the theme of the fascist in us and among us.

In my concluding remarks I will then ask: why did the analyst decide to write such an email to the candidate, with such veiled hostility? Why did he become a fascist *de facto*? I will propose that the theory of complexes and counter-transference is not enough to explain his attitude. I will claim – following Beebe – that it is a matter of integrity, which the analyst lost in his actions. Perhaps he lost his integrity because he is trapped in a complex (of course!), but this does not excuse his attitude. Such an attitude can traumatize (again!) the candidate. And another problem adding insult to injury is the fact that reparation never happened. Reparation outside of the analytical context is not possible.

AS: I like the way you interweave 'real' politics, professional politics, and personal experience.

SC: In 1985 you edited a book titled *The Father* and in 1993 you wrote again about the father in your book titled *Political Psyche*. In fact, there are chapters on the father in most of your books. Why the interest on the father (when psychoanalysis always looked at the mother)? This was so innovative and challenging.

AS: When I started in the mid-70s, the senior people in the (Jungian) Society of Analytical Psychology in London said it was due to my mother complex! When writing about the father, I avoided the mother who was regarded as the way more important parent developmentally. I think they got their ideas from a mis-reading of Winnicott. Or maybe it was an accurate reading! Then I got attacked for apparently saying there was no difference between the parents of the two sexes (which I never said). It has been an uphill struggle.

Also, therapists prefer to look at the negative father rather than at the positive father. Specifically, the benign role of the father's body is simply overlooked. Fathers are indeed about sex and aggression – but sex and aggression are not only malevolent.

I am interested in the male father but I do not idealize him. 'The good enough father of whatever sex' is targeted at those who idealize the male father. Women heading families on their own, or with another woman, can do a damn good job of 'fathering'. This can be tweaked to open the psychoanalytic doors to an acceptance of two men heading a family together.

SC: You wrote about the *plural father*, the *father of whatever sex*, and doing so you also wrote about *gender confusion* and you claimed that there is a value in the confusion. You also wrote about the *wounded father* (as something to be healed) and about the *father's desire to be loved* (and not only as an a-emotional or un-emotional security provider). You wrote that if the popular phrase *the new man* meant anything, then it surely referred to a 'loving and attentive father' and a 'sensitive and committed partner of whatever sex'. Andrew, how are men today and how are fathers today?

AS: In the West, I'd say that the changing role of the father, and of men generally, is the most potentially generative and healing development in society. I mean from a psychosocial perspective.

SC: When writing about the father you underlined that it is time to look at the new father. I propose – following Robert Moore – that we need to look at the mature masculine and feminine to move beyond the *struggle* of genders. What is your take on this? There is still too much friction between sexes on the collective as well as on the individual level and – I propose – too much immaturity and anger (instead of mutuality).

Psychoanalysis in the twenty-first century

SC: I now want to look at psychoanalysis in the twenty-first century. According to many, psychoanalysis is *passé*. In an article published by *The Guardian* in January 2012,[6] you wrote that 'This could be Carl Jung's century'. Is it still so? Or is Jung/psychoanalysis *passé*?

AS: Clinically, the standing of Jungian analysis is high because it combines the rigour of psychoanalysis with wider existential and humanistic perspectives. Also, Jung was a pioneer of relational psychoanalysis and his work enables a combination of interpersonal and intrapsychic dynamics to be addressed. The alchemical metaphor captures that well.

SC: Do you believe that psychoanalysis should have a central role in shaping society? If so, which?

AS: Such a role is only possible if analysts also behave as activists and make alliances and a common cause with political groupings of all kinds. On our own, we are useless. We need to be humble and aware of our limitations. Allied to other disciplines, and inside other (academic) frameworks, we have a role. An analyst on every committee or commission – but, please God, not a committee of analysts!

SC: Thank you Andrew! This is a good place to bring this interview to a close.

Notes

1 I base this model on the following nine pillars: (1) It connects theory and clinical work (therefore helping to prove the accuracy and efficacy of analytical work with patients); (2) It is transdisciplinary; (3) It is pluralistic (Samuels, 1989) and demonstrates an attitude of inclusion (to replace the split and separation typical of the history of psychoanalysis); (4) It 'starts from the premise that the individual is born into a set of social and psychological circumstances' (Orbach, 2014: 16); (5) It 'investigate[s] the ways in which psychic and social processes demand to be understood as always implicated in each other' (Frosh, 2014: 161). (6) It has an 'emphasis on affect, the irrational and unconscious process, often, but not necessarily, understood psychoanalytically' (Frosh, 2014: 161); (7) It offers a conflict-relational approach (Orbach, 2014) and stresses the need for continuous adaptation in the process of becoming who people authentically are; (8) Becoming (who people authentically are) is seen as a liberation (Watkins, 2003); (9) Analysis is framed as 'accompaniment' (Watkins, 2013) based on 'the co-construction and multiplicity of meaning' (Hargaden and Schwartz, 2007 quoted in Orbach, 2014).
2 Samuels (2015).
3 Which evolved into the publication of 'A New Therapy for Politics?' (Samuels, 2015).
4 Thus Giddens, Beck and Beck-Gernsheim, but I would also add Bauman (2000).
5 San Francisco 2020.
6 Retrieved from the Internet on 30 September 2019: https://www.theguardian.com/commentisfree/belief/2012/jan/25/carl-jung-century

References

Albright, M. (2018). *Fascism: A Warning*. New York: Harper.
Bauman, Z., (2000). *Liquid Modernity*. Cambridge: Polity Press.
Bernhard, T. (1988). *Heldenplatz*. Frankfurt: Suhrkamp Verlag.
Frosh, S. (2014). 'The Nature of the Psychosocial: Debates from Studies in the Psychosocial' in *Journal of Psycho-Social Studies*, 8(1, November).
Heller, J. (1961). *Catch-22*. New York: Simon & Schuster.
Lorenz, H. and Watkins, M. (2003). 'Depth Psychology and Colonialism: Individuation, Seeing-through, and Liberation' in *Quadrant*, 33, 11–32.
Orbach, S. (2014). 'Democratizing Psychoanalysis' in D. Loewenthal and A. Samuels (Eds), *Relational Psychotherapy, Psychoanalysis and Counselling: Appraisals and Reappraisals*. New York and London: Routledge.
Progoff, I. (2013 [1955]). *Jung's Psychology and its Social Meaning*. London: Routledge.
Samuels, A. (1989). *The Plural Psyche*. London: Routledge.
Samuels, A. (1993). *The Political Psyche*. London: Routledge.
Samuels, A. (2001). *Politics on the Couch*. London: Profile Books.
Samuels, A. (2014). 'Appraising the Role of the Individual in Political and Social Change Processes: Jung, Camus, and the Question of Personal Responsibility – Possibilities and Impossibilities of "Making a Difference"' in *Psychotherapy and Politics International*, 12(2), 99–110.
Samuels, A. (2015). *A New Therapy for Politics*. London: Karnac.

Watkins, M. (2003). 'Dialogue, Development, and Liberation' in I. Josephs (Ed.), *Dialogicality in Development*. Westport, CT: Greenwood.

Watkins, M. (2013). *Accompaniment: Psychosocial, Environmental, Trans-Species, Earth*. Retrieved 11 November 2018 from: http://mary-watkins.net/library/Accompaniment-Psychosocial-Environmental-Trans-Species-Earth.pdf.

Contributors

Mary Addenbrooke, PhD is an accredited Training Analyst at the Society of Analytical Psychology and a member of the Association of Jungian Analysts in London. She has coordinated a Substance Misuse Service in the NHS and works as a Jungian analyst and supervisor in private practice in West Sussex. She has been a supervisor for the IAAP in Belgrade since 2005. She published *Survivors of Addiction: Narratives of Recovery*, Routledge in 2011 and is currently working on a book relating to therapeutic approaches to addiction. She has lectured widely on working with addicted people and their families and those who have left addiction behind.

PhD Title: An enquiry into psychological aspects of recovery from dependence on psychoactive substances

PhD Abstract: Literature on 'life after addiction' is scant. Traditionally, longitudinal studies have concentrated on quantifiable variables, for example, health or forensic outcome, using large cohorts of subjects rather than investigating psychological perspectives of recovery or continuing addiction. My study is based on the qualitative analysis of a set of tape recorded interviews of twenty-seven ex-patients of a local substance misuse service formerly treated for dependence on alcohol or injectable drugs, primarily heroin. In the majority of cases, abstinence had lasted between five and twenty-four years whereas six informants, who were originally treated in the 1970s were still addicted, providing a comparison group. I examined precursors to the cessation of drug and alcohol use and the mode of their quitting. For them, a step out of isolation occurred away from dependence on the substance. They sought and accepted help on an ongoing basis. A process of psychological rebuilding then commenced, which involved an altered relationship between the self and the ego, and going closely alongside this, altered relationships with others. I reflected upon the significance of Jung's link with the founding of Alcoholics Anonymous and examined first, the challenges of the first five years after quitting, and then the experience of people who had been abstinent for between twenty-five and thirty years. I found psychological stasis or deterioration in those still addicted, whereas those who had remained abstinent demonstrated intricate and fascinating processes of change.

James Alan Anslow, PhD is a Visiting Fellow of the Department of Psychosocial and Psychoanalytic Studies at the University of Essex, UK, where he researches the psychology of journalism. He is also a London-based freelance journalist. He received his doctorate in Psychoanalytic Studies from Essex University in 2017. He is single-authoring Jung and Journalism for Routledge as part of its 'Jung: The Essential Guides' series, and is writing The Tabloid Trickster for the same publisher, based on his PhD thesis, and on forty years of experience as a British national newspaper journalist. He also lectured in journalism at City University of London for several years. His other works include (with Helena Bassil-Morozow) Faking individuation in the age of unreality: Mass media, identity confusion and selfobjects in *Analytical Psychology in Conversation with a Changing World* for Routledge in 2014, and Myth, Jung and the McC women for *British Journalism Review* in 2008.

PhD Title: The tabloid Trickster: A post-Jungian evaluation of early twenty-first century popular British newspaper journalism characterised by that of *The Sun*.

PhD Abstract: At the beginning of the twenty-first century, British tabloid newspapers, whose circulations were already in steep decline, faced twin existential challenges: a growing tendency by consumers to access free information and entertainment content from the Internet, and demands for more stringent regulation of 'print' journalists, particularly those employed by, or servicing, 'tabloid' titles. The latter challenge was characterised in 2012 by the report of the Leveson Inquiry (Part 1) into the culture, practices and ethics of the press, ordered by the UK government as 'phone-hacking' revelations triggered the closure of the tabloid *News of the World*, then one of the most read English language newspapers in any country, and led to a string of high-profile court cases, one of which culminated in the conviction and imprisonment of the title's former editor Andy Coulson. For decades, influential media theorists had condemned many aspects of British popular newspaper journalism, a critique fuelled by the Leveson Inquiry and associated criminal investigations. Some analysts argued that Britain would be psychosocially healthier if newspapers such as *News of the World*'s sister publication, *The Sun*, either ceased to exist or were radically revised. However, this work uniquely explores the proposition that British tabloid journalism is driven archetypally by what Carl Jung identified as the Trickster, a collective shadow reflecting an ambiguous but necessary principle portrayed in myths, folklore, literature and contemporary media as a disruptive, lascivious, liminoid troublemaker. This thesis investigates and amplifies earlier explorations of the Trickster—notably, but not exclusively, by post-Jungian thinkers—and applies its conclusions to a depth-psychological assessment of contemporaneous popular British newspaper journalism. By revealing the archetype behind the tabloid stereotype, I suggest that UK statutory press regulation would 'castrate' the tabloid Trickster, rendering it unable to perform its psychosocial function, to the detriment of a society already challenged by a fragmenting post-modern media landscape.

Elizabeth Brodersen, PhD is an accredited Training Analyst and Supervisor at the CGJI Zürich. She received her doctorate in Psychoanalytic Studies from Essex University, UK, in 2014, and works as a Jungian Analyst in private practice in Germany and Switzerland. She published *Laws of Inheritance: A Post Jungian Study of Twins and the Relationship between the First and Other(s)*, Routledge in 2016; co-edited with Dr Michael Glock *Jungian Perspective on Rebirth and Renewal: Phoenix Rising*, Routledge in 2017, and is author of *Taboo: Personal and Collective Representations, Origin within Cultural Complexes*, Routledge, 2019. Her latest publication is an edited work with Pilar Amezaga entitled *Jungian Perspectives on Indeterminate States, Betwixt and Between Borders*, Routledge, 2020. Elizabeth is former Co-Chair of IAJS board of directors and currently a member of the English Research Commission at the CGJI Zürich. She is also a member of the International Journal of Jungian Studies (IJJS) editorial board as well as an editorial board member of Brill's Contemporary Psychoanalytic Studies series.

PhD Title: Laws of inheritance: On the psychology of the relationship between the first and other(s) – A post-Jungian perspective.

PhD Abstract: I speculate that imbued in interdisciplinary cross-cultural perspectives of mythic, socio-economic, literary, pedagogic and psychoanalytical representations, two archetypal, creative, developmental inheritance laws interact as 'twins': Eros (fusion/containment/safety) and Thanatos (division/separation/risk) as dividers, multipliers and mixers of cultural heritable forms. By 'twins' I include the intra-psychic as well as the interpersonal domain. I hypothesize these 'twin' laws as matrilineal (Eros) and patrilineal (Thanatos): matrilineal as communal/horizontal inheritance belonging to earlier kin clan forms; patrilineal, hierarchical inheritance, coinciding with the Genesis Creation Myth c. 3000 BCE in the Middle East, as one source, to rationalize the onset of primogeniture. Primogeniture gave the exclusive right of the first-born male to protect property from diminution and 'fixed' gender properties, specifying 'masculine' as territorial dominance. Horizontal 'feminine' specificity defined as passivity and nurture became subjugated, losing all heritable, creative value. This study of 'twins' reveals why cross-cultural forms including gender traits are not fixed but influenced by earlier flexible matrilineal forms. I argue that implicit in inheritance laws is a psychological 'twin' dilemma which developed under primogeniture, namely, how can one inherit as 'first' without betraying that original source (including matrilineal) and not be blamed for treachery as inheritance passes through the generations. I suggest that this double bind is re-enacted by splitting one 'twin' aspect into 'good/safe' and the other into 'bad/divisive,' depending on cultural developmental requirements. Twins personify this dilemma so well because as a single social unit, one twin can be saved, the 'other' damned without anyone noticing any vital loss or having to acknowledge the subtle, splitting mechanisms at play. With the recent movement away from the importance of patrilineal primogeniture, cultural forms have been re-defined to fit a modern landscape that now acknowledges earlier matrilineal kin structures. I offer a unique forum to show how each inheritance law competes for primacy as the 'first' and the 'other(s)': although one twin has been sacrificed, this twin simultaneously overlaps and usurps the 'first' by stretching the margins in between them by allowing tabooed, disassociated traits to enter the realm of conscious acceptability.

Index words: inheritance laws, archetype, twins, shadow, gender, cultural forms.

Stefano Carpani, MA, MPhil is an Italian sociologist (University of Cambridge) and psychoanalyst trained at the C.G. Jung Institute, Zürich. He graduated in Literature and Philosophy from the Catholic University of Milan. He works in private practice in Berlin (DE).

He is the initiator of the YouTube interview series "Breakfast at Küsnacht. He is among the initiators of "La prossima generazione" (The next generation) a think-tank dedicated to the under40, asking them to imagine and tell the ideas, projects, initiatives, policies about the—post Covid-19—"new" Italy; He is among the initiators of "Psychosocial Wednesdays", a digital salon moulded on those Freud´s Wednesdays meetings in Vienna and on Jung´s meetings at the Psychological Club, and feature speakers from various psychoanalytic traditions, schools, and associated fields.

Stefano is also the editor of *Breakfast at Küsnacht: Conversations on C. G. Jung and Beyond* (Chiron, 2020), *The Plural Turn in Jungian and Post-Jungian Studies: The Work of Andrew Samuels (Routledge, 2021)*, *The New Ancestors: Anthology of Contemporary Clinical/Theoretical Classics in Analytical Psychology* (Routledge, forthcoming 2021), and *Freedom after Freedom: Psychosocial Perspectives on Individuation and Liberty in a Globalized World* (Routledge, 2022). In 2006 he published with Prof. Mauro Magatti (Milano: Vita & Pensiero) an interview with John B. Thompson titled *Sociology in the 21st Century*.

He is the author of the following papers: The Consequences of Freedom (in *Jungian Perspectives on Indeterminate States: 'Betwixt and Between' Borders*, Routledge, 2020), 'The Numinous and the Fall of the Berlin Wall' (in *Jung's Red Book for Our Time: Searching for Soul Under Postmodern Conditions* – Volume

4, Chiron, 2020). He is also the editor of the forthcoming book *The Plural Turn: The Development of Jungian and Post-Jungian Studies and the Work of Andrew Samuels* (2020) and *Breakfast at Küsnacht: Conversations on C.G. Jung and Beyond* (2020)

PhD Title[1]: 'THE I+I': Individuation in a 21st century advanced and individualized society

PhD Abstract: In my work I propose a comparative study of Swiss psychoanalyst C.G. Jung's Individuation process and German Sociologist Ulrich Beck's Individualization theory, which will lead to merge the two into a new concept: the "I+I". The "I+I" (the concept of individuation in an individualized society), takes Beck's individualization theory as a valid picture of second modernity and merges it with Jung's individuation process. The "I+I" is an attempt to claim that to become free in late modernity, therefore to fulfil one's destiny, people need to individuate once being individualized. The novelty of such research might support current social theory and psychoanalytic research as well as to reinforce the discourse undertaken by psychosocial studies since the 90s and by relational psychoanalysis since the 80s. Therefore, a comparison as such can serve as a rejuvenation of Psychosocial studies (where Jung takes into account the psychic and Beck the social) and an opportunity to explore further the importance of the relational approach in contemporary psychoanalysis. I intend to underline that Jung's Individuation theory is a possible frame (not the only one, nor the best) to ascertain the lacks within Beck's theory of individualization (therefore traditional sociology). My conclusions will underline that: (i) Beck's research is fundamental to portraying and understanding second modernity; (ii) to claim that a renewed look at Jung's individuation process is fundamental in any attempt to examine our current epoch; (iii) it could be beneficial to employ relational psychoanalysis and psychosocial studies into current investigation, therefore to move to a relational-psychosocial approach.

Laner Cassar, PhD is a registered Clinical Psychologist, an IAAP Jungian Analyst and Gestalt Psychotherapist. He received his doctorate in Psychoanalytic Studies from Essex University, UK in 2016. He currently heads the Psychology department at the Gozo General hospital in Malta. He also works in private practice as an analyst in Malta. He is president of the Malta Developing Group within the IAAP as well as the president of the International Network for the Study of Waking Dream Therapy (INSWDT). He is author of the book C.G. Jung's Active Imagination and Robert Desoille's Directed Waking Dream: Bridging the Divide (Routledge, 2020).

PhD Title: Bridging imaginal pathways: The Jungian technique of active imagination and Robert Desoille's 'Rêve éveillé dirigé' method.

PhD Abstract: This theoretical study brings together Carl Jung's active imagination and Robert Desoille's "rêve éveillé dirigé/directed waking dream" method (RED). Such a rapprochement is twofold. First, it aims to study the historical development of these two approaches in Central Europe in the first half of the twentieth century. Second, it aims to explore their theoretical similarities and differences and proposes implications for a hybridised and integrated framework of clinical practice. The first section of the study contextualises Jung's active imagination and RED in the broader psychotherapeutic currents practised at the time. Furthermore, this work analyses them through the geo-historical background of twentieth-century France and Switzerland. It also goes on to investigate key historical intersecting points where Jung and Desoille, as well as their disciples, crossed paths. The second section of this study is a theoretical comparison between C. G. Jung's active imagination technique and Robert Desoille's directed waking dream method (RED). This work compares the spatial metaphors of interiority used by both Jung and Desoille to describe the traditional concept of inner psychic space in the waking dreams of Jung's active imagination and Desoille's RED. This study also attempts a broader theoretical comparison between the procedural aspects of both RED and active imagination by identifying commonalities and divergences between the two approaches. The comparison is built on a comparative methodology based on five operatively important categories chosen from the literature review. These are related to the therapeutic practice and procedures of both waking dreams and include: setting and preparation of the body, structure and directivity by the analyst/therapist, transferential and counter-transferential relationship, narratives, and interpretation. Such a comparison also helps to explore the implications for an integrated-hybridised framework of clinical practice, that is, a RED-based approach to active imagination that fills an important gap in post-Jungian writings on active visual imagination as well as offering a long-awaited acknowledgement of the RED method.

Martyna Chrzescijanska, PhD, a Lecturer at London Metropolitan University, School of Social Professions (UK) and author of *Psychogeotherapy. Revision of Therapeutic Space* (Routledge, 2020).

PhD Title: Psychogeography, psychotherapy and psychogeotherapy: A critique of containing space in therapeutic work

PhD Abstract: The thesis offers a critical exploration of the roles played by ideas of space and containment in psychotherapy. A wide range of existing approaches to the notion of therapeutic space in depth psychology is presented (particularly Freudian, post-Freudian, Jungian and post-Jungian perspectives). The dominant models of containment in psychotherapy are then interrogated. The thesis discusses these models from different perspectives, drawing on various disciplines, such as art, social studies, cultural studies and philosophy. Specifically, the thesis aims to employ approaches derived from psychogeography, with a focus on the praxis of 'aimless walking', in order to shed new light on classical concepts of therapeutic space and containment in depth psychology and psychotherapy. It is asked whether and how we can progress to consider alternative models of therapeutic space, leading to the proposal of what the author terms 'psychogeotherapy'. This fresh approach is not offered as an instant solution to the problems noted with existing approaches, nor are such approaches inappropriately dismissed. A feature of the thesis is its analysis of various psychogeographical personal testimonies. The thesis is to be considered not only a critical piece of writing, but also a fresh and creative account of the work of psychotherapy.

Clare Crellin, PhD is a United Kingdom Council for Psychotherapy Registered Psychoanalyst and retired Consultant Clinical Psychologist who was awarded her PhD in Psychoanalytical Studies by the University of Essex, UK, in 2012. During her career in the National Health Service UK, she served a three-year term of office as Chair of the Site for Contemporary Psychoanalysis, London, and subsequently served as External Examiner for the psychotherapy training of Re-Vision, London for seven years. Her current work is as psychotherapist and supervisor with Hospice Care Isle of Man. In her work and her range of interests, the practice of psychotherapy has always taken priority, balanced with theoretical and academic writing. She has a long-standing active interest in the History of Psychology and is on the Editorial Board of the British Psychological Society's periodical *History and Philosophy of Psychology*. She is the author of *Jung's Theory of Personality: a modern reappraisal*, Routledge 2014, and has published papers on historical topics.

PhD Title: Re-appraising C. G. Jung's personality theory

PhD Abstract: Outside Jungian analytical psychology, Jung is categorised as a personality theorist. Because, historically, evaluations of Jung's personality theory have given rise to myths, misrepresentations and misunderstandings about Jung's work, a reappraisal of his reputation as a personality theorist is long overdue. The resulting marginalisation of his theory of personality restricts Jung scholarship, limits opportunities for research, and minimises the public accessibility of Jungian psychotherapy. My approach is hermeneutical. By surveying more than is usual in what is defined as Jung's personality theory I reveal a far wider scope to his ideas on personality than is generally appreciated. I discuss criteria for evaluating theories of personality and develop a broader set of subjective and objective criteria that reveal the relevance and value of Jung's theory. I argue that Jung restores the sense of unity of personality and brings a transcendent angle, broadening the scope of personality theory. In the first section, I examine the place of religion in Jung's theory. I consider the close connection between Jung's work on alchemy and his key concepts: individuation and the self. I explore the links between Jung's use of active imagination in Liber Novus

(Jung's Red Book) and his typology, and examine the function of Jung's concept of the archetypes in the formative and transformative processes of personality development. The second section focuses on evaluation. I critically review the presentation of Jung's theory in textbooks of personality from the 1930s onwards and identify significant flaws in the representation of his life and theoretical ideas. I discuss their impact on Jung's reputation among psychologists. Finally, I apply my criteria to re-evaluating Jung's personality theory with particular focus on consciousness and the unconscious, and archetypes. I suggest possible directions for a programme of further evaluation and research.

Sukey Fontelieu, PhD attended the University of Essex and Pacifica Graduate Institute and is currently a Professor in the Jungian and Archetypal Studies Program at Pacifica. She has published a book, *The Archetypal Pan in America: Hypermasculinity and Terror* (Routledge 2018), and a number of papers on depth psychology. She has a private practice in Santa Barbara, CA.

PhD Title: Pan stalks America: Contemporary American anxieties and cultural complex theory

PhD Abstract: This study contributes to a better understanding of contemporary anxieties in American culture by applying meanings derived from mythology to panic inducing cultural phenomena. It asks if the Greek god Pan metaphorically exemplifies the archetypal core within an American cultural anxiety complex. The principal technical device used is Jung's method of amplification, rendering cultural material at a more psychologically substantial level. This hermeneutic research interprets primary sources and commentaries for three historical events. A pattern of escalating anxiety in America is posited as underlying the bullying and scapegoating that led to the 1999 Columbine massacre. In 2001, American reactions following the terrorist attack on 9/11 congealed into panic-driven legislation and escapism. Currently approximately 26,000 military personnel are raped by their peers, aided by apathy that allows a persecutory element within the military to remain in command. These problems fall within the mythological purview of Pan. Manifest destiny, exceptionalism, the historical domination of the Mideast, bullying in public schools, and the chain of command in the military are all examples of a dominant group negatively projecting onto an outgroup. This thesis found that the best predictor of the birth of a cultural complex is if a dominant group or culture has inadequate means to examine its own projections. Pan and his companion nymphs are envisioned here as both a defensive shell of "exceptionalism" and a core naiveté in American culture. Pan's compulsion into life is a symbolic expression of an archetype that was once alive in the bold spirit of America, but has rusted into paralysis due to a lack of initiative towards contemporary problems. Where the US once unconsciously identified with the most courageous and expansive in the Pan archetype, now the archetype of panic stalks America.

Kevin Lu, PhD is a Senior Lecturer and Director of the MA Jungian and Post-Jungian Studies in the Department of Psychosocial and Psychoanalytic Studies, University of Essex. He is a former member of the Executive Committee of the International Association for Jungian Studies and a member of Adjunct Faculty at Pacifica Graduate Institute. His publications include articles and chapters on Jung's relationship to the discipline of history, Arnold J. Toynbee's use of analytical psychology, critical assessments of the theory of cultural complexes, sibling relationships in the Chinese/Vietnamese Diaspora, racial hybridity, and Jungian perspectives on graphic novels and their adaptation to film.

Phil McCash, PhD is an Associate Professor in the Centre for Lifelong Learning, University of Warwick, and Course Director for the MA Career, Education, Information and Guidance in Higher Education. He is also a Fellow of the National Institute for Career Education and Counselling, and currently edits the Journal of the National Institute for Career Education and Counselling. He is interested in the re-imagination of career development in the workplace, education, and wider community and has pioneered a research-informed approach to this subject. His work focuses on career theory, cultural and transformative learning, career education, coaching, career coaching, narrative theory, and depth psychology.

PhD Title: Career development at depth: A critical evaluation of career development theory from the perspective of analytical psychology

PhD Abstract: In this thesis, it is argued that Jungian and post-Jungian perspectives, in contrast to those of Freud and Adler, have been neglected in classic and contemporary career development theories. This omission is addressed by undertaking a critical evaluation of career development theory in relation to analytical psychology. The primary research strategy adopted is a systematic and critical comparison of the two literatures. Canonical and contemporary texts from within career studies are selected, focusing on seven areas of career theory: cultural systems, personality, career types, career strategies, narrative, life course development, and learning. These are critically evaluated using concepts from analytical psychology. Specifically, the work of Jung and post-Jungian scholars is deployed in relation to individuation and the key themes of: projection, persona, typology, archetypal image, personal myth, vocation, and transformational learning. The original contribution is a post-Jungian evaluation and reimagination of career development theory. It is suggested that cultural career theory can be enhanced by considering the role of projection. In addition, it is argued that self-concept career theory is enriched by Jung's structural model of the psyche; and the literature on career types can be broadened to include typology. It is further proposed that individuation offers a more critical take on career strategies; and personal myth extends the narrative turn in career studies. Finally, it is claimed that developmental theory is illuminated by an analytical psychological view of vocation; and career learning augmented by transformational learning theory. Overall, it is argued that 'career' means to carry life, and through personal myth, weave together the golden threads that connect us all.

Andrew Samuels has, for almost 40 years, evolved a clinical blend of post-Jungian, relational psychoanalytic and humanistic approaches to therapy work. He is recognised internationally as one of the leading commentators from a psychotherapeutic perspective on political and social problems. His work on the father, sexuality, spirituality and countertransference has also been widely appreciated.

He is a Training Analyst of the Society of Analytical Psychology and was chair of the UK Council for Psychotherapy 2009–2012. He is a co-founder of Psychotherapists and Counsellors for Social Responsibility. He was Professor of Analytical Psychology at Essex (until 2019) and holds visiting chairs at New York, London Roehampton and Macau Universities.

Samuels' books have been translated into 19 languages and include *Jung and the Post-Jungians* (1985), *A Critical Dictionary of Jungian Analysis* (1986), *The Father* (1986), *The Plural Psyche* (1989), *Psychopathology* (1989), *The Political Psyche* (1993), *Politics on the Couch* (2001), *Relational Psychotherapy, Psychoanalysis and Counselling: Appraisals and Reappraisals* (2014), *Passions, Persons, Psychotherapy, Politics* (2014) and *A New Therapy for Politics* (2015). A selection of video lectures may be found on www.andrewsamuels.com.

J.A. Swan, PhD, trained formally as a painter, and later qualified as a Psychologist in clinical and transpersonal modalities. She studied at the University of Pennsylvania, PAFA, and Moore College of Art & Design in the United States and received a research PhD from the Centre for Psychoanalytic Studies in England. She has worked as a university lecturer and as a therapist in private practice. Her research interests combine Archaeology, Architecture, Religious Art, and Jungian Theory. She currently works as a writer and visual artist.

PhD Title: On the spirit and the self: Chagall, Jung, and religion

PhD Abstract: The thesis, now a similar-titled book (Chiron, 2019), compliments and extends the current scholarship surrounding the Russian-French artist, Marc Chagall's (1887–1985) place in the history of twentieth-century art as a religious artist. Central to this study is the psychic process of individuation and the ways in which images created by artists appear to depict the deeper changes in our collective human existence. A new perspective on Chagall's well-documented creative output is presented through the application of Jungian theory: Jung identifies a separation between the cultural and historical underpinnings of natal faith, or creed, and the presence of an internal, personal spirituality, or religious attitude. Applying this theoretical approach defines Chagall's creative connection to his own natal Hasidic faith whilst clarifying the interiority of his religious experiences on a universal level. That creative development may be explored through the visual patterns of sacred transformative imagery is, too, a new approach in Chagallian scholarship, elevating two original key concepts: the 'Chagallian sacred-secular binary', illustrated potently in the Artist's lifelong treatment of crucifixion imagery; and, the 'Chagallian temenos sites', architectural structures and their settings that function in space to celebrate Biblical-themed art and religious life. An emphasis upon the use of primary source materials – including letters, journal articles, speeches, and autobiography – provides the Artist's personal voice on the topics of faith and religion across the twentieth century's historic and social changes. The study is illuminated by 90 reproductions of Chagall's paintings, Bible Series etchings and lithographs, stained glass installations, and the author's photographs of architectural sites, to support the perspective that, like Jung, Chagall is among the most prolific and significant religious communicators during the twentieth century.

Huan Wang, PhD graduated from PPS University of Essex. She was a Psychotherapist for five years in the clinical department of a hospital in Wuhan, a city in China. At present, her research interests mainly focus on the effects of political interventions on relationships within family, and how to address the individual position in a collectivism setting.

Her PhD dissertation is on femininity and masculinity in romantic relationships in contemporary China. The study is mainly from Jungian and post-Jungian perspectives, and focuses on how young Chinese couples have been affected by traditional values, Westernization and the One-child policy.

PhD Title: Clinical aspects of traditional and contemporary narratives of femininity and masculinity in intimate relationships in China today: Jungian and post-Jungian perspectives

PhD Abstract: To understand and deal with difficulties of contemporary marriages in China, I investigate the notions of masculinity and femininity as they are related to intimate relationships, from depth psychological perspectives. I argue that these notions are not universal, but are, rather, culturally/socially assigned. By interviewing Chinese couples and amplifying a Chinese opera – Peony Pavilion – I point out that, in China, the feminine and the masculine aspects of emotional behaviours are not as clearly divided and opposite to each other as they are in the West. I address how sexuality and aggression have played an active role in romantic relationships and fostered the process of individuation for both men and women, and how relationships with one's own mother and father have influenced this process.

An examination of clinical materials offers further proof of these arguments. My conclusion is that the Chinese psyche today is experiencing a transition from the compliance of collectivism to the awareness of individuation, and that the rediscovery of the notion of integrity will make young Chinese people independent individuals and bring a new approach to their marriage.

Note

1 Proposed title.

Index

A.A. (Alcoholics Anonymous) 6, 181, 231; recovery 15, 16, 18, 19, 20, 21, 22, 23, 24
abortion 159, 164, 175
abstinence 15, 17, 24, 53n3, 231; in the first five years 20; long term 20–23
academic supervision xiii, xiv; *see also* Part II
acceptance 7, 21, 23–24, 58–59, 106, 166, 228
acculturation 87
active imagination 8, 71–82, 111, 192, 193, 207n3, 222, 235–236, 237
Adam and Eve, allegory of 60–61
Adams, Michael Vannoy 117, 122
adaptation 65, 67, 161, 229n1
addiction 5–6, 16, 20, 21, 22, 23–24, 182
Adler, Alfred 60; reception/adoption of his ideas by Jung 129–131, 133–134, 139, 203; theory of fictions of 132–133; triangulation with Freud and Jung 131–132, 139
Adler, Gerhard 215, 222
Adorno, Theodor W. 7, 57–69
agency 9, 29, 46, 68, 129, 138, 140, 163
agriculture 40, 41, 42, 48, 52–53n1
alchemy 3, 8, 79, 100–111, 147, 198, 199, 220, 237
alcohol dependence 5, 15–24, 231
Alcoholics Anonymous (A.A.) 6, 181, 231; recovery 15, 16, 18, 19, 20, 21, 22, 23, 24
alienation 61, 78, 118–119, 120
altitudo 76–77
Amazon 31, 35n2
American culture 113, 120, 122, 238
amplification technique 102, 103, 105, 110, 238

analytical psychology 50, 183, 191, 193, 199, 202, 209, 215, 221; and personal myth 129–140; Samuels' personal contribution to 222–225
anima and animus 50–51, 53n5, 77, 226
anthropology 78, 87; archetypal twinning process 6, 38–53; evolutionary 40, 47; feminist 47, 49; matrilineal line 39–46
Anti-Apartheid Movement 213, 217
anxieties 78, 115, 118, 167, 208; cultural complex 113–124, 238
aphorisms, of Theodor Adorno 58, 59, 60, 61, 64–65, 66
appearance 76–77, 146, 147, 152, 161
Appraising the Role of the Individual in Political and Social Change Processes 3
archaic identity 60
archetypal expression 143, 152
archetypal imagery 105, 147, 150–151, 239
archetype of the Self 152
archetypes, Jung's theory of 10, 69n13, 114, 115, 116, 237; alchemy and individuation 103, 105, 110; Chagall, Jung and religion 146–147, 148, 150
ascents 76, 77, 78, 80
assimilation 87, 105, 161, 174
Astrum 109
Augustine of Hippo 72, 73, 74–75
authenticity 76, 148, 163, 167, 175, 209, 229n1
authoring 138–139
authority 7, 73, 166, 172, 221, 222; and Adorno 58–59, 62, 68

Index

autonomy, personal 3, 5, 10, 68, 109, 115, 219; and containing space 89–93, 96; and marriage in China 163, 164–165

Bachelard, Gaston 75, 76, 79
Bachofen, Johan Jakob 40, 42
barbarism 40
Bassil-Morozow, Helena 26, 29, 30, 31, 183, 232
Beck, Ulrich 3, 4, 66, 219, 235
Beck-Gernsheim, Elisabeth 3, 4, 66, 219
becoming 8, 76, 77–80, 80–81
Beebe, John 189, 209, 227; and marriage in China 162, 163, 164, 166–167, 171, 172
being 8, 74, 76, 77–80, 80–81
being in the world 65, 67
Benjamin, Jessica 7, 58–59, 64, 68, 168, 215
Bible, the 7, 51, 72, 149
binary gender 45, 168
Bion, Wilfred 91, 93
blogs 27, 30, 34
borders 8, 86–89, 93, 143
boundaries 8, 10, 23, 43, 46, 163, 169; and containing space 86–89, 92, 93, 94, 95, 96, 97
bride price 48–49
Briffault, Robert 40, 42, 48
broken individualisation 4, 11n8
Burckhardt, Titus 100, 101, 110

Calhoun, Cheshire 163, 164
cannibalism 43, 48
capitalism 2, 58, 67
carrier of life 137–138
castration 39, 42–43, 50, 59, 61
Centre for Psychoanalytical Studies, Essex University 1
Ceppa, Leonardo 58, 59, 60, 64, 65, 66–67, 68
C.G. Jung Institut, Zürich 186, 189, 234
Chagall, Marc 9–10, 143–153, 155–158, 206, 240, 241
China: female images in 161–162; integration in 160–165; integration and integrity 171–176; integrity in marriage 165–167; marriages as relationship beyond gender difference 167–171; psychotherapy training and qualification 159–160; reproduction policy 159
Christ, Jesus 10, 72, 78, 106, 149, 151, 152
Christianity 73, 89
'civilisation' 39, 40–41, 44, 50
clarification 7, 59, 61, 62, 65, 66, 68
clinical psychology 198, 235, 236
Collected Works 77, 78, 102, 106, 130, 136, 147
collective unconscious 8, 115, 117; and Adorno 66, 67, 69n13; alchemy and individuation 100, 103, 104, 105, 106, 108–109; Chagall, Jung and religion 147, 150, 151
collectivism 10, 161, 164, 171, 175, 241
colonisation 87, 92, 96
Columbine High School shootings 114, 118–121, 122, 238
combination 161, 173, 174, 228
communal systems of exchange 40
communism 2, 45, 174; matrilineal 41, 43, 45; primitive 41
compensation 5, 7, 62, 66, 130
competition 43, 166, 215
complementarity 215
complexes: castration 50; cultural anxiety 113, 114, 117–122, 123, 238; inferiority 64, 129, 132, 189; male supremacist 48–49; mother 50, 173, 227; Oedipus 39, 43, 132; saviour 94; superiority 60, 132; theory of 116; *see also* cultural complex theory
Confessions 72, 73
conflict 2, 10, 52–53, 64, 68, 134; and contemporary American anxieties 114, 116, 117; in marriage in China 160, 161, 166, 168, 169–170, 173, 174; and twenty-first century psychoanalysis 220, 224, 229n1
consciousness 58, 60, 61, 67, 69n13, 104, 105; and archetypes 114; disturbed state of 114; ego- 22, 50; false 67; higher level of 97; and life-lines 133; and linearity 137
Consequences of Freedom, The 62, 234
constructivism 15
containing space in therapeutic work, critique of 86–97
containment 8, 24, 42, 75, 171, 196; and contemporary American anxieties 119, 120; in PhD abstracts 233, 236

contamination, of therapeutic process 96, 97n2
contemporary American anxieties 113–124
contractual supervisory style xiii
Corbin, Henry 109, 110
cosmology 8, 91, 100, 101–102, 103–104
counselling 4–5, 95, 184, 214
counter transference 186, 222, 225–228
Creation myths 7, 38, 101, 102, 233
creationism 7, 39, 40, 42–43, 44, 45, 46, 50, 51, 52
creative writing 147, 149
critical theory 58, 59, 65, 68
Crucifixion, the 10, 147, 150, 151–152, 240
cultural anxiety complex 113, 114, 117–122, 123, 238
cultural complex theory 9, 113–124
cultural complexes 9; in America 117–122; post-Jungian theory of 116–117
cultural history 8, 91, 100
cultural materialism 44
cultural norms 40
Cultural Revolution 164, 170, 172
cultural unconscious 116, 117
culture: dominant 113, 118, 123; golden threads of 129, 138–139, 140, 239
Curran, James 29, 31

Daily Mail 31–32
daimon 68
dangers 79, 81, 87–88, 95, 96, 103, 120, 138
Darwin, Charles 40; *see also* evolution
death 18, 39, 45, 107, 109
defence mechanisms 20, 87, 88, 95, 168, 216–217
defensiveness, and uncontained states of mind 93–97
degradation 21, 22, 53n3
delimitation, of borders and boundaries 87
dependence, on psychoactive substances 5, 15–24, 231
depth psychology 2, 8, 110, 115, 146, 160, 183; containing space 86–87, 89, 90–91, 92–93, 94, 97; PhD abstracts 236, 237, 239; tabloid trickster 32, 34, 35; twenty-first century psychoanalysis 222, 223, 224
depths 8, 74, 76, 77–80, 80–81

Der Sturm 1920 155
descent: rules of 44, 47, 49; into the unconscious 8, 81; into the underworld 77, 78–79, 81
desegregation 161
Desoille, Robert 8, 71, 72, 74–75, 76–77, 78–79, 80, 81, 235
destiny 68, 118, 120, 235, 238
detoxification 19, 20
dialectics 45, 72, 76–77
dialogue 10, 63, 140, 167, 171, 173, 192, 202
diffusionism 43, 44
directed waking dream 80, 235
directional supervisory style xiii
disagreements 10, 161, 162, 166, 167, 170, 174, 208
disinheritance, psychological effects of 49–51
displacement 49, 52–53n1
Divine spark 109
doctoral supervision xiii, xiv; *see also* Part II
dominant culture 113, 118, 123
dream interpretation 103, 105, 160
dreams 2, 64, 93, 115, 143, 205, 207n3, 222; and alchemy and individuation 104, 106–107; waking 75–77, 79, 81, 236
drug dependence 16, 24
drug use 5–6, 17, 20, 182
dualism 91
Durkheim, Émile 3, 64, 69n13
dynamic unconscious archetypes 105

eclecticism 1–2, 223
ecopsychology 92, 97
ego 63, 65, 81, 116, 137, 231; and alchemy and individuation 104, 105; and containing space 90, 92, 93, 97n1; and marriage in China 166, 169; psychology of 67
ego-consciousness 22, 50
emancipation, to liberation from 7, 57–69, 168, 226, 229n1
emergence, in work of Chagall 149–150, 151, 152
emotions 4–5, 17, 20, 74, 88, 136, 143–144, 221; and contemporary American anxieties 114, 116, 118, 119–120, 121, 122
enantiodromia 19, 23, 132, 136

Engels, Friedrich 40, 46, 47, 49
enjoyment 58
entertainment 19, 27, 28, 33, 35n10, 232
epistemology 71, 77, 136, 139, 171
equal opportunities 51
Eros 6, 80, 233; and laws of inheritance 38–39, 41, 42, 44, 45, 46, 49–50, 52, 52–53n1, 53n4, 53n5
escape 17, 18, 24, 28, 80–81, 121
essence 76, 90
Essex School 1
ethics 9, 95, 96, 162, 163, 171, 226, 232
evolution 40, 44, 47
exogamy 43
extended family 46, 165, 169
extroversion 64

Facebook 27, 28, 29, 30, 31
false consciousness 67
family 41, 43, 44, 47
fantasy 4, 11n6, 80, 81, 115, 119, 166; and critique of Adorno 64, 67; and containing space 87, 88–89, 90, 91, 93, 96, 97
fatalism 9, 17, 129, 138, 140
fate 34, 68, 138, 195
father, the 1, 39, 40, 41, 42–43, 43–44, 46, 47, 48, 50
fear 8, 20, 23, 39, 52–53n1, 61, 78, 81; and containing space 87, 88, 94; and contemporary American anxieties 118, 120, 123, 124
female images, in China 161–162
female line, passing of lineage and inheritance through 38, 39–46, 47
'feminine' agency 46
feminine principle 169, 170, 215
femininity 46, 168, 241
feminism 7, 45, 47, 49, 86, 189, 215, 223
fictions, Adler's theory of 132–133
filtering 10, 27, 29, 148–149
'first' and 'other(s), relationship between 38–39, 51
first-born 6, 38, 40, 47, 48, 51, 233
Foucault, Michel 71, 73
fourth gender 46
fragmented self 90–91, 92
Frankfurt School 3, 7, 58, 60, 62, 64, 68, 219
freedom 4, 65, 111, 121, 122–123, 187; and laws of inheritance 41, 42, 48, 51

Freud, Sigmund: and Adorno 7, 57–69; on the father 39; on incest taboo 42–43; on individuality 92; and neuroses 4; on psycho-sexual development 39; triangulation with Adler and Jung 131–132, 139
friendship 166
functionalism 43–44

gender 38, 39, 42, 44, 45, 46, 50, 51, 52, 168
Genesis Myth 7, 51
Giaccardi, Chiara 4, 11n8, 189–190
Giddens, Anthony 3, 4, 219, 224
God 24, 134; active imagination and *Rêve éveillé dirigé* 73, 74, 78, 80; and Adorno 60, 63, 67, 68; and alchemy and individuation 101, 102, 103, 106; and laws of inheritance 40, 47, 50, 52
Goethe, Johann Wolfgang von 74, 79, 82n5, 104
golden threads of culture 9, 129, 138–139, 140, 239
grounded theory 5, 16
group identity 117
guiding fictions 129, 130, 132, 133–134, 139

happiness 4, 7, 106, 165; in critique of Adorno 57–58, 61, 62, 64, 65, 68
Harris, Eric 119, 120
heart, the 67, 72, 73, 74, 77, 102, 148
heights 8, 76, 77–80, 80–81
hermeneutics 33, 104, 106, 133, 237, 238
heteronormativity 46
Hibiscus Town 170, 171
hierarchical primogeniture 51
Hillman, James 2, 129, 220; active imagination and *Rêve éveillé dirigé* 75, 78, 79–80; in critique of Adorno 64, 65, 66
Hogg, Michael A. 87
Horkheimer, Max 68, 68n2
human agency 9, 29, 46, 68, 129, 138, 140, 163
human rights 39, 89
hypermasculinity 9, 120

Id 60, 93, 97n1
identity 8, 29, 224, 232; archaic 60; autonomous 89–93; dreaming 93; gender 168; group 117; and integrity

163; Marxian predetermined
'objective' 66; modern 73; national 87,
89; psychotherapeutic 88; self- 188;
self-contained 89–93; self-invented 3,
4, 219; social 88; uncertainty- 87
Iliaster 109
image hyper-saturation 10, 148–149
image-making 147, 149, 150, 151
imagery, visual 10, 143–153, 155–158
imaginal world 64, 75, 235; and Chagall,
Jung and religion 10, 143–144,
144–145, 146, 148, 149
immortality 8, 100, 101, 107, 109
impingements 90–91, 93, 94, 96–97
In Front of the Picture, 1968–1971 156
inauthenticity 76–77, 164, 172
independence, psychological 41, 42, 49,
167, 170, 172, 175
indigenous cultures 41, 42, 45
indignation 175–176
individual complexes *see* complexes
individual psychology 58–59, 130, 134,
203, 204
individualisation 4, 5, 11n8
individuality 65, 89, 90, 92, 104–105,
134, 162
individuation 9–10, 80, 184, 185, 209,
222, 226; and alchemy 8, 100–111,
199; and Adorno 58, 63, 65; and
containing space 91, 92; and Chagall,
Jung and religion 147, 149, 150, 151,
152; and marriage in China 160, 170,
174, 175; and personal myth 133, 134,
137, 138, 139
inferiority complex 64, 129, 132, 189
infinite diversity 109
inheritance, laws of 6, 38–53, 53n4, 186,
233, 234
inner self-knowledge *see* interiority
inner space/inner world 2, 72, 75–76, 91,
96, 167, 220
instinct 57, 59, 60, 67, 109, 151
integration 1–2, 64, 67, 68, 86–87, 88,
91, 93, 94; Chinese notion of 10,
160–162, 165; and integrity 171–176;
intercultural 87
integrity: in depth 172; and integration
171–176; in marriage 165–167;
psychological notion of 163–165
interiority 8, 66–67, 91, 145–146, 236,
241; and active imagination and *Rêve
éveillé dirigé* 71–72, 72–81, 82n1, 82n2

internalisation 7, 58, 59, 62
Internet 148, 173, 174, 232; and tabloid
trickster 27, 28, 30, 31, 32
interpretivism 33, 104, 106, 133, 237, 238
intimate relationships 10, 160, 163, 165,
166, 167, 171, 241
intrapersonal anxiety 115
Introductory Lectures 59
introjection 88, 93
introversion 64, 203
invasive aggression 49
inwardness 64, 71, 73, 74
isolation 20, 23–24, 202, 231

Jameson, Fredric 76
Jesus Christ 10, 72, 78, 106, 149,
151, 152
journalism 6, 28, 30, 32, 34, 183–184;
popular newspaper/tabloid 27, 30,
32–33, 34, 232, 233
Jung, Carl Gustav: and Adler's ideas
129–131, 133–134; on alchemy 8,
100–111; archetypes theory of *see*
archetypes, Jung's theory of; complex
theory of 116; on cosmology 8,
101–102; on myth 9, 113, 114–116; on
personal myth 134–139; personality
theory of 8, 100, 107, 108, 110, 111,
199, 237; and religion and Chagall
9–10, 143–153, 155–158; triangulation
with Adler and Freud 131–132
Jung and the Post-Jungians 1, 202, 223
*Jungian Perspectives on Indeterminate
States* 1
Jungian psychology *see* analytical
psychology

Katabasis 77, 78–79, 81
Kimbles, Samuel 113, 114, 116–117, 122
Klebold, Dylan 119, 120
Klein, Jessie 120
knowledge 7, 33, 117; in critique of
Adorno 59, 60, 61, 62, 65, 66, 68;
self- 8, 73, 163; universal 91; *see also*
interiority
Kristeva, Julia 50, 87, 91
Kurgan tribes 48

laissez-faire supervisory style xiii
Laws of Inheritance (book) 39, 46
laws of inheritance (concept) 6, 38–53,
53n4, 186, 233, 234

Leveson Inquiry 27, 28, 32, 232
Lévi-Strauss, Claude 44
liberation, from emancipation to 7, 57–69, 168, 226, 229n1
libido 133
life course development 137–138, 239
life-lines 133, 139
lifespan 143, 145, 146, 149, 151
lifestyle 20, 23, 24, 29, 41, 48, 214
L'Obsession, 1943 158
localisation, of psychotherapy 160–161, 174
love 1, 5, 50, 59, 102, 166, 168, 170, 171, 173, 228

madness 50, 124, 175
MailOnline 28, 30, 31–32
male supremacist complex 48–49
mandalas 94, 97n2, 103, 108, 110
Marcuse, Herbert 4, 68n2
marital difficulties 10, 161, 167, 169
marriage in China, as psychological relationship 10, 159–176
Marx, Karl 43, 45, 49, 66, 67, 160
masculinity 49, 168, 241
mask 134, 172 *see also* persona
mass media 29, 30, 31
materialism 17, 40, 43, 44, 59, 137
matrilineality 38, 39–46, 46–49
matrilocal descent rules 47
Mayan civilisation 49
meditation 62, 73, 110
Memories, Dreams, Reflections 79, 81, 129, 135, 136
mental disorders 9
mental health 159, 172, 175
mentoring, by Andrew Samuel 1, 188, 189–190, 193
Mercurius Britanicus 30
methodology, research 15–16, 192, 236
methods: research 33, 34, 111; therapeutic 160, 192; waking-dream 71, 72, 75, 76
millennial anxiety 118
mind 35, 60, 69n13, 73, 87, 91, 92, 93, 109; states of 15, 93–97
Minima Moralia 57, 59, 69n4
misogyny 7, 9, 42, 52–53n1, 53n3
modern identity 73
monotheism 38, 45, 48, 51
moral imagination 10, 173

Morgan, Lewis Henry 39, 40, 41, 42, 44, 45, 46
mother, the 42, 45–46, 47, 50, 64, 173, 227
mutuality: and acceptance of authority 7, 58–59, 62; in psychoanalysis 15, 65; in relationships 23, 24, 228
mysticism 73–74, 110
mythology 115, 135, 200, 238
myths: creation 7, 38, 101, 102, 233; Genesis 7, 51; of Pan 120, 122–124, 238; personal 9, 129, 134–139, 139–140, 203–204, 239

Narcotics Anonymous (N.A.) 6, 20, 21, 22, 23–24
narcotics use 5–6, 17, 20, 182
natal faith 147, 149, 152, 241
national identity 87, 89
natura primitiva 7, 60, 61
Negroponte, Nicholas 31
Nekyia 77–78
neo-conservativism 9
neo-evolutionism 44
neo-Jungian psychology 1, 10n2, 189, 223; critique of Theodor Adorno 7, 57–69
Neolithic era 6, 40, 41, 42, 45, 46, 47, 48–49, 49–50, 51, 145
neuroses 4, 69n13, 105, 130, 131, 164, 168
neurotic constitution, The 130
New Testament 72
New Therapy for Politics, A 2, 11n4
news 27–28, 30, 31–32, 33, 34, 119
News of the World 32–33, 34, 232
night sea journey 77–78
9/11 terrorist attacks 114, 118, 121–122, 238
1984 170, 171

Oedipus complex 39, 43, 132
Old Testament (OT) Genesis myth 7, 51
one-child policy, in China 159, 164, 165, 166, 173, 241
oneness, of the psyche *see* unity, of the psyche
ontology 68, 89
order 49, 87, 91
OT (Old Testament) Genesis myth 7, 51
'other', the 4, 7, 63, 87, 165, 226

pain 10, 21, 24, 80, 87, 88, 93, 121, 152, 162
Palaeolithic era 40, 41, 42, 44, 45–46, 49, 51
Palaeolithic–Neolithic kin structures 6
Pan, myths of 120, 122–124, 238; *see also* contemporary American anxieties
panic 9, 113, 114, 116, 121–122, 123, 124, 238
Papadopoulos, Renos 1
Paracelsus 101, 102
pastoral society 41, 48
pastoral supervisory style xiii
pathology 50, 59, 75, 124, 164, 216
patrilineality 6, 46–49, 234
pedagogy 132, 139, 233
Pentagon, 9/11 terrorist attack on 114, 118
persona 23, 117, 162, 172, 203, 239; and critique of Adorno 64, 69n13; and personal myth 133, 134, 139; *see also* mask
personal autonomy 3, 5, 10, 115, 163, 164–165, 219; and containing space 89, 91, 92
personal myth 9, 129, 134–139, 139–140, 203–204, 239
personality theory, of C. G. Jung 8, 100, 107, 108, 110, 111, 199, 237
phantasy *see* fantasy
philosophy 8, 22, 72, 91; and alchemy and individuation 107, 109, 110; and personal myth 132, 134, 138
pleasure principle 58
Plural Psyche, The (book) 2, 143, 148, 202
plural psyche (concept) 2, 223–224
pluralism 1–11, 57, 66, 132, 173, 192; and twenty-first century psychoanalysis 215, 216, 221, 222, 223–224, 229n1
pluralistic psychology 131, 139
Poetics of Space 75
political agency 29
Political Psyche, The (book) 2, 183, 216, 227
political psyche (concept) 2
politics 1–11, 33–34, 64, 183, 207; and containing space 86, 87, 88; of Jungian studies 221–222, 224–225, 227; and twenty-first century psychoanalysis 214, 216, 218, 219, 220

Politics on the Couch 2
popular newspaper journalism 27, 30, 32–33, 34, 232, 233
positivism 15, 136
post-Jungian theory of cultural complexes 116–117
Postmodernism (book) 76
postmodernism (concept) 76, 82n7
pragmatic logic 107
precipitating depths 77–81
press regulation 28, 32, 34, 232, 233
primitive communism 41
primogeniture 6, 7, 233, 234; and laws of inheritance 38–39, 40, 42, 43, 45, 46, 48, 49–50, 51, 52
'prize fighter' metaphor 18–19
projection 137, 146, 239; and alchemy and individuation 102–103, 107, 110; and containing space 87, 88, 95; and contemporary American anxieties 115, 117, 119, 120, 121
property ownership 6, 41, 48–49, 49–50, 52
psyche: plural 2, 223–224; political 2; spatial 93; unity of the *see* unity, of the psyche
psychic islands *see* complexes
psychic laws 67
psychic qualities 67, 75
psychoactive substances, recovery from dependence on 15–24
psychoanalytic research 16, 235
psychological independence 41, 42, 49, 167, 170, 172, 175
psychological interior *see* interiority
psychological relationship, marriage in China as 159–176
psychology: analytical *see* analytical psychology; clinical 198, 235, 236; depth *see* depth psychology; eco- 92, 97; ego 67; individual 58–59, 130, 134, 203, 204; Jungian *see* analytical psychology; pluralistic 131, 139; *see also* Jung, Carl Gustav
Psychology of the unconscious 135
psychosocial studies 2, 3, 5, 63, 189, 235; and twenty-first century psychoanalysis 217, 218–219, 223
psychotherapeutic identity 88
psychotherapy, and alchemy 105–106

quitting, of alcohol and drug misuse 15, 18–23, 231–232

Rangell, Leo 164
rape 'epidemic', in United States military 114, 122
reason 57, 58, 63, 68, 73, 74, 105, 107
recovery, from dependence on psychoactive substances 15–24
Red Book, The 72, 74–75, 77, 78, 80, 81, 202, 238
redtops 27–28, 29, 30, 31, 32–33, 34, 232; see also *Sun, The*
reductionism 110, 132
Reed, Evelyn 40, 42–43, 44, 46, 48, 49
regeneration 45, 105, 145
regulation, of the press 28, 32, 34, 232, 233
relatedness, principle of 169, 170, 215
relational psychoanalysis 65, 189, 235; and twenty-first century psychoanalysis 216, 218–219, 223, 228
relationships: of addicts 17–18, 22, 23, 24; intimate/romantic 10, 160, 163, 165, 166, 167, 171, 241; with Samuels *see* Part II; social 4, 5; therapeutic 95, 96, 110
religion 64, 66, 67, 105–106; and Chagall and Jung 9–10, 143–153, 155–158
Renaissance 89–90, 91, 101, 102
repetition, in work of Chagall 149, 151
reproduction, Chinese government policy on 159
research methodology 15–16, 192, 235–236
research methods 33, 34, 111
Rêve éveillé dirigé 8
rewards 21, 22–23, 24, 80
romantic relationships 10, 160, 163, 165, 166, 167, 171, 241

sacred archetypal images 147
sacred geometry 89, 91, 97n2
St. Augustine 72, 73, 74–75
St. Teresa 72, 74
salvation 78, 89, 170
same-sex twins 38
Samuels, Andrew: as activist 213–214, 217; contribution to analytical psychology 222–224; on anti-Semitism 216–217; books that have influenced 218–219; on complementarity 215; emotionally constrained background 214–215; on the father 225, 227–228; influence of feminism 215; on good-enough all-rounders 220–222; attraction to Hermes 215, 216; and humanistic and integrative psychotherapy 217; on Jungian analysis 222, 223, 228; on neo-fascism 225–227; on neo-Jungians 223; parents of 214, 227; on plural psyche/pluralism 215, 223–224; and politics 214, 220, 224–225; on post-Jungian analytical psychology 215; principles stemming from his personal psychology 215; on contribution to psychoanalysis 222–224; on psychoanalysis in the twenty-first century 228; on psychosocial studies 219; Psychotherapists and Counsellors for Social Responsibility 214; as relational-Jungian 218–219; relations between women and men 214–215; on societal role for psychoanalysts 220; as student radical 214; in Swaziland 213–214; on themes that continue to preoccupy him 218; attraction to the Trickster 215–216; on the unconscious 220, 224, 226, 229n1
savagery 40
saviour complex 94
second-born twins 38
security 1, 42, 60, 118, 160, 167, 172, 228
sedentary fertility 49
self, the 58, 63, 73, 74, 102, 224, 231, 237; and alchemy and individuation 103, 105; archetype of 152; autonomous 89, 92, 93, 96; and containing space 87, 89, 90, 91, 92, 97n1; fragmented 90–91, 92; and mandala symbols 108; and marriage in China 163, 165; and personal myth 136, 137–138; on the spirit and 9–10, 143–153, 240–241
Self Portrait with a Clock 157
self-containment 88, 89–93
self-curation 31
self-identity 188
self-invented identity 3, 4, 219
self-knowledge 8, 73, 163
separation 66, 105, 108, 150, 223, 229n1, 233, 240; and laws of inheritance

38, 41, 42, 49, 53n5; and marriage in China 160, 164–165, 169, 174
setting, therapeutic 15, 87, 94–95, 96–97, 97n2, 236
Shamdasani, Sonu 65, 135, 136, 202
Singer, Thomas 113, 114, 116, 117
smartphones 27, 30
soaring heights 77–80, 80–81
social adaptation 65, 175
social agency 29, 46
social identity 88
social laws 67
social media 27, 28–29, 30, 31
social relationships 4, 5
Society of Analytical Psychology 181, 217, 227
sociology 3, 4, 5, 6, 15, 33, 188, 219–220, 234, 235; and critique of Adorno 57, 59, 60, 64, 67, 68, 69n13
soul 67, 89, 90, 101, 189; and active imagination and *Rêve éveillé dirigé* 73, 75, 76, 77, 78, 79–80, 82n6
spatial metaphors, of interiority 8, 71, 75–76, 87, 236; *altitudo* 76–77; precipitating depths 77–81; soaring heights 77–80, 80–81; Theatre of Memory 89–90, 91
spatial psyche 93
spatial vertical dialectics 76–77
spirit, and the self 9–10, 143–153, 155–158
spirituality 8, 23–24, 66, 67, 214, 223, 240, 241; and active imagination and *Rêve éveillé dirigé* 72–73, 74, 82n2
spiritus contra spiritum 182
splitting 52–53n1, 119, 168–169, 221, 229n1, 234
Stages of life 7, 60
states of mind 15, 93–97
Stories about the Ming Dynasty 174
strengths 21–22, 23, 24, 164, 169
structuralism 43, 44
structure, provided by an academic supervisor xiii
subjectivity 5, 73, 90, 93, 121, 167
sublimation 59, 60, 61, 62
substance use 15–24
suffering 8, 51, 87, 93, 115
Sun, The 26–27, 27–28, 29, 30, 32–33, 34, 35, 184, 232
superego 21, 164
superiority complex 60, 132

supervision, doctoral xiii, xiv; *see also* Part II
surface 76–77
symbolic, the 10, 50, 144, 146, 152
symbols 10, 45, 63, 67, 114; and alchemy and individuation 106, 107, 108–109; and Chagall, Jung and religion 144, 145, 146, 153n12
Symbols of Transformation 78, 103, 135

tabloid trickster 6, 26–35, 184, 232, 233
taboos 42–43
technology 6, 10, 44, 51, 72, 118, 148, 160–161; and tabloid trickster 27, 30, 31–32
temenos 91, 94, 97n2, 145, 206, 241
Teresa of Ávila 72, 74
Thanatos 6, 38–39, 41, 42, 44, 45, 46, 49–50, 52, 52–53n1, 53n4, 53n5, 53n6, 233
Theatre of Memory 89–90, 91
therapeutic frame 95
therapeutic methods 160, 192
therapeutic practice 96, 236
therapeutic process 94, 96
therapeutic relationships 95, 96, 110
therapeutic setting 15, 87, 94–95, 96–97, 97n2, 236
therapeutic space 93, 94, 96, 97, 97n2, 236
therapeutic womb 94
therapy 3, 8, 100–111, 160, 219; containing space 92, 93, 94, 95
third gender 46
time out of joint 188, 189
Tinder 30
totalitarianism 170, 175
totemic law 43
transcendence 61, 76, 80
transference 24, 38, 58, 107, 182, 186, 222
transformation 30, 71, 75, 90, 121; and alchemy and individuation 101–102, 104, 105, 106, 108, 111; and Chagall, Jung and religion 143, 145, 147, 149; and critique of Adorno 61, 65, 66; metaphor of 10, 147
Trickster 232–233; Samuels as 183–184, 185, 186–187, 192–193, 215–216; tabloid 6, 26–35
Trump, Donald 9, 87, 175, 224, 225
Twelve Steps 23–24

twins, an archetypal study of 38–53
Twitter 27, 28, 29
two-children policy, in China 159

uncertainty-identity theory 87, 88
unconscious: collective *see* collective unconscious; cultural 116, 117
uncontained states of mind 93–97
United States military, 'epidemic' of rape in 114, 122
unity, of the psyche 2, 8, 76, 80, 114, 116, 192, 224; and alchemy and individuation 100, 102, 108, 109
universal knowledge 91

vessel 88, 90, 91
violence 9, 39, 43, 87, 137, 164; and contemporary American anxieties 113, 114, 116, 117, 120, 123
visions 43–44, 73, 74, 90, 115, 136, 138; and alchemy and individuation 102, 107, 109
visual imagery 10, 143–153, 155–158

void, in an addict's life 24
vulnerability 6, 19, 20, 21, 24, 60, 96, 164

waking dreams 71, 72, 75–77, 79, 81, 236
warfare 2, 48–49, 51, 105, 118, 214
Watergate scandal 164
Watkins, Mary 7, 57, 61, 63–64, 74, 226, 229n1
Westernisation, in China 162
wholeness 71, 80, 108, 116, 146, 150; and containing space 91, 92, 97n1
wider life 135–137
wishes 4
workers' rights 52
World Trade Center, 9/11 terrorist attack on 114, 118

'Yin' and 'Yang' 168
young couple case study 4–5
YouTube 27

Zoja, Luigi 175, 176
Zweig, Stefan 61–62, 64

9780367525064